VASECTOMY, FRESH FLOUNDER
and GOD?

AN ANTHOLOGY
by

HARRY SARAZIN

ISBN: 1481003445
ISBN-13: 9781481003445
Library of Congress Control Number: 2012921555
CreateSpace Independent Publishing Platform
North Charleston, South Carolina

For Ann and Jim
And for Marilyn who's memory
rests softly with me always

CONTENTS

INTRODUCTION

An introduction is supposed to introduce the book, tell you what it's about, it's overall theme. I can't do that. There is no overall theme, unless you consider chaos to be a theme. Perhaps that's the wrong word. Diversity might be more appropriate. Look at the title. Those three things in the title are the titles of three of the essays in the book. Not much connection among them is there, and that's about as diverse as it gets.

With that as a disclaimer, I can say that this book is about the thoughts that have been swirling around in my head for a number of years: funny thoughts, sad thoughts, angry thoughts, religious thoughts, political thoughts, and sweet thoughts. I have set these down as essays. And, since this is an anthology, I've scattered among the essays some poems; some short stories; and one very, very short play (*Countertop Confrontation*) written on a dare: Betcha can't write dialogue between two inanimate objects and make it a play. Betcha I can. If you can avoid it, don't ever grow up. Finally, there are seven Christmas letters. Yes, I know, a little strange, but you'll understand when you get there.

I need to mention that this book would not have come into being were it not for the encouragement (that's a euphemism—incessant haranguing is more accurate) of my daughter, Ann Felter, and my son, Jim Sarazin. Finally, I want to acknowledge the help, support, and encouragement of the St. Croix Writer's Group, of which I am a proud member.

There you have it. The best I can do by way of introduction, with a little acknowledgement slipped in. If you get a sense that journeying through this book might be fun, I hope you're not disappointed.

Harry Sarazin
November 13, 2012

VASECTOMY

This is a delicate subject, and one which I think cannot be fully appreciated unless you're a man; as childbirth can't be fully appreciated unless you're a woman. But, I will try to explain this in such a way that all will understand, and there will be no unresolved questions dangling loosely unanswered.

In the days before the pill, noninvasive contraception was limited to condoms, abstinence, or the rhythm method, more fondly known as Catholic roulette. I hated condoms, and the other two choices were less than acceptable, so it remained to be decided: a tubal ligation or a vasectomy. I didn't have much of a leg to stand on since the vasectomy is far less invasive than the ligation, so it was settled; I would get a vasectomy.

My appointment was set for Friday, March 26, 1976, at the office of Dr. Fernando Lopez in Havre de Grace, MD. Lopez was the only urologist in town. Marilyn and I had met with him a week before, as was protocol for a vasectomy, and although he was nice enough, I was a little concerned by his heavy accent. Does he have a medical degree from an accredited US medical school or from some third-rate school in a third-world South American backwater? After all, I don't want just anyone entering the sacred zone.

Let me take just a moment to explain the term "sacred zone." For those of you who have spent some time with a man, you understand that the area surrounding Billy and Bobby, the Ball brothers, and their little sack house is sacred. No human (except by specific or implied invitation) is invited in, and certainly no foreign object is allowed. To violate this zone is to court serious bodily harm.

All right, back to March 26. I was ushered into Lopez's examination room by a cute young assistant. I suppose she'll hand him his scalpel and scissors, or saw, or hatchet, or whatever he uses, as she gazes down at my sure-to-be-shriveled little thing. This is going to be awful. In the room, slightly off center, was an examining table resembling tables I'd seen in the medical examiner's office where they perform autopsies. Oh God, this is really going to be bad. "Take off your trousers and underwear," she said with a smile. "Yeah, and are you coming back as soon as I'm naked to check me out?" I thought. I could feel the shrinkage starting.

After lying on the slab for a few minutes, Lopez came in, and mumbling something, taped my now almost nonexistent willy to my abdomen with surgical tape. I guess he didn't want to risk slicing it off. That's thoughtful; me either. Then he left. A few more minutes passed and in waltzed Miss Cute Cheeks ostensibly to get something, but it was clearly a mission to have a look. More shrinkage.

The anesthetic was administered, with the cute chick in attendance (by now nothing left to shrink), and when everything was numb, the first of two cruel cuts in the scrotum was made, and out through the slit Lopez pulled one of the vas deferens. I could feel the tug deep in my lower abdomen, then a snip and the same for the other side. It was at this point that I wished, like Adolph Hitler, I had just one ball. The incisions were sutured, and I was told I could get dressed and be on my way. "Take it easy for a couple of days," Lopez said. "There'll be some swelling, and you'll have some pain when the anesthetic wears off. Here's a prescription for pain pills if you need them." And with that I was out of there, neutered and humiliated. I could picture the cute assistant getting together with her friends after work: "An FBI agent came in today for a vasectomy, and you should have seen it. Not much there." This statement was then followed by shrieks of laughter. Perhaps I should ask for a transfer to Philadelphia.

There was a lot of swelling and when the anesthetic wore off, a lot of pain, particularly when I tried to walk or get in any position where my legs were even remotely close together.

The phone rang. It was the night duty agent in Baltimore. There was a fugitive staying at a cheap motel in Aberdeen. She had a long criminal record, mostly for fraud and embezzlement, and had at least nine aliases. Her true name was Mary Magdalene Vezzani, white female, fifty-three years old, five feet six, and 200 pounds. She has been known to resist arrest on previous occasions. Go get her.

"Oh shit. Why today?" I thought. But duty first, so I called Wayne, my partner, and asked him to pick me up. En route to the motel I explained my delicate medical condition and instructed him to let her have it square between the eyes with his .38 if she gave even the slightest hint of coming near me. Wayne, in his compassionate way, offered to make a sign I could hang around my waist – "Recent vasectomy. Do not touch." Very goddamn funny.

It took me a few minutes to walk from the car to Vezzani's motel room door, since I had to walk with my legs spread about four feet apart, reminding me of Shakespeare's line referring to bowlegged men: "Lo, what manor of men are these that hang their balls in parenthesis?"

The arrest went without incident, and after Vezzani was safely lodged in the Harford County Detention Center, I went home to garner as much sympathy as I could. After all, it was I who took the bullet for Marilyn on the autopsy table.

SNOWSHOES

Hanging on the wall in my living room, here in the north woods of Wisconsin, is a pair of very old, very used, beat-up snowshoes. Below is their provenance.

❧

The snowshoes you see hanging on the wall have a rich and sordid history involving gambling, theft, and even murder.

The story begins with Pierre LePouff, an eighteenth century French fur trapper. LePouff happened to be at Ft. Frontenac, a French trading post and fort, in what is now Kingston, Ontario, on August 27, 1758. It was during the height of the Seven Years' War. The English attacked the fort that day, and a bloody battle raged until the fort fell, but LePouff managed to escape with a few tools, a musket and some traps. He headed north on foot deep into the Ontario woods. When he felt he was safe, he settled on a suitable piece of land on which to build a shelter for the winter. Once the shelter was complete, he found a prime ash tree from which he constructed the frames for a pair of snowshoes. For lacing he made rawhide from the hide of a deer he harvested for food.

LePouff's snowshoes served him well that winter and for a number of years thereafter. One day during the winter of 1767, LePouff traveled to Smiths Falls, Ontario, to sell his furs. That night he visited the Deadeye

Saloon and got into a poker game with the nefarious gambler Big Nose Jake Crawford who was rumored to have murdered seven men. LePouff lost all his money, and in a last desperate measure to recoup, he gambled and lost his snowshoes.

Big Nose Crawford was a city guy, not given to trekking through the woods on snowshoes. But he kept them for many years. One night, an itinerant blacksmith and part-time burglar, Moose Garrigan, broke into Crawford's place. Big Nose confronted Moose, they fought, and Garrigan stabbed Crawford in the throat with a ten-inch hunting knife. He fled with the snowshoes and some other valuables. He was eventually captured, tried, and hanged.

The snowshoes were sold at auction to an accountant, Mortimer McPherson. But seemingly mild-mannered, McPherson had a dark side. He was a serial killer who only killed in the winter. He wore the snowshoes to drag his victims deep into the woods where they were eaten by animals and never found. After years of killing, his evil secret was discovered. Like the previous owner of the snowshoes, he was tried and hanged. They were again sold at auction.

The next owner was a young logger and farmer, Norbert Sarazin, my great-grandfather, who walked from Ontario to the Upper Peninsula of Michigan on the snowshoes, settling in Lake Linden where he married and raised a family. The snowshoes were passed to his son Frank, my grandfather, then to my father, and finally to me. You can see they are well-worn, but I won't repair them because that would diminish the mystique of their provenance.

What you have just read is completely untrue. I wrote the provenance some time ago then set about finding snowshoes to fit the story. It was a long task, over a year, then one day in the fall of 2011, while in Berlin, Maryland, I spotted the perfect snowshoes in the window of an antique store. I bought them, and now the snowshoes and story are united in perfect harmony.

JIM

Jim and I met in high school. We were friendly, but not friends. He had his circle, and I had mine. Jim was tall and gangly, and he was shy, mainly because he was deeply embarrassed about his acne. I don't remember the acne, but then that sort of thing is always more painful for the victim than the observer. Although the word didn't exist then, Jim was a geek. He was very bright, and his natural bent was toward math and science.

We graduated high school and went our separate ways. He went to school for a while, but lacking funds had to drop out. He enlisted in the Air Force intending to be a pilot, but his eyes weren't good enough, so he became a navigator.

He met Dolores in Germany where he was stationed and where she taught in the Air Force school system. They married and Jim resigned his commission. Now, armed with the GI Bill, he returned to school and got a degree in physics. He landed a job with Collins Radio, later to become Rockwell International, and he and Dolores moved to California where she was from and where his work was. They had two kids, Patty and Jim IV. Life was good for Jim and Dolores. They settled in Mission Viejo. He prospered at Rockwell, getting an MBA along the way, and Dolores went back to teaching after the kids got older.

I don't remember which high school reunion it was, perhaps the all-school reunion somewhere around the middle '90s. It doesn't really matter. My wife and I and Jim and Dolores attended. We happened to be sitting at the same table, and a conversation quickly broke out. Things were different now. Jim and I had matured. Our outlooks had changed, and a considerable amount of water had passed under our keels. We hit it off instantly. We discovered we had similar interests and largely similar views. Our conversation lasted well into the night and continued the next day at some other reunion event. I found Jim to be an engaging, funny, very bright, brutally objective (the scientist in him), gentle guy. We agreed to stay in touch.

Thus began an exchange of e-mails through the years; thousands of thoughtful long e-mails setting out complex positions on politics, philosophy, economics, and religion; light and frivolous e-mails about the travails of daily life; and poignant e-mails about sad or moving events. At one point his daughter suggested that he should save our e-mails because the exchanges reminded her of the spirited exchanges between Shaw and Churchill. I replied that she was, of course, right, and I would be Shaw. He agreed. I think he rather fancied being Churchill. Jim later compiled the more interesting e-mails in a series of three-ring binders, which he titled *Harry and Me*.

Jim and I were both raised Catholic. He practiced his religion; I did not. One email I wrote raised some serious religious issues he was unable to adequately respond to. So, in characteristic fashion, he enrolled in an adult religious education class sponsored by the Diocese of Los Angeles. He was so taken with the class that he enrolled in another and another. This regular religious education went on for years.

In addition to the e-mails, Jim and Dolores began visiting us at our cabin in Barnes each summer. Those were wonderful, rich visits, full of stimulating conversation, stimulating spirits, and good food. I looked forward to them as a child awaits the arrival of Santa at Christmas.

Two years ago Jim had heart bypass surgery; fairly routine nowadays, it went well. A few months later, during a routine follow-up, they discovered a spot on his lung. It was malignant, and it was removed. It wasn't long before other symptoms began presenting, all complicated by his long struggle with diabetes. Jim and Dolores didn't make it to Barnes in 2006; he just wasn't well enough. Earlier this year the cancer metastasized, and a grueling, debilitating round of chemotherapy began.

In August he changed doctors, and the chemo was replaced by radiation. In late September he was hospitalized because he could neither walk nor talk. Bypass surgery was done on his legs because of circulation problems caused by the diabetes. On October 6 Jim came home; on the 8th he died.

There won't be any more e-mails. There won't be any more visits. There won't be any more lively, intellectual exchanges. There is a hole in my life. The gangly kid with acne was my dear friend. I shall miss him.

MISSED OPPORTUNITY

It was a gorgeous day. The bitterness of winter was mostly over, and spring was trying to claw its way through layers of clothing still worn more of habit than necessity. Old gray snow, winter's fading legacy, lay unevenly on the ground while the streets and sidewalks were clear. That was a long time ago, but I remember that day with unflinching clarity.

Patty and I were riding our bikes home from school together as we often did. Ahh, Patty. She and I were both twelve, and I was in love. I don't mean that silly kid stuff. No sir, this was the real thing. This was love as no one in the history of the world had ever experienced it. I was pretty sure of that. And why not. Patty was a slight, gentle girl. Gentle mixed with a fair measure of toughness. She had grit. That combination did not seem to me unnatural; rather it defined feminine.

Patty's face demanded staring. She was Venus intact. Her smile was wide and easy. Her deep blue eyes, soft and sweet as a breath, locked my young soul in a state of perpetual ecstasy. Her dark blond, shoulder-length hair flowed from under her brightly colored wool cap and framed her gorgeous face as exquisitely as anything in the Louvre. Yes, I was smitten, hooked, head over heels, rubber-kneed in love, and, I discovered, there's a lot to love about love.

We chatted twelve-year-old chat as we rode along. Soon her house came up, and we stopped and continued talking. So sweet the day. Then suddenly, without even the hint of a preamble, she said, "Are you wearing long underwear?" Oh my God. How can I discuss my underwear with the woman I love? I could feel my face flushing as my throat slowly twisted into a speechless knot. After a moment I regained enough composure to manage a trembling, "Yes." With that word my face was now in full flush, and my hands began to sweat. Then, with a smile and the ease of a ballerina, Patty said, "Me too. I'll show you mine if you'll show me yours."

What happened next isn't as clear in my mind as the events leading up to it. I am told sudden shock followed by a huge dose of adrenaline will do that. I can tell you, however, that I mumbled something incomprehensible and rode off.

I have spent the past fifty-eight years fantasizing about that day and what might have happened if I had agreed to share my underwear with my love, but I didn't, and I missed an opportunity never to come again.

A SAILOR'S SONG

I was called into the boss's office one afternoon in March and told I had been transferred. It was expected—in fact, it was inevitable—because that was the way the organization worked. I was a little sad about leaving New Orleans, but there was a whole country out there full of places I could be transferred to, so the thought of a new adventure held a certain appeal.

He smiled, holding the letter so only he could see. This was in character. There was something about him that delighted in inflicting minuscule levels of torture. It wasn't that he was mean-spirited exactly, but knowing him compelled one to believe he would rather pull the wings off a fly than swat it cleanly dead.

"Well, where to?" I said, in a way designed to convey only mild interest.

"Where would you like to go?" was the response, complete with finely atomized spit. Joe had an unfortunate combination of odd lip structure and overactive saliva glands, which resulted in visible moisture whenever he tried to talk and smile at the same time.

"Doesn't matter, I guess. Anywhere'll be OK," I lied.

"How about Baltimore?" And with that he thrust the transfer letter into my hand.

I had been through Baltimore a couple of years before, and I wasn't impressed. In fact I made a mental note to never go back if possible. Now it wasn't possible, and I was beginning to alternate between panic and serious depression."Sounds great. Thanks Joe." And I left. He probably knew I was lying, but there's no way I was going to admit the organization had gotten to me.

That was twenty-eight years ago. I went to Baltimore, submerged in morbidity and self-pity. Then a funny thing happened. I fell in love. I fell in love with Baltimore (even though I live in Havre de Grace, I still carry on a secret love affair with Baltimore), and with Maryland, and most especially with Chesapeake Bay.

In 1968 I read a piece in the *National Geographic* by Robin Graham—the first of three installments describing his singlehanded voyage around the world in a small sloop, beginning when he was sixteen. I don't know what it was about that first article, ghost written I presume, but it caught my fancy and fired my imagination. What an adventure, what freedom, what nearly absolute control over one's destiny, and this kid's only sixteen. I'd never sailed before—well, there was that afternoon on the Sunfish in Florida, but that doesn't count. I'd never sailed like Robin Graham, over the horizon toward distant and unknown lands, into the vortex of an adventure, propelled only by the wind, and personally responsible for the outcome. I had to be part of this.

The first step was to visit the public library and check out every book I could find with the words "Sailing" and "How to" in the title. I read them all, some good, some not so, but all interesting. This sailing stuff didn't seem all that complicated, but the terminology. I hadn't reckoned on having to learn a new language. (Two years of French had resulted in being served beer one morning in a restaurant in western France after I had asked for more butter.) A pulley is a block, downstairs is below, behind is abaft? What kind of nonsense is this? Oh well.

The next step was to try it. I visited the Havre de Grace Marina under the new ownership of Arvid Scherpf. "I'd like to rent (I wasn't sure if the proper word was "rent" or "charter") a Flying Scot for the day. What's your rate?"

Arvid was a tall, blond, Nordic-looking sort of fellow, the kind you'd expect to be at the helm of an ocean-going sailboat bound for anywhere distant. "Twenty-five dollars for the day. Have you sailed before?"

I was ready for this. "Sure, nothing big, just daysailers, but I've done a good bit of that." My voice wasn't quite as confident as I would have liked. *Don't blow it. If he finds out, you'll never get the boat, and you'll be forever trapped in one of those catch-22 things.* He was silent for a moment, studying me with that look you get from your kid at Christmas just about the time he's old enough to figure out the truth about Santa Claus.

"OK, the boat's over there in that slip. You go ahead and rig the sails, and I'll be down in a bit to take you out for a check." PANIC! This wasn't in the scenario. Well, there's no turning back now. What was it George Burns said about show business? Sincerity is the most important thing, and if you can fake that, you've got it made.

I rigged the sails, correctly it turned out, and off we went. We sailed around for a few minutes, then headed back in. "I guess you have sailed before," said Arvid with a smile. "Have fun." And with that he turned his back, and I was left alone to experience my first sailing adventure.

That was a long time ago. Arvid and I have been friends since that first day and have shared some marvelous sailing adventures together. When I told him years later that the day he rented the Flying Scot to me was the first time I had ever been in a sailboat, he admitted the reason he checked me out was because there was something that didn't quite ring true (probably the new deck shoes), but the ride convinced him he was wrong.

Getting Marilyn and the two (then young) kids interested in sailing was a little more difficult than I expected. Spending hours sailing back and forth on the Susquehanna in a small daysailer under a broiling summer sun was not their idea of a great time, much less an adventure. Clearly we had to have our own boat so we could go somewhere, but convincing the more rational half of the partnership was another matter.

The following summer Marilyn was called home (to Wisconsin) for a family emergency that fortunately turned out all right. She decided to spend a few extra days there, and while she was gone a plan formed.

"Arvid, I'm looking for a good little used boat. I can't spend much, but I want something we can go out on overnight. You have anything?"

"As a matter of fact I do." It was an Islander 21, and when I saw it I knew it was the right boat. We negotiated (Arvid's better at that than

I, but I got a fair deal) my bank-approved a loan over the phone, and the deal was done. But there was a small hurdle.

"Hi, how's it going up there?" The small talk lasted for a few minutes, then, "I've been talking to Arvid about a nice little 21-foot sloop he's got for sale. It's in good shape, and the price is really right. What do you think?" I don't recall the exact words Marilyn used—I have a habit of purging my memory of unpleasant things—but my recollection is that the reaction was milder than I had anticipated, which, to a somewhat twisted mind, represents an affirmative response. The deal stood.

That little gray sloop, named *Carina* after a constellation in the Southern Hemisphere (I couldn't find a constellation in the Northern Hemisphere with a nice-sounding name short enough to fit on the transom alongside the outboard) became my magic carpet, my Rosinante, and the windmills I tilted at were Annapolis, St. Michaels, Oxford, and a long list of other exotic "foreign" ports.

In all fairness, there are those (family) who will tell you without much urging, that those early days on *Carina* could be trying. They will site my insistence on the "purity" of sailing; that is, real sailors don't turn on the motor except in cases of life-threatening emergency, and then only sparingly. Sitting under a white-hot August sun in no wind, they will say, qualified as life-threatening. I caution you to view these remarks with some skepticism. We know what heat stroke can do to the judgment. In 1982 *Carina* was sold and replaced by a beautiful Sabre 28 we named *Cyrano*. Soon we will have had *Cyrano* ten years. What a marvelous ten years that has been. She has traveled the length of the Chesapeake Bay and as far afield as Newport. *Cyrano* has been a sturdy companion, and I could ask for no better. The kids are grown now and have their own interests, and Marilyn has become a seasoned sailor, as eager (nearly) as I to set out any day the forecast doesn't call for snow or a hurricane.

But what happened to the adventure? What became of that Robin Graham germ that invaded my psyche back in 1968 that demanded I set out across an unknown ocean to visit exotic tropical islands? I am happy to report it hasn't been lost. Modified perhaps, but not lost. I have never actually sailed to exotic places (four races to Bermuda comes close). Responsibilities have mainly limited me to Chesapeake Bay. But through an accident of genetics I have been blessed with a marvelous imagination and an inability to grow up. Never Neverland has always occupied a corner of my sea bag, so a weekend overnighter to some quiet anchorage still fires the imagination. Never mind that it isn't Tonga or the Torres Strait; Worton Creek will do very nicely. Each venture is an adventure, and if there's fog, or too much wind, or driving rain, then this Magellan just has to handle it, because that's what we adventurers do. The years have not diluted the excitement I felt that first day on the Flying Scot. Time has only managed to make sailing and the Chesapeake so much a part of me that they define me, and I feel blessed. This is my song.

Thank you, Mr. Graham; thank you, Mr. Burns; and thanks for the transfer, Joe.

AN ARRESTING COINCIDENCE

I was assigned to New Orleans after completing training at the FBI Academy. New Orleans—not a bad place to start an FBI career; not a bad place indeed; quite a few notches over Butte or Omaha.

I was assigned to Bud Gaskell's squad, as were all first office agents (FOAs). Poor Bud, a truly nice and gentle man, having to put up with first office agents who generally didn't have a clue about how to be FBI agents, and rarely realized it.

I found a place to rent (we were only going to be in New Orleans for a year) in the suburb of Metairie, while Marilyn wound things up in Maine, where we had lived for four years. Soon she and the kids joined me, we settled in, and life was good. I jumped into my work with the enthusiasm of a logger in town on a Saturday night. I quickly learned two things. First, training school ill prepared one for the realities of being an FBI agent, particularly the complexities of the paperwork, and second, there was a pecking order in the office, with first office agents at the very bottom. At the top was the "Palace Guard," the seasoned old guys who could do pretty much as they pleased, because they had long ago made their bones. Guys like Joe Peggs and John (I've forgotten his last name). All the rest occupied various rungs of respect and seasoning somewhere in between we FOAs and the Guard.

The first few cases I was assigned were simple violations, one small crime, one subject, a little evidence and just a few witnesses—simple, but still a bit daunting for one so green.

The days became weeks, and the weeks a full month, then a month and a half. I was beginning to find a groove, still a little shaky with the paperwork, but just beginning to find a tiny slice of comfort level. It was at this point that I got the call.

I had been home from work for about an hour when Bud Gaskell called. "Harry, this is Bud. Do you want to go on an arrest?" *Do I want to go on an arrest? My God! Are you kidding? Do I want to go on an arrest? Ask me if I want to spend the night with Marilyn Monroe, ask me if I want to get into the astronaut program, and you'll see less enthusiasm. Be cool Sarazin. Don't let on you're excited.*

"Sure Bud. I'd be glad to. What do you want me to do?" I said, a little embarrassed that the pitch of my voice replicated one who had recently been castrated. I was directed where and when to meet the arrest team. Bud explained that we were going to arrest Ralph Francis Gaudio, an escapee from a maximum security prison—a very bad guy considered armed and extremely dangerous. The New Orleans office had located Gaudio about three weeks before through an informant, but they delayed arresting him because they thought he might lead them to Alfred Oponowicz, his good friend, who was on the FBIs Ten Most Wanted list. It seems The Bureau (FBI Headquarters in Washington) was getting nervous about Gaudio being free, so it ordered New Orleans to snap him up. *WOW! I mean, WOW! This is a big deal, and Bud asked me to go along.*

The plan was simple. It was evening of a clear, hot day in May. Lots of people were in their yards barbecuing or playing with the kids. An agent in scruffy clothes had driven past Gaudio's triplex and spotted him in a T-shirt and shorts, barbecuing in his yard. His girlfriend, Carol Fish, was apparently in the house. The plan was to pull up en masse and take him in the yard, or if he was in the house, we would go in the front door and get him. His escape from the yard was somewhat limited by a high fence, and his escape from the house would be limited because it would be immediately surrounded. My assignment was to remain in the front yard in case he, for whatever reason, might emerge from one of the other triplex units. It didn't dawn on me at the time that the translation of this assignment was to stay the hell out of the way.

Jack Miller was the lead agent, so, according to FBI custom, he would make the arrest in the yard, or be the first through the door. The plan was set, we had our assignments, and it was time to go. We piled into several cars and arrived at Gaudio's place in a few minutes. The grill, with thin wisps of smoke curling up from it, was in the front yard, but Gaudio wasn't. The place was immediately surrounded. As I approached my assigned position, I paused momentarily to peek through a small space in the drapes at the end of Gaudio's unit. I was looking into a bedroom and through the bedroom door into the living room. There, standing in the living room, was Carol Fish, a gorgeous, curvaceous young woman—completely naked. Completely buck naked—not a stitch. I motioned for Jack to come over. He did, looked, then motioned for Bud, who did the same. Lest you get the wrong idea, this was necessary FBI reconnoitering, nothing more, of course.

With guns drawn we took our positions. Jack knocked loudly on the front door, and was prepared to kick it in, when it flew open and there stood the naked Carol. She took a step back and began to scream. It was a bloodcurdling, deep from the swamps scream, clearly heard for blocks. She wouldn't stop screaming, which caused the neighbors to come out, and the confusion level grew. One neighbor, in the unit adjoining Gaudio's, came out with a shotgun in his hands. He was a young fellow, with wide eyes and the look of someone about to rescue a damsel from something, and he was going to use his shotgun to do it. He was now in my territory—the front lawn. I identified myself, pointed my gun at him and, in a surprisingly calm voice, ordered him to put the shotgun down. After a moment of hesitation, he did. I then ordered him to get back in his house, which he did.

By this time the yard was filling with curious neighbors. After a reasoned request and a little threatening, I got them to return to their houses, and the scene in the yard returned to normal. Meantime, the arrest team searched the house, but Gaudio wasn't there. This was crisis time. Bud had been telling the Bureau we could pick Gaudio up any time. Now, when the Bureau said do it, he was gone. Bud could see his career evaporating before his eyes. Gaudio couldn't be far away. We had to find him. We would get in our cars and start fanning out.

"Bud," I said, "I live about six blocks from here. I can get my personal car and start looking. It'll be another unit with another set of eyes," I reasoned.

"Sure kid," he snapped, then went back to other business.

I ran home. I didn't want to ask for a ride, because I didn't want to tie up a search car, so I ran home. I ran into the house with a breathless explanation to Marilyn, then into my car, and off I went, looking for Ralph Francis Gaudio.

My car was a 1964 white Chevrolet Impala with red interior. It was getting dark now, and I turned my headlights on. I searched beginning near Gaudio's house, then slowly expanding. Finally I got to Jefferson Downs Race Track. I decided to cruise the parking lot just in case. My windows were down; I was as wound up as a tiger stalking its prey, and I was ready. If Gaudio was anywhere on the planet, he was mine. I was a highly trained, seasoned member of the premier law enforcement organization in the world. Well, scratch seasoned, but you get the idea.

As I drove slowly through the now dark Jefferson Downs parking lot, a sharp whistle to my right startled me. I turned the car and there, in my headlights, emerging from behind the bushes at the edge of the parking lot, was Ralph Francis Gaudio.

I have to pause here to explain something. Mr. Hoover, or "The Hoov" as we fondly referred to him, decreed that FBI agents will never make arrests alone. The idea was to always outnumber the bad guy. This policy worked fairly well, since almost all FBI arrests are planned. It's not like the cop on the street who responds to emergencies. But occasionally, FBI agents find themselves in situations where they must make an arrest alone. Now, on my very first arrest, I found myself in that situation, with an armed and very dangerous escapee from a maximum security prison. *Shit.* To make matters worse, because Mr. Hoover said it wouldn't happen, FBI training never included the procedures for making a felony arrest alone. *Shit.*

I stepped out of the car, gun drawn, being careful to stay behind the headlights. As Gaudio ran toward me, he motioned for me to cut the headlights. I held my ground. When he got to the front of the car, I said, in the sternest voice I could muster, "FBI, Gaudio. You're under arrest. Hands on the car." Actually, I was quite surprised at how well it came out. I really sounded convincing. Gaudio froze for a moment, then in a voice quietly whispering complete despair, he said, "Aw shit," which I thought pretty eloquently summed up his situation.

I had the bad guy up against the car, feet well back and spread to keep him off balance as I patted him down. There aren't many hiding places when you're wearing a T-shirt and shorts. He wasn't armed. Now came the time to handcuff him. But what do I do with my gun? I can't handcuff him while holding a gun, but if I holster it, and he knows, he may turn, and we would find ourselves in one hell of a fight. I was pretty sure I would win, but I'm not big on violent confrontation, so avoiding a fight was the best approach. I got his upper body lying on the hood, arms straight out in front of him. I slowly, and very quietly, holstered my .38 special snub nose. In a flash, I got his hands behind him, and he was handcuffed. Whew.

Grabbing him securely by the arm, I got him upright, led him to the passenger side of the car, and put him in. After I got in the car, I turned to Ralph Francis Gaudio, and in what I thought was a really cool federal cop voice said, "Gaudio, you give me any trouble and you're going to be in a world of hurt."

He turned to me, and with what I thought was the slightest hint of a smile, said, "Don't worry kid. I won't give you any trouble. You're too nervous."

Aw shit, I thought. Which pretty eloquently summed up my situation.

Thus was my first arrest. I found a pay phone, called the office, and asked them to radio Bud that Gaudio was in custody. We met, and Bud and Jack took him off my hands. I wasn't sure, but I thought I saw a tear welling in Bud's eyes.

Several days later I learned Gaudio had spotted the agent who drove by to check the place. He told Carol to strip, and when the cops hit the place, to scream her head off, figuring it would cause enough confusion to give him some extra time. He was right. When he got to Jefferson Downs he found a phone booth, called a friend, and asked him to pick him up in the parking lot in about an hour. The friend had a 1964 white Chevrolet Impala with red interior.

A CHRISTMAS PRAYER

Hello, God. You and I don't talk anymore, but it's not you, it's me. I just don't know if you exist. OK, I understand that most people on earth "know" you're real, but you and I understand that no one can really know you exist; they can only believe you do, and there's a big difference. I'm pretty sure you don't take offense at my stand; after all, you endowed your humans with the ability to reason and question. Exercising that gift, it seems to me, is part of your overall plan and must please you.

I know you don't really intervene, at least not in the big stuff, so it seems to me that prayer operates more as a mental salve for the one who prays than it does to accomplish its stated purpose. How many millions prayed to no avail during the Holocaust? How many thousands prayed before and during the hurricanes that destroyed so many families and so much property over the years? How many millions throughout the world pray, but starve to death anyway? How many millions pray, but still fall victim to HIV and other diseases which in the developed world barely exist? It's pretty obvious you let events unfold in their own natural way, so if it's arrogant of me to call this a prayer, I apologize, but I don't know what else to call it. Maybe I'm just a kvetch.

I guess you know we have a president who is a good and decent man, who desperately wants to do the right thing, but who is in a job that's a few intellectual and temperamental pay grades above his capacity. He got us into a disastrous war in Iraq, saying you told him to do it. I don't think so. We've now lost nearly 2,200 young American lives and 30,000 Iraqi civilians, and our national coffers are being drained at the rate of $177 million per day. But we can't go back and undo that any more than we can un-ring a bell. We cannot, from a moral standpoint, invade and nearly destroy a nation, then walk out leaving it in shambles. We have to stay in Iraq until it can take care of itself. My prayer is this: while we're there, keep our troops safe, and please hurry things along.

Kim Jong-il, part of Mr. Bush's "Axis of Evil," is a far more evil dictator than Saddam Hussein ever dreamed of being and far more dangerous. He's a guy who would probably score 9 on a 10-point nut scale. I pray two things regarding North Korea. First, that Kim, who is well on his way to developing a nuclear weapon, restrains himself, and second, that Mr. Bush restrains himself. We, and the world, can ill afford a reckless adventure in North Korea.

The third leg of the Axis of Evil is Iran, another soon-to-be nuclear power. Its president, Mahmoud Ahmadinejad, a guy who would also score 9 on the nut scale, says the Holocaust was a hoax, and suggests moving Israel to Europe, Canada, the United States, or Alaska (I'm not sure what he thinks Alaska is). Same prayer here, God. Restrain him from harming his neighbors or us, and restrain our president.

It's a dicey world, God, but when hasn't it been? I guess you've watched your creatures destroy themselves needlessly since they evolved into thinking creatures, which perhaps makes the word "thinking" an oxymoron.

I love my country, and I have always been proud of what it stands for. America has been the gold standard by which all other nations judged human rights. But that gold has begun to tarnish. Memos from the White House, the Justice Department, and the Department of Defense, either setting out how torture should be conducted or condoning it, have sullied our reputation and placed any American who serves overseas, and falls into the hands of a foreign power or group, in greater jeopardy. Abuses at Guantanamo, Abu Ghraib, and secret CIA prison sites in Central and Eastern Europe, where we farm out torture, are abominations and mock what we stand for. Torture is morally wrong. If that doesn't resonate with our faith-based president, then the practical side of torture should: it simply doesn't work. Senator McCain, no stranger to torture, has proposed simple, straightforward legislation that would eliminate these practices, but the White House has refused to accept it. During Condoleezza Rice's recent European tour, she was asked repeatedly about US policies on torture. Her replies were so tortuously legalistic and evasive they were an embarrassment. My prayer is that Mr. Bush comes to realize the futility of his policy and accepts Senator McCain's amendment.

The Kyoto Accord has been ratified by 141 countries, which account for 55 percent of the world's greenhouse gas emissions. But one country, which accounts for 25 percent of all greenhouse gas in the world, refuses to come on board, saying compliance would be too expensive. That country is the US. The Bush administration and the Clinton administration before it both balked. You probably understand better than I the stranglehold that industry has over government, Republican and Democrat, but expense isn't the real issue here; the well-being of planet Earth is. I'm not a tree hugger, God, far from it, but I am a pragmatist, and global warming isn't a myth. I pray that this administration, and Congress, bite the bullet and do the right thing for the generations to come.

And speaking of Congress, God, wow, what a mess. Divisions are as deep as at any time since the late eighteenth century, and the backbone inside the Beltway is sadly lacking. If Congress, and indeed the press, whose responsibility it is to take any administration to task, had asked more tough questions and held the administration's feet to the fire a little more in 2003, we likely wouldn't be embroiled in Iraq. We bleed money there and through massive pork-barrel projects, while Congress wants to cut spending by cutting social programs, including Medicare; at the same time, it wants to cut taxes. Never before have taxes been cut during a time of war. Our national shame is that forty-five million Americans are without health insurance. Wasn't it your son who said, "Whatsoever ye have done unto one of the least of these my brethren, ye have done unto me?" My prayer is that Congress becomes a little more congenial, compassionate, and a lot more responsible.

OK, God, that's all. Actually there's more, and I could have been more detailed, but you know the details, and I've bent your divine ear quite enough. If you're there, thanks for listening. I know you don't intervene, but if you decide to bend your rule just a little, we here on earth sure would be grateful. If not, we understand. Oh, by the way, Happy birthday to your son.

Sincerely,
Harry Sarazin

FAIR MAIDEN
A Short Story

The following document was found buried in the wall of an old castle, hard by Dingle Bay, in County Kerry, Ireland, in 1987 by the famous anthropologist Margaret Leakey O'Toole. It became lost for a time until it came into my possession recently at a yard sale put on by an itinerant garage door salesman who had fallen on hard times. I'm not sure what to make of it. Here it is, translated by me from the Celtic:

"Once upon a time, in a land far beyond the sea, there lived a maiden so fair the flowers in the fields blushed in her presence. Not only was she fair, but she possessed qualities unheard of in the land in which she lived, so very far away.

"There was, in the land, a knight who knew the fair maiden from earlier days when she worked for the Town Crier and before the knight became old and cantankerous. In those early times the knight and the fair maiden talked and laughed and happily drank mead together. They had a common understanding and a common view of things weighty and trivial, and this commonality bound them in spirit.

"By and by the fair maiden moved to another land and gained for herself much respect and admiration because she was competent and accomplished. Meantime, the knight retired from the knighthood midst much fanfare and adulation. He then cast about to discover new pursuits, but being a knight suits one for very little. Eventually he became a used saddle merchant. But a life of doing battle with dragons had jaded the knight, and it took more than selling saddles to stimulate his interest. So, before the seasons had changed a half score of times, he became restless.

"One day a messenger arrived at the castle with a missive from the fair maiden. The knight was thrilled. He sent a courier with a return message, and as the days passed they exchanged more messages, light and full of laughter, as in their early days.

"You must understand, gentle reader, that although the knight is truly a kind soul, he can, on occasion, be an old fart (from the French, *farteaur*, meaning not a pleasant thing to be around), so as time passed, he began to send more and more contentious messages to the fair maiden. He did so not out of a conscious effort to be contentious, but simply because he was what he was.

"The knight, an incredibly introspective and sensitive person—some of the time—eventually sensed that the fair maiden was miffed (from the German *mifzelwachen*, meaning pissed off). He felt badly about this, and in an extraordinary act of contrition had only a spinach salad for lunch on Thursday. He did other knightly acts of atonement, far too numerous to occupy this story, hoping the fair maiden would again warm to him.

"The days and weeks passed, and their messages to each other gradually regained their light and playful tone. Slowly, ever so slowly, the knight began to realize that which he had so long denied. His feelings for the fair maiden were more than friendly, and they always had been. He wondered if she shared his ardor, and he prayed she did.

"Then one day a courier arrived with another message from the fair maiden, but this one was different. It was written on a particularly delicate and decorous piece of parchment. As he held it, he detected the delicate odor of jasmine. With trembling hands he broke the seal, and opened the message.

"'Dearest Knight,' it began. 'I have been blessed for a very long time by your friendship; pray you have been blessed by mine. It has survived stormy difficulties, and like steel in a forge, has been tempered by them. Now, dear knight, I must reveal to you...'"

The story apparently went on, but this is all that survived.

A CLOSE SHAVE

Before we begin, let me explain. Those of you who are guys don't need this. Those of you who aren't may benefit from the explanation.

Guys don't get their hair styled; they get it cut. Guys don't go to Fluffy Duffy Unisex Hair Salon; they go to a barber. There's a reason for this, and it rests somewhere in the DNA of the first Homo erectus who discovered that his hair was getting in his eyes, and he needed to do something about it.

When I was a kid, I got my hair cut at Lee Russell's Barbershop. I used to ride my bike to Lee's, and going there was a thrill, because a haircut was only a tiny part of the package. I reveled in sitting on one of the hard chairs lined up against the wall and choosing a guy magazine: *Esquire*, *Popular Mechanics*, *Field and Stream*, and a bunch of others. But what I craved most was the conversation.

I tried to time my visits to Lee's to correspond with his busiest time. That way I could sit and listen to the men talk. When you're eleven or twelve or thirteen, you don't say a lot in Russell's Barbershop, but if you listen carefully, you hear a lot of guy talk. There's stuff about politics, sports, hunting and fishing, and even a little homespun philosophy, and of course the occasional dirty joke. I sat mesmerized by the "guys" talking, and secretly, down deep, felt I might be one of the guys. They talked about "stuff," not people like girls talk about, but "stuff." How much pulling power a Ford pickup has; how the administration is, or is not, screwing everything up; how the Packers are going to do in the upcoming season, and what the walleye are biting on. I'm talking stuff—important stuff, real guy stuff.

There aren't many barbershops left. Most of the barber colleges have closed. What you have out there are a bunch of young girls who have been trained in "hair styling," not barbering. They cut your hair, but don't have a clue what they're doing, and generally make it look like, well, not like a real haircut. It's not their fault. They haven't been taught that a man's haircut is a special thing and requires special skills.

There are two barbershops I go to. One in Maryland, run by a guy named Tom, and the other in Wisconsin, run by Dennis. Each is owned by a genuine barber—an old-time genuine barber—the kind of guy who cuts your hair, then puts shaving cream on the back of your neck and shaves it with a straight razor. God, I love that.

And that brings me to the point of this essay. I went to Tom's today to get a haircut—my last before going to Wisconsin for the summer. The name of his shop is "Barbershop." Not too imaginative, but functional. Tom and his brother Jerry are the barbers, although Tom runs the show. It's a real old-fashioned barbershop, complete with all the required magazines, but with a nod toward modernity, as the selection includes *Rolling Stone.* What's not to love about that?

Tom and Jerry both had customers in their chairs when I walked in. Jerry was cutting some old gent's hair. Turns out he was president of Harford Bank around the turn of the century. He talked a lot—a whole lot—and apparently he's deaf, because when he spoke, the framed cartoons on the wall vibrated on their hooks.

Tom was cutting a young guy's hair, probably around thirty years old. It was obvious that Tom would finish first. When he did and the customer got out of the chair, I got up to take my place. But they weren't finished. They went to the shampoo chair. The guy sat down, extended the back of his neck over the trough leading into the sink, and closed his eyes; it was sort of like he was getting ready to be guillotined. Actually, he was about to be prepped for a shave. Let me interject something here, ladies. A shave, with a straight razor, in a barbershop, by a professional barber, ranks up there with the two best feelings in the world, and depending what you just did last, it may be number one.

Tom placed hot wet towels on the guy's face to soften his beard—standard procedure. Then he lathered the customer's face with exquisite dexterity. I went back to my *Esquire*. A few minutes later Jerry finished, and I was next up. As I walked to the chair, I glanced at Tom and his customer. The guy had a smile of sublime contentment on his face, as his head was stretched back over the sink. But all was not well in the barbershop. His neck was glistening with blood, like he had been attacked by an Al Qaeda terrorist, and even more blood was trickling down from a slash just below his lower lip. I was fairly certain I wasn't witnessing a homicide, but it was obvious that my favorite barber, the guy I had decided I would get a shave from one day, had nearly rendered his customer forever silent.

The remarkable thing was that Tom seemed entirely unfazed by the carnage—sort of like a butcher accustomed to cutting fresh meat. Tom applied wet towels to the bloody areas as he chatted calmly with the victim. Most difficult was the slash just below the guy's lower lip. Mere pressure was not enough here; it required a styptic pencil, which of course, Tom had ready. It was clear at this point that this was not Tom's first experience with fresh blood.

With most of the bleeding stopped, and the evidence removed, Tom led his patient back to the barber chair for a few final clips. The guy sat in the chair, facing the mirror, with a big smile on his face, obviously pleased by the fine shave he had just received and totally unaware how close he had come to decapitation. The only trace of red was a tiny spot just below his lower lip. Tom noticed it too, and with a smile and the casual manner of someone about to brush a crumb off his shirt, he said, "Oops, looks like I nicked you." Then he applied another layer of constriction with the styptic pencil.

I'll rethink the shave.

CONNECTIONS

What I've done in my chosen profession and personal life, although vitally important at the time, had, in reality, all of the earthshaking rumble of a fly stomping his way across a picnic table. I don't presume to diminish my role as husband, father, or friend, but when I say I have made no great contribution I'm referring to that which will ensure one's place in history. Now, in this seventy-first year of my life, as I think about that, I'm quite comfortable.

So what does an average man reflect on in the last quarter of the game? The first reflection is, of course, mortality. And it's thoughts of one's mortality that drive the soul to mine the essence of a life well lived, if not great. What is worthwhile in an ordinary life? If I did not mold the past like clay in the potter's hands for all to see and admire, then perhaps it is simply my place in the past that lends meaning. If not the star, then why not the starlight. And it is thoughts of my place in the past that have revealed to me a connection that guarantees I will not, like Updike's Bech "…up in smoke—cease to exist."

I was born and raised in northwest Wisconsin. At twenty-three I moved away to seek my fortune, got married, and started a family. For many years I have lived elsewhere, several elsewheres, all many miles away, but I have remained connected to my Wisconsin roots. Each summer all accumulated vacation time was spent at "The Lake." The Lake is a cabin nestled in the Wisconsin woods, hard by a beautiful lake, in the township of Barnes, twenty-three square miles larger than Baltimore, but with just 600-plus registered voters.

My first memory of anything in my life is a few seconds of mental video of me at four walking across the subfloor of the cabin as it was being built. I have later images of my dad spending therapeutic hours in the yard "puttering," an activity that accomplished little, but eased his business-taut nerves and cheered his soul.

I remember rowing *Kitty Foy*, a beautiful lead-heavy, 18-foot mahogany, plank-on-plank rowboat, to all the secret inlets and places on the lake until my hands were raw and my bottom blistered—places I was sure only I knew of, including the honeybee log on the point.

I remember planting a little Norway pine down by the lake when I was about nine, a little tree about my height. It now stands a healthy fifty-plus feet.

I remember introducing my girlfriend Marilyn, later to become my wife, to the lake and praying she would begin the same kind of love affair with it I so sensuously enjoyed. I remember bringing our babies, then children, then young adults to the lake from afar. I remember the joy I felt when, as they grew older, they talked of the lake not only glowingly, but possessively. Now the cycle repeats with grandchildren. The continuum so established, I will live forever.

A few years ago, I retired again, for the second time, but this time permanently. I was freed of saluting any master but my own reflection, and we decided to spend entire summers at the lake. It was a decision taken easily—a decision I had been hoping to make for a very long time, and the making of it was a soothing release. So here I am, at the lake, the place I so dearly love, sitting quietly on a gray, drizzly afternoon with a fire in the fireplace, thinking thoughts of mortality and my place in the cosmos as an ordinary man, and my thoughts draw me inexorably to connections.

I have a loving and nurturing family, and that is, of course, the most important connection. But it's like the connection one has with one's hand or eye; it's always there, not to be taken for granted, but so much a part of you, it is you. The kind of connection that dances across my mind now at this stage of my life, in this quiet place, still and beautiful as a lover's whisper, is a connection to something else, something beyond the family that defines me, something shouting to the world who and what I am, something that, like a long-forgotten infantile need, provides mother's milk to the soul.

I envy the cultural heritage of American Indians that inexorably connects them to places—a heritage mocked in a world of throwaway houses, throwaway jobs, throw- away families, and often throwaway lives. Orville Looking Horse, the nineteenth generation Keeper of the Pipe for the Lakota, said this a few years ago upon returning to the Black Hills: "In this place there is everything that is." I am humbled by the beauty and profundity of that thought. My connection, my place where there is everything that is, where my life establishes its most profound meaning, is here in this cabin nestled in the woods hard by a beautiful lake. It is here that I am whole. It is here that as an ordinary man, I am a giant.

HARRY

I t's entirely understandable. He's a handsome twenty-seven-year-old bachelor who comes from a good family, for the most part. There are a few black sheep hiding in the family tree. Uncle Henry VIII was a bit of a scoundrel, but that's not Harry's fault. His only job, as an Army Air Corps helicopter pilot, doesn't pay much. But not to worry, he's got a tidy income, living for the most part on the public dole. So young Harry finds himself one night recently in the posh and very expensive Encore Wynn Resort in Las Vegas, in their largest suite with a few friends. By the way, don't worry about the bill. Steve Wynn waived the nearly $48,000 tab. Anyway, Harry and his friends notice there's a pool table in the suite, so naturally they engage in a game of naked pool. A perfectly logical thing to do, especially if there are young ladies present, and there were. It don't get no better than that.

Let's step back for a moment and consider Prince Harry's position, not on the pool table, but in life generally. He's a lieutenant in the British army, but his grandmother is the boss so, let's face it, he gets a little wiggle room. He's also third in succession to the British throne. That sounds impressive at first glance, but actually it isn't. The British monarchy reigns, but they don't rule. Essentially they have nothing to do, so they spend a great amount of time at public functions, shaking hands, making small talk, and having their pictures taken. They also adopt favorite causes that they devote time and energy to, and this sort of makes it all right that they really produce nothing at all. We don't know what Harry's favorite cause is, but we can guess. In order for him to become king, his grandmother, a nice and very proper old lady, who carries a rather boring handbag as though it has been surgically attached to her forearm, has to bite the dust. Then his father, a somewhat stiff gent with extraordinarily bad taste in second wives, has to die. Then Harry's older brother, another handsome young man in robust good health, with extraordinarily good taste in first wives, has to pass on to wherever kings go. It's not likely Harry will have to man-up and assume the throne any time soon, so what the hell, have some fun.

Unfortunately, one of the guests at the naked party brought a camera and took some pictures of Harry with the crown jewels on public display, in close proximity to a sweet young thing similarly unclad. Then this despicable miscreant put the pictures out in the ether for all to see. A quick disclaimer; sadly, I wasn't there, so this is speculation, but I suspect a bit of alcohol might have been involved in this little debauch.

We now get inextricably to the delicate question of Harry's culpability. I can only guess, but I suspect Grandma is pissed. I assume Harry's commanding officer is likewise pissed—unbecoming conduct and all that sort of thing. But wait. Harry was not in public; he was in a private room with (he thought) friends. Shouldn't one be able to let one's hair and pants down in one's own private room for which one is paying thousands of pounds a night? OK, he didn't pay for it, but you know what I mean. It seems to me the real culprit here isn't young Harry who dangled his dong, but the dork who took the pictures of the dangle and published them. And where were the two bobbies from Scotland Yard who accompany Harry everywhere? Shouldn't they have demanded everyone check their cameras and cell phones at the door? I think so.

As you consider what happened, don't be too judgmental. Poor Harry is a guy who doesn't have anything productive to look forward to in his life, who has, no doubt, had his ass reamed by granny and his CO, and who likely feels sheepish and betrayed. He's probably so distraught he can scarcely concentrate on the three or four babes fawning over him at whatever exclusive club he happens to be visiting. The life of a royal isn't all that great. I wouldn't trade places with him for anything—yeah, right. And Pippa is in the family.

I'M READY

We went to the doctor's office a while back. It was my wife's appointment, so I sat in the waiting room shuffling through magazines until I happened upon an old issue of *Sail Magazine*. I don't generally read sailing magazines anymore. I did for over thirty years, but I stopped a few years ago because we stopped sailing and sold our boat. It wasn't an easy decision, but one born of necessity; we were getting too old and creaky for the physical part of sailing. So we sold the boat, sold our house in Maryland, and moved to the pine woods of northwest Wisconsin where we used to vacation and where we now live. It is an old family property, which we dearly love and which is a wonderful palliative for the loss of sailing.

As I thumbed through the magazine, now even more slick than when I last read it, I noticed an article about the 2006 Newport - Bermuda race. It marked the one hundredth anniversary of the race, and there were 263 sailboats entered. They ranged from just over 30 feet to the 98-foot *Maximus*. The fleet included high-tech racing boats like the 50-foot *Gyphon Solo*, with a carbon fiber hull and mast, water ballast, and a hydraulically operated movable keel and *Dame of Sark*, a beautiful forty-five-year-old wooden Concordia yawl—a true classic.

In the spirit of the race's one hundredth anniversary, the article mentioned some of the famous old yachts that helped make the Newport - Bermuda race world famous—yachts like *Dorade, Baruna*, and

Bolero. Bolero, my gosh; I was navigator on *Bolero* on a passage from Ft. Lauderdale to St. Croix, USVI in 1996. She had been meticulously refurbished, and being aboard her was not only a privilege, but pure delight.

As I read the piece, my mind wandered back, back to some of the blue water passages I've made to Bermuda, the Caribbean, and New England. I recalled the passage from upper Chesapeake Bay to Newport, RI, on my own little 28-foot sloop, *Cyrano*. It was a leisurely trip in fine weather, mostly in sight of land, until we approached Montauk Point as darkness fell. Then the fog rolled in—dense, all-enveloping, cotton-like fog. The only navigation equipment aboard was a compass, knotmeter, depth sounder, and a somewhat useless handheld RDF (radio direction finder). GPS hadn't arrived yet, so navigation out of sight of landmarks was by dead reckoning, but we made it; we fetched The Great Salt Pond on Block Island, dead on, despite the fog. My God, but that felt good.

I remember beating for nearly three days into 40 knot winds on the way to Bermuda in a less than structurally sound boat that began to come slightly apart during the storm, and I remember how good it felt to land at St. George's, go ashore, and sip a dark and stormy in the White Horse Tavern.

I remember racing flat out from Marion, MA, to Bermuda in 1979 aboard *Argonaut,* an Allied 42-foot yawl. We had a fine, seasoned crew. Our cook was Stormy Donaldson, a wisp of a girl, barely five-foot-three and cute as a button. But she was a tough, world-class blue water sailor and a classically trained chef. The galley was directly opposite my nav station, and when the boat heeled to port, my dividers, with their needle points, would occasionally slide off the nav table and fly into Stormy's butt as she prepared a meal. There was some loose talk aboard that I might have prevented those unfortunate accidents if I had secured the dividers properly, but that was just loose talk. I thought the only decent thing to do was to offer to kiss the wounded area to make it all better, but Stormy declined.

The last day out, dinner was filet mignon with béarnaise sauce, among other things. This, and the rest of the extraordinary meals Stormy made, was prepared on a gimbaled three-burner propane stove while heeled over 20° or more and often pitching wildly.

We won our class, and I won the navigator's trophy in our class. That trophy sits proudly on my mantle here in the Wisconsin woods as a reminder of...well, you know what of.

My mind returned to the article, and I read that the 2006 Newport - Bermuda race was characterized by light winds. It spoke of the real challenge in every Bermuda race—the Gulf Stream. It might be useful to point out that the Gulf Stream is an ever-changing oceanographic phenomena. It doesn't flow at a constant speed and in a fixed location. Rather it varies in drift (speed) from under 2 knots to often over 3, and it meanders, changing position like a giant snake. It also throws off eddies—doughnut-shaped swirls of moving water—often many miles in diameter. Warm eddies are found to the north of the stream, spinning clockwise and cold eddies to the south, spinning counterclockwise. The trick is to figure out how to avoid the eddies where the current is foul (flowing against you), utilize those where the current is fair (flowing with you), and enter the stream itself to either maximize a fair current or minimize a foul one. All of this has to be done in conjunction with an analysis of the high seas weather forecasts. The skipper, navigator, and tactician, if there is one, put their heads together before and during the race, and, based on the data available and their experience, decide on a plan of action. Making this decision is agonizing, and it's usually based on one part science and two parts intuition.

The 2006 Newport - Bermuda race posed an intriguing set of choices. Would it be better to go east of the rhumb line (straight line to the destination) and catch a meander in the stream with a fair current for some miles—a longer route—or would it be better to go west of the rhumb line, cross the stream at a more or less right angle, and catch the fair side of a cold eddy—a shorter route than the first choice? Some very seasoned skippers and navigators chose the first option; the first yacht to cross the finish line chose the second.

My juices began to flow as I read. Every time I've made an extended blue water passage I swore a few days out that I would never do it again. And every time, once ashore sipping the product of a distiller's art in the warm womb of a friendly saloon, I and my shipmates would plan the next passage. That's just the way it is: love/hate, but a little more love than hate.

I haven't sailed blue water since the trip on *Bolero* in 1996. But I keep my navigation skills fine-tuned. I regularly take celestial shots with my sextant; I check the latest Gulf Stream data on the computer, and using it, along with NOAA high seas weather forecasts, plan imaginary passages on imaginary yachts. I have to guess if I planned right, because there's no execution to verify the decisions. Of course my friends think I'm a bit nuts; perhaps they're right.

I have voice mail on my phone. I get messages regularly, but I haven't had any for a long time asking me to navigate an ocean passage. I guess no one needs an old celestial navigator. With GPS and all the rest of the electronic wonders available now, a twelve-year-old could successfully navigate around the world. That must be the reason I don't get the calls anymore—yup, that's it; electronics has done me in; that's got to be it.

In truth, that's partly it. The other part is that I now occupy geezer status, so besides being an obsolete celestial navigator, I'm obsolete. That's all right. I'm going to continue to check my voice mail anyway—just in case. I'm ready.

AN OLDER VIEW

It's a pity, I think,
As the years drift on by,
That life becomes viewed
Through maturity's eye.

Three score and four
Have slid under my keel,
And I find myself slowly
Less able to feel

The silly and wild
Anticipation of youth;
More measured, more cautious
More concerned with the truth.

Time, as all know
Weathers badly the face.
But what of the spirit,
Why must it keep pace

Can't I reach in my soul
To a dim distant past,
Where the flush of each sunrise
Was a thrill that would last?

The uncluttered beauty;
The pure expectation:
Where went the child
Of laughing elation?

GOD?

It is a tenant of faith among most of the religious of the world that all events are part of a grand design. From the blossoming in spring of a tiny wild flower to the cataclysmic clashing of nations, everything that happens occurs as part of a master plan, controlled, or allowed to unfold, by power or permission of a higher being. The nature of that being is considered a mystery, and belief in Him/Her is dependent on faith. There is, of course, nothing wrong with faith. Much in our lives is driven by faith. We don't understand the world around us, other than to understand that it is very complex. We accept on faith that the sun will rise each morning; that the love of our loved ones will persist; that the union of sperm and egg brings life and with it a unique, unmatched human being; and that we are capable of thought, although we can neither see nor measure thought, or for that matter, adequately define it.

Faith is wonderful, and if left alone it is perhaps enough to sustain spirituality. But man, in his never-ending quest for truth, attempts to define God, and in so doing unhinges the delicate bridge faith gives us to spirituality.

I am a product of a Catholic education begun in the '40s. Those were the "good old days" when authority was respected, kids obeyed, crime was something only rarely read about in the paper, and religion solved all problems.

I recall three things the good nuns drilled into our little Catholic heads. One, God loves us all, like a benevolent father; two, it was a mortal sin to question the existence of God and the fundamental teachings of the church as revealed by God through His disciples, including Peter's duly designated successor, the Pope; and three, that the only path to salvation was through the Catholic Church. That's a heavy load for a little kid, and at some point it began to bother me. I don't honestly recall how old I was when I began to question (a euphemism for doubt and probably not clever enough to immunize me from eternal damnation). I suppose it was early in high school. I was particularly troubled by the prohibition against questioning. "Always question," Sister Alvera, the science teacher, told us; that is the scientific way and the path to truth. How come we can't question religion; are they hiding something? We can't question because we must accept our religion on faith was the reply. That seems a bit circular and self-serving, and I didn't buy it. If God created all of us, and loves us all as His children, how come He singles out one sect (Catholics) for salvation, to the exclusion of all others, many of whom worship Him in good faith, and many others of good faith who know nothing of the Catholic Church because of geographic isolation. I seriously questioned that bit of nonsense. It wasn't long before I became an agnostic.

If God is so good, and loves us so much, like a father, how come He lets things like the Holocaust occur? How can He allow a million men, women, and children to be shot and hacked to death in Rwanda? How can he allow tens of thousands of His children to be slaughtered by the Janjaweed in Darfur? The answer is that these events are part of His master plan, and we don't need to understand it. Huh? What kind of sense does that make? It doesn't answer the question; rather it sounds like a copout. Richard Dawkins said, rightly I think, "One of the truly bad effects of religion is that it teaches us that it is a virtue to be satisfied with not understanding." The traditional Christian definition of God creates another problem for me. God, we are told, is the Unmoved Mover. He is not a being that possesses attributes such as goodness, love, and power—He *is* those things: goodness, love, power, and more. To possess an attribute implies a quantity of that attribute, therefore, a finite limit. God has no limits; therefore, God is all things, and nothing can exist without God, and nothing exists that is not God. If that's true, I asked a young Jesuit instructor in college, how can there be evil? If you accept the premise that nothing exists that is not God, and that evil exists, it follows that God is evil as well as good. How can that be? Simple, was the reply. St. Augustine had the same question in the fourth century, and he resolved it by concluding that evil is not a thing, but rather the absence of good, just as darkness is the absence of light. We are punished, therefore, not for evil, but for the omission of good. We don't go to hell for murder; we go to hell for failing to not murder.

I have real trouble with this. It smacks of an attempt to explain away the obvious. Genocide and the murders of 3,000 innocent people on 9/11 are not the absence of good; they are the face of evil. Evil does indeed exist in a world where, by definition of God, it cannot.

But this is only the tip of the questioning iceberg. There is something even more fundamental that troubles me greatly. But before I go on, let me state that I do not deny the existence of God; although I think it is likely He doesn't exist, and I don't see how our definition of God is consistent with the facts.

We are taught that God has no beginning and no end and that He created the cosmos and that his greatest creation is man whom He formed in His own image and likeness. We are told that God is knowledge, and power, and love and that he loves all mankind and that all He demands is that we love Him back and obey His rules. Why? If there is a force so great as to have no beginning and no end and so powerful as to be able to create the enormity and complexity of life, how is it that He needs our love and adoration? How is it that He needs anything we can give Him? How is it that He needs anything at all?

And what about the human condition? The world is full of suffering and unfairness and cruelty, as well as love and beauty. We journey along our rocky path and the only guideposts are those set up by our religious beliefs. If we follow these and lead a "good" life, we will be rewarded in the end with heaven, which is being with God. But, if we reject the proper path, we are condemned to eternal damnation to suffer the absence of God. Why? What's the point of this all-powerful, supreme being toying with His creatures, causing them pain and suffering and constantly testing their loyalty? It almost seems that this being needs something from us, and if this is true, He isn't really a supreme being because there is something He lacks, specifically, our loyalty and love. In other words, the definition of God doesn't square with the reality of our existence. The myth of the Garden of Eden and the fall from paradise further complicates the dilemma. The myth of the Garden harbors an inconsistency, because God, by definition, needs nothing, including our obedience. It seems to me that it's easier to imagine an Eden where there are no wrong decisions, where God has truly created a world in His image and likeness, full of love and goodness, and devoid of that which is incompatible with Him—evil.

Does that mean there is no God? I don't know. It does mean that God as we know Him is our creation. Look at the two Gods in the Bible. The God of the Old Testament is vicious, unforgiving, small-minded, homophobic, homicidal, racist, genocidal, and paranoid. But the God of the New Testament is a bit more mellow. Which one is it? It means that we really don't know who or what God is. I am perplexed by the Aristotelian argument for God as the "Unmoved Mover" and that all actions that occur in the universe are caused by previous actions in the universe. That linkage seems to stop with God, because He is the Unmoved Mover. As Voltaire pointed out, those two statements are contradictory. Put another way, our universe is so complex, a higher force had to have created it. The logical succession of that argument is that the higher force that created it (God) is so complex that a higher force must have created it. Of course, the argument goes on ridiculously to infinity. What we have done by using God to explain our universe is substitute one mystery for another.

It seems fair to say that there is a force in the cosmos, and an argument for that might indeed be in its complexity and order, although chaos also seems to be part of our existence. I have trouble when man anthropomorphizes that force to create a supreme creature in man's own image and likeness. So what's really behind creation? Let's just say it's a mystery. I am honest enough to say I don't have the answer. But I refuse to make one up just to explain what I don't understand.

Where does this leave us? Spirituality and the practice of some sort of religious belief seem to be a part of the psyche of man, probably because no matter what tribal unit or culture man exists in, his need to explain his existence, and the world around him, has caused him to create a force greater than himself to satisfy that explanation. His need to bring order to the species and ensure its future existence has caused him to shift the mystery that surrounds him to a mystery in the sky with not a bit more insight.

Millions of human beings have been killed over the millennia in the name of God, and extremists today murder in God's name. Blaise Pascal put it succinctly when he said, "Men never do evil so completely and cheerfully as when they do it from religious conviction." So is religion a positive force in life? Is the practice of religion a good thing? It can be, but I'm inclined to believe that in the grand scheme of things, religion is not the positive force we think it is. Do people in general need religion? Many think they do. The problem is that religion really has less to do with God than it has to do with a hierarchical structure of men who anoint themselves with the power to tell us what God thinks.

I have no quarrel with religion, although I have a quarrel with how it is often practiced, and I certainly have no quarrel with God, if there is one. I have a quarrel with, and sympathy for, those who are blinded by faith. I saw a news clip of a man in New Jersey looking at the rubble of what was his home following Hurricane Sandy. He said, "God was good to us. He spared us." If vandals had destroyed his home but left him and his family unharmed, would he have said they were good to him, or would he be mad as hell and want them prosecuted? Why isn't he mad at God for destroying his home? My quarrel is with any religion that claims it is the only path to salvation, and my quarrel is with those who confuse faith with fact, then condemn all who don't think as they do. Charles Bernard Renouvier, the nineteenth century French philosopher wrote, "There is no certainty; there are only people who are certain."

GOING HOME

I don't believe you can't go home. No offense, Mr. Wolfe. You're a very bright fellow and a marvelous writer, but not everything you said is true, at lease in my case, and I would like to make a case for my case.

Fifty-six years ago my father bought two and a half acres of land, rich with pine, red oak, and poplar, on the Upper Eau Claire Lake, in a remote area of northwest Wisconsin called Barnes. He paid $600 for the property and in 1938 put up a two-bedroom log cabin with a huge living room and split rock fireplace. I was about four then, but I have small flashes of memory about those early days, like fireflies in the night. I remember walking across the subfloor one golden summer afternoon before the log walls were up. I remember later after it was finished, that great, grand living room with log rafters from which hung what seemed to me to be the largest oxen yoke ever made. I remember that beautiful split rock fireplace with the bluish-green "man in the moon" face cemented in the center, high above the heavy oak mantle.

"The cottage," or "The Lake," as we called it, was my parents' summer getaway. We lived about fifty miles to the north, in Superior, and escaping to The Lake on weekends was their way of keeping balance.

As a youngster I spent long, marvelous hours on the water in an 18-foot mahogany rowboat named *Kitty Foy* after my paternal grandmother. I was not allowed out of sight, but the spirit of Magellan burned in my soul, so the rule was breached at every opportunity; grownups don't understand those things. How I loved that boat. There weren't many cottages on the lake then, and the number of permanent residents there wouldn't have filled a small car. Wherever I rowed (the old Johnson 6 hp outboard died when I was about seven) I fancied myself a Viking, rowing for the first time to the stark, deserted shores of North America. The inlet under the little bridge led to a lily pad pond then to a mysterious canal connecting the Upper Eau Clair Lake to Birch Lake then Robinson Lake. Things don't get much more exciting than that.

To a young mind aching with curiosity, the woods surrounding the cabin were as full of mystery and intrigue as any described by the Brothers Grimm. Wandering through them for hours watching the birds, squirrels, and occasional deer captured me totally and helped cement forever the emotional bond I have with that place.

A call came one August morning in 1941 from the Forest Ranger in Minong, informing my mother that the cabin had been struck by lightning during a particularly violent thunderstorm the night before. The nearest fire equipment was twenty-five miles away, and by the time it arrived in the dark of that violent night, the cabin had burned to the ground. Only the rain kept the surrounding woods from being destroyed. Later that day we drove to The Lake to see if it was really true or just a cruel joke. I'll never forget the sight of my mother sobbing quietly and the emptiness I felt when I saw nothing left but smoldering ashes and the black skeletons of the stove and icebox. The fireplace stood, but was mortally wounded, and the man in the moon had vaporized, leaving a charred, grotesque indentation where it once was.

This happened right before the war, and by the next spring when rebuilding was to have begun, materials were frozen. Dad fixed up the large room over the boathouse so we could use it until the forces of good overcame the forces of evil and we could build a proper place.

It was 1948 when he rebuilt the cabin. I was thirteen then, and during the winter of '47-'48, I took a shop course in the eighth grade. Naturally, by that summer I knew all there was to know about drafting, architecture, structural engineering, etc., so I drew the plans for a new cottage, submitted them to my father, and was astonished when they were accepted with only minor modification. John Desrosiers, a "local" who could do nearly anything with a trowel, hammer, and saw, was hired to build the place, and in short order it was up. This cottage was different from the original. Instead of logs, it was built of conventional materials and half-log siding. The new fireplace, like the old, was made of split rock, but my old friend, the man in the moon, was sadly missing. The biggest change was indoor plumbing with hot and cold running water. No more outhouse and hand pump. We had slid, courtesy of the REA, into the twentieth century, and perhaps lost a little in the doing. In an effort to stay connected to the north woods, the interior walls and ceiling were all finished in knotty pine.

As I grew from boyhood to near manhood, spending most weekends at The Lake with family and friends, I continued to explore in the *Kitty Foy*, a little further afield each year. I planted trees and watched them grow, trees that are still there, strong, tall, and peaceful as sleep. I knew where all the good fishing spots were, and some secret places I feel obliged not to discuss even now. The Lake had become a part of my soul.

In 1955 I met Marilyn, also from Superior, and in 1958, after navy preflight training in Pensacola, Florida, we were married. Much of our courtship was spent at The Lake, and in the process it captured her as it had me.

Jobs have kept us living more than a thousand miles from The Lake since 1958, but we have raised two kids who know it and love it, because each summer, no matter what, all accumulated vacation time has been spent there.

In 1977 while we were there, our daughter met the nephew of some old friends who were among the few permanent residents there. It was love at first eye flutter, and two years later they were married. Although they too now live far from Barnes, the family connection to The Lake has been strengthened by their union.

Now we have grandchildren—Brad, our daughter's child, and Katie, our son's. It's no accident that their parents bring them to The Lake at every opportunity. Their little minds are being filled with the sweet intoxication of that place, and I feel the gentle warmth that thoughts of succession bring.

I write this from The Lake. This morning a small red squirrel chased a big gray up a tree and across the branches to another. Later, a pileated woodpecker drummed a new hole in a nearby poplar, and early this afternoon two magnificent bald eagles glided by a few feet above the water out front, fishing. A few moments ago the mournful tremolo of a distant loon floated through my open window on warm afternoon air.

Yes, Mr. Wolfe, you can go home—I am home.

NO CRITICAL THINKING

In early June of this year, the Texas Republican delegation met in Ft. Worth to approve their 2012 platform, parts of which zero in on the state's educational system. In the platform they oppose the teaching of "higher order thinking skills" which teach and encourage critical thinking. The platform argued that critical thinking might challenge "students' fixed beliefs" and "undermine parental authority."

I think they have a point. Why would we want our kids to get in the habit of actually questioning a position, weighing it in the face of evidence pro and con, and coming up with a decision? What possible value could that have? Isn't it far better to fill their malleable brains with things we believe? Things like Obama is a Muslim who wants to destroy America. Things like the earth is only 6,000 years old and humans were created intact, as they are today, and evolution is a cruel, left-wing hoax. Things like global warming at the hands of man is another hoax; just trust the coal and oil industries, they'll tell you the truth.

I can imagine critical thinking becoming so dangerous that some people might be persuaded that all races are equal—how ridiculous is that? What if critical thinking resulted in people believing homosexuals were born that way and that they actually have rights, including the right to marry and to be parents? Think how dangerous that sort of thing would be. It would take all the fun out of taunting, bullying, and even killing all those queers, and no good Christian, God-fearing person wants that fun taken away.

Those Republican platform builders, united by a bond of mediocrity, break into a cold Texas sweat at the thought of their issue ever accepting science over the ranting of a preacher in cowboy boots and a ten-gallon hat, whose credentials are a certificate from a mail-order Bible school in Mississippi and a diploma from a Texas high school where the Texas School Board has banned any reference to Darwin or the fact that condoms actually prevent pregnancy,

Better to tell our kids quaint stories like the one about the fifteen-year-old virgin who got knocked up by a ghost while engaged to a much older carpenter. In order to protect her from scandal, the carpenter decided to hide her. But while he was thinking about it, a spirit appeared to him in a dream and told him his fiancé's pregnancy was OK, so he bought it, and life went on. Nine months later she gave birth to a boy. Here's where it gets complicated. Turns out the boy is part of a trio, including the ghost who got his mother pregnant, that is described as both one entity and three at the same time (if you find that irrational, the explanation is that it's a mystery—get over it). So, technically, the virgin was knocked up by her own son. By the way, she remained a virgin even after giving birth. I'm not sure why that's important. You certainly wouldn't want any youngster questioning that little tale, and that's precisely what critical thinking might lead to.

Here's another story you don't want your kids to question or challenge. There is this 600-year-old guy who has a wife and three sons with wives. The story doesn't say what gym the guy belonged to, or how he ate, or what medical plan he was on, but it must have been spectacular to be 600 years old; I'm impressed. A spirit, the same one or ones who pulled off the stunt with the virgin, says to the guy that he should build a boat, called an ark, about 450 feet long and seventy-five feet wide, roughly the size of a small freighter. The spirit says he's going to destroy the earth with a huge flood and that the guy and his family should gather two by two (male and female) every creature on earth, along with food for everybody (that some creatures dine on others wasn't mentioned in the story). Now that's a pretty tall order. There is wide disagreement among scientists as to how many species of land animals exist on earth, but many believe it's around 7.7 million, give or take a few million. The story of the ark takes place thousands of years ago when the only means of transportation was the ass, (which members of the Texas Republican delegation can identify with), the horse, the camel, or very slow sailing vessels. Most of the world was unknown. Despite this, as the story goes, the guy and his small family were able to go to every corner of the earth. (I say corner because the earth was flat then—the Bible says so—but that changed, and now it's round). They gathered all the species of animals, two by two, including a bat the size of a raspberry, found only in the foothills of the Andes, and every one (two by two) of the approximately 750,000 species of insects, and brought them all back to the ark, along with food for everyone. Imagine how hard that would be today even with modern transportation and GPS, and yet they did it with only eight people. According to the story, the rains came "on the seventeenth day of the second month." The ark floated aimlessly because it had no means of propulsion. On the seventeenth day of the seventh month, as the waters receded, the ark came to rest on a mountaintop. But the guy, his wife, his three sons, and their wives, and all those animals stayed aboard until the spirit told them to go ashore on the twenty-seventh day of the second month, one year and ten days after they all went aboard the ark. Wow, I wonder what it smelled like on the ark. Besides the smell from the animals and humans, there was a year's worth of food for eight adults and fifteen million animals, with no refrigeration.

That's an even bigger whopper than the story about the virgin, and it's part of the "fixed beliefs" the Republican delegation doesn't want kids to challenge. Why? Because they're afraid. As long as man has existed, he has created myths as a bridge between the world he understands and that which he doesn't understand. From those myths comes religion. All religions are based on myths. Myths in a religious context give us great comfort because they create a roadmap to explain the inexplicable. That they are untrue is irrelevant. They are believed and they give comfort, and that's all that matters. As man has progressed through the eons, and his knowledge of the world and universe around him has increased, some of these myths have toppled in the face of reason and discovery. The important thing is that as we see more and more rational explanations for the world around us, the world that used to frighten us, we no longer need to rely on myths to explain that which we don't understand. The ancients believed that when the sun began to grow dark in stages during the middle of the day, it was a sun-eating dragon that was responsible. That was their myth to explain something they didn't comprehend. Today we call it an eclipse, and we know how it works. We know there is a logical explanation for everything; we haven't found all those explanations yet, but we know all phenomena in the universe have rational explanations. There are, however, some who can't bear to have their myths challenged because they lack the capacity to understand the truths that evaporate those myths or the capacity to understand that all things have a rational explanation, or, and probably most important, they cannot bear the emotional devastation of being wrong. Rocking the belief boat is terrifying for them. That's why the Texas Republican delegation doesn't want "students' fixed beliefs" challenged.

DREAMS

I dream a lot—I always have.
Dreams, like tiny creatures flitting to and fro,
Silhouetted in the dusk of evening sky,
Swarm around the secret places of my mind
Bringing sweet memory of things past,
And sweet anticipation of things yet to be.
Among the past and yet to be
Are memories and thoughts of you,
Soft and gentle,
Caressing my heart and soul.
And as they do the little creatures of my dreams
Become fireflies, jewels of the night,
Jewels because they are of you.
I love you now and evermore.

FIVE DOLLARS
A Short Story

Mike Corrigan's life was a mess. His company had been bought by a huge corporation, and the new company didn't need two directors of IT, so Mike was downsized. Downsized—what a stupid word. He was fired. He fell into a deep funk. Although he knew that losing his job had nothing to do with anything he had done, it still hurt, and it was humiliating.

Then, two months later, Maureen, Mike's wife of fourteen years, announced that she had made a huge mistake fourteen years ago and didn't want to be married anymore. He hadn't seen it coming. Sure, there were some lumps in their marriage, but then all marriages have lumps. It's something you work through, and you move along. But divorce...he was devastated and confused. Maureen had asked him to leave, and in a state of numbness he agreed. Later, with his lean six-foot frame slouched in a worn, overstuffed chair in the tiny, broken-down apartment he rented, he thought, "Why should I have to leave my home when it's she who wants out?" But it didn't matter; Mike was too exhausted to fight. Maybe later, but not now.

The days passed, and Mike began to realize if anything was going to happen in his life to make it better, it was up to him to make it happen. He began networking, sending out resumes, and searching the trade journals. He would find another job, he felt certain of that, but it might take some time. Meanwhile, he tried to reason with Maureen, but she was determined to end their marriage. Mike didn't think there was another guy, so why? Had the entire fourteen years been a lie? Had she been seething with discontent, even hatred, all those years? He didn't understand. Perhaps he never would.

Maureen, tall, slender, beautiful, and accomplished, hadn't wanted children; Mike did, but she was adamant, so they didn't have any. Mike felt that you can't successfully raise kids when one parent doesn't want the role, so the "no" always has to trump. Now here he was—no job, no wife, and no kids. Mike Corrigan, big, strong, athletic, intelligent Mike Corrigan, with soft blue eyes and thick brown hair, at the age of forty-two, in the prime of his life, was a mess.

Two years passed, and during the course of that time Mike found a job, a very good job as a matter of fact, better than the one he lost, and he moved into a decent condo. His divorce was behind him and wasn't as messy as he anticipated. All their assets, his and Maureen's, were evenly divided, including the equity from the sale of the house. He hasn't spoken to her since that final day in court, and there's no reason to ever speak to her again. The initial shock and pain have largely faded, and he understands that in some perverse way she may have done him a favor, because after she announced she wanted out, he saw a side of her that he had been blinded to, a side he didn't much like. So on balance, the mess that was his life has evolved into a stable, comfortable existence, albeit a bit lonely.

It was a clear, warm, sunny Saturday in April when Mike decided to do his weekly grocery shopping. He had always been a good cook, so the transition to bachelorhood, on the culinary level at least, was a breeze. He hated having to shop on Saturday because of the crowds, but he hated even more doing it after work when he was usually exhausted. The market was particularly crowded this Saturday, mostly women, many with kids, and a few old couples.

He completed his list, and found a checkout line a little shorter than the others. The woman directly in front of him, second in line, was a particularly attractive late-thirties mother with a little girl around nine or ten. Mom had her long blond hair in a ponytail stuck through the hole in the back of a Baltimore Orioles baseball cap. She was tall and lean, with a kind face and intelligent eyes. The little girl was clearly her daughter, with the same comfortable face, beautiful eyes, and a smile full of sunlight as she stole glances at Mike. Both mother and daughter carried themselves with dignity, but there was something just a little off. They looked, well, just a little shabby.

When it came mom's turn to check out, she had just a few things, all basic: milk, bread, eggs, chicken, some vegetables, two potatoes, an onion, etc.

"That's $36.72," said the pimple-faced kid at the cash register. Mom dug into a slightly battered purse from which she pulled two ten dollar bills and a fistful of ones, which she began to carefully lay out on the counter, counting slightly above a whisper as she did so.

"Thirty, thirty-one, thirty-two, thirty-three." Then she stopped. She had no more ones, and apparently no more money. Her face flushed with embarrassment. "I, ah I'm sorry. I guess I'm a little short. I'll put something back."

Mike acted impulsively, and without even thinking he said, "Hey, we all run short from time to time. Here, take this." He offered a five-dollar bill.

"Oh I couldn't..."

"No, please," Mike interrupted. "It's only a five, and you can help someone else next time you're in line and the person ahead comes up short. Please take it. It's not a problem."

Slowly the woman reached for the money, and looking Mike directly in the eyes, she smiled and said very quietly, "Thank you."

Two Saturdays later Mike was back at the market, searching for the molasses, when he saw the mom and daughter at the end of the aisle. He approached them. "Hi. Nice to see you again."

She looked puzzled for just a moment then smiled. "Hi. Thank you again for what you did. That was very kind. I want to give you your five dollars back," she said as she reached into her purse.

"No, please. I don't want it back. Consider it a small gift to a damsel in distress."

"Well then, let me at least buy you a cup of coffee," she said with a firm level of insistence.

"Fair enough. Coffee would be wonderful."

They checked out, put their groceries in their cars, and met at a small coffee shop next to the market. Her name was Barbara McClarren. Her husband, a successful engineer, packed his bags one Saturday morning three years ago, announced he was leaving the marriage, and disappeared. He had quit his job the week before. Neither she, nor his friends or family have heard from him; he just disappeared. She had been a stay-at-home mom with a degree in economics; now she was forced suddenly to get back into the job market. She did, eventually, but with a short job history and a large gap when she stayed home, her resume was a little thin; good jobs were hard to find. She finally landed a low-paying office job. Meanwhile, she lost the house and was forced to move with her daughter, Katie, into a low-rent apartment. It had been a struggle these last three years, but she was making it, and she had started night classes to earn her master's. Katie, who was nine, was a very bright, gentle child with a quick wit and a giving nature.

Something happened that day in the coffee shop, something Mike never believed possible; he and Barbara connected. It was almost as if they had known each other for years. They agreed to meet again, all three of them. The meetings became dates, and after a year or so, Mike knew he was in love, and he knew Barbara was too. They married on June 3. It was a small, quiet wedding, just family and a few close friends, but it was beautiful, and it had a feeling of permanence.

One year later, on June 3, their first anniversary, Mike awakened early. He was going to fix breakfast for Barbara and serve it to her in bed. He crept out of bed, carefully avoiding waking her, and went into the kitchen. There on the kitchen table was a small gift-wrapped package with a card taped to it bearing his name. He opened the package. It was a crisp, new five-dollar bill set in a beautiful wooden frame. Below the bill was an inscription: "Here are the first five of the million reasons I love you. All my love, Barbara."

LIFE LIST

I was reading the Sunday *New York Times* recently when I came across a piece in the Sunday Styles section about life lists. Life list—what's a life list? So I read the piece. I quickly learned that I may be the only person on the planet who has never heard of a life list. A life list, as you undoubtedly know, is a list of things you want to do before you die—a bucket list. It never occurred to me to actually list the things I want to do before I die. That somehow seems so, so anal. The piece told about a preschool teacher in Salem, Oregon, named Rachael Hubbard, who has a life list of seventy-eight items, including build a house for Habitat for Humanity, read *Pride and Prejudice*, earn a master's degree, and become quadrilingual. Wow, that's heavy-duty, but then she's only twenty-four.

I got to thinking about life lists, and it led me, of course, to review my own life which, up to this point, has been blissfully devoid of lists. When the full impact of this delinquency landed on me, I found myself awash with guilt and shame. I've never had a life list, I thought. I've never even heard of a life list. Does that mean I have no focus, no ambition, no master plan, no goals? Am I just a worthless, lazy lout— life listless? Has everything I've done so far been nothing more than a series of happy accidents, recklessly un-driven by a list? Then I began to sweat. What if my friends and family find out I've navigated a little over seven decades without a list, without goals? Will they ever speak to me again? Will I be ostracized from society with a scarlet tattoo on my forehead—NLL: No Life List? Now the sweating turned to trembling and fear. I've got to do something, I thought. I've got to extricate myself from the morass I've built by neglect. I'll make a life list, and I'll let everyone know I have one, but they can't know this is my first, so I'll number each goal starting with seventy-two. When they ask what the first seventy-one goals were, I'll be casually vague, emphasizing that it isn't so much what you've done, but what you plan to do. That's the very soul of a life list. It's more about the list than the accomplishments. But I'll have to be careful. If I include the simple and mundane they'll wonder why those weren't part of the first seventy-one items on the list. Of course I'll have to include those important things I haven't already done. But there's a problem. I'm not sure I can think of any important things I haven't done. I'm not sure I can think of seventy-one important things I have done in my life. I'm not even sure I've even done fifteen. OK, don't panic, think. The first seventy-one items don't all have to be important. The whole point of a life list is to lay out those things you want to do, not the things you have to do. The have-to-dos are the important things; the want-to-dos can be silly or important. Ah, that puts it in better focus. Now I think I've got the hang of it. All right, let's see what we can come up with:

72. Spend two weeks in Manhattan doing nothing but visiting restaurants, pubs, art galleries, the theatre, the Met, and spend some quiet time at the Algonquin Hotel introducing my muse to the ghosts of Dorothy Parker, Alexander Wolcott, Robert Benchley, Harold Ross, Robert Sherwood, and the rest of the round table gang.

73. Visit Ireland again, this time with a driver. Driving in Ireland scared the hell out of me. Same for the restaurants and pubs, but scratch the art galleries and theatre and add a couple of castles.

74. Visit the Andalusia region of Spain again. Ditto restaurants and pubs, and add bull fights, sherry distilleries, and swimming in the Med.

75. Visit Bangkok. Once again, food, but add orangutans, long-tail boats, and ancient ruins.

76. Learn to scuba dive.

77. Take courses at the CIA (Culinary Institute of America).

78. Drive a Formula 1 race car.

79. Take a balloon ride.

80. Take a glider ride again.

81. Do more cooking with my granddaughter.

OK, there's a list of ten. I'll add to it as time goes by, but it's a decent start, and I think it will impress my family and friends. They will now see that I actually have a plan; I have goals; I'm grounded and focused, unlike the loose cannon nare-do-well they might have found me out to be had they discovered I had no life list. The pressure is off.

You will notice that none of the items on my list is substantive. None holds the promise of real accomplishment. None will get me nominated for the MacArthur Award or a Pulitzer Prize. That's all right. A little lack of substance in one's life from time to time is the stuff that gives it spice.

MORALITY

How do moral concepts become established in a society? Does religion inform morals? How are religions established? It is commonly accepted that a nation which strongly adheres to religious principles is a nation with a settled, functional, moral society. What religious principles? It may be useful here to examine what Joseph Campbell, the renowned mythologist and philosopher, has to say about religion. All religions, throughout the history of mankind, and in every society, arise from myths. Myths, he says, are the stories developed in a society to act as an interface between what can be known and what is unknowable. Myths are a society's guideposts to help it understand that which cannot be understood. How did we as a species get here? How did the universe come to be? Who or what is the force of nature? So the myths a society develops to explain that which we cannot know through our senses or reason become the bedrock of that society's religion. It is remarkable how societies existing in vastly different times or places, societies who have had no contact with one another, develop astonishingly similar myths. The virgin birth exists in societies predating the birth of Christ and in societies that have never heard of Christ. In his book, *The Hero with a Thousand Faces*, Campbell points out a common thread running through the myths of vastly divergent societies. That is, the appearance of a "hero" or savior, his subsequent violent death to save the society from ruin, followed by his ascendance into another world, or the spirit world. This is an important point. Campbell, rightly I think, attributes these similarities to the fact that all human beings, no matter what their race, or when they lived, are more similar psychologically, intellectually, and physiologically than they are different. So we tend to come up with the same or similar myths to explain that which we hunger to know, but never can in an empirical way.

It is probably useful at this point to define morality. The common definition is the quality of the rightness or wrongness of an action. This can be a bit misleading. A "right" action for an embezzler is to embezzle as much money as possible from a victim, then get away with his crime. But is that moral? Hardly. Right, in moral terms, refers not to the self, but to the larger society we live in. That is, does the right action positively or negatively affect society? In the case of the embezzler, his personally ordained "right" action negatively impacts the society he is a part of; therefore, it is not moral. This discussion may seem painfully obvious, but it is central to any discussion of morality.

Are all commonly held truths always true? Any discussion of morality is, in the end, nothing more than man's attempt to articulate his higher behavior in rational terms. Those with a religious bent will say that all morality flows from God—their God, of course, and they are certain of it. Voltaire said, "Doubt is not a pleasant condition, but certainty is absurd." He also said, "If God did not exist, it would be necessary to invent him." In terms of morality, I don't think it really matters if God is real or created. Man has always managed somehow to devise a workable moral model. Here now, is the crux of morality. Man's existence as a species is only assured so long as he devises a workable moral code; otherwise, he would wipe himself out.

Aristotle thought that morality was the subordination of senses and lower tendencies to rational rule and principle. This is a powerful argument, and it is consistent with the Golden Rule as a source of common sense morality. Now here's where it gets really interesting. Joseph Campbell in his books *The Power of Myth* and *The Hero with a Thousand Faces* beautifully demonstrates that disparate cultures, many existing before the birth of Christ, worshiping a variety of gods, and separated by geography or time, almost always devise a code of conduct similar to the Golden Rule. This supports Aristotle's argument about morality, which was expressed more than 300 years before the birth of Christ. Aristotle also said that the higher good for man is not in the moral life, but in "the theoretical inquiry and contemplation of truth." That's a seductive argument for anyone possessed of the two traits necessary for a writer or scientist—curiosity and objectivity. Although Aristotle separated morality and truth, it seems to me you cannot have truth without morality, nor morality without truth.

In a 2005 article by Gregory S. Paul published in the *Journal of Religion and Society*, a publication of Creighton University, a Jesuit University, Paul reports on a study done to see if there is a correlation between religiosity and social dysfunction. Religiosity, for the purposes of the study, was defined as a measure of absolute belief in God, literal belief in the Bible, attendance at worship services, regular prayer, and a rejection of evolution. Social dysfunction was measured by homicide rates, STD rates, teenage pregnancy, juvenile mortality, and juvenile suicide.

Sixteen prosperous developed democracies and one second-world democracy (Portugal) were studied. The results were remarkable. Japan, Scandinavia, and France have the lowest rates of religiosity, but they also have the lowest rates of social dysfunction. The highest rate of religiosity, far higher than any of the other sixteen nations, was in the US. But the US also had the highest rates of social dysfunction. Even when regions of the US were compared the same correlation existed. The South and Midwest tend to have higher rates of religiosity than the Northeast. The South and Midwest also have higher rates of social dysfunction than the Northeast.

It may be bad science to draw a causal effect from the data. For example, it could be that those countries with the highest rates of social dysfunction also have the highest rates of religiosity as a reaction to that dysfunction. A lot more work has to be done. But the fact is, there seems to be a clear statistical correlation that tends to debunk the popular belief that religiosity is socially beneficial, that is, that the more religious the nation the more morally stable it is. Another curious finding is that life spans tend to be longer in the more secularized and less religious nations.

Now, consider the question of religion informing moral values from a slightly different point of view. For centuries the church endorsed slavery. Why not? The Bible endorses slavery in multiple passages.

Popes, bishops, and priests had slaves. Our forefathers had slaves. Anyone who was not a slave had slaves. It was part of the culture in all civilized nations and in most that were not. Revered church fathers like Thomas Aquinas and Augustine said that slavery, rather than being intrinsically evil, was part of "natural law." But then in Europe, secular society began to question the morality of slavery around the beginning of the nineteenth century. Later, in the mid-nineteenth century it ended in the US. During this process the church took tentative steps toward a declaration of abolition, but never completely articulated it. It wasn't until 1965, toward the end of the Second Vatican Council, that the church formally denounced slavery. For thousands of years slavery was accepted as natural and moral by the church. So what happened to change that? Nonreligious sectarianism decided it was evil, and the church scrambled to catch up.

One more brief example. The Bible clearly and unequivocally condemns usury, and usury in this case is defined as charging interest on the loan of money. Again, the church fathers resoundingly said usury was contrary to natural law, condemned by the Bible, and thus a sin. Meantime, economies emerged, and it became apparent in the marketplace that charging interest on the loan of money was a legitimate monetary enterprise, beneficial to both the lender and the borrower. The church finally capitulated. Once again it was secular moralists that set the bar, not the church as the earthly representative of God.

So, does religious dogma drive morals, or does a more fluid, sectarian need to exist in harmony with one's fellow man drive morals? When you consider that question, consider the religious dogma of the crusades and the inquisition and the religious dogma of the fundamentalist Islamic jihad. Does religious dogma inform morals in those cases? I guess it depends on how you define morals.

Now we come full circle. In our culture we live generally by a moral model, the Golden Rule, articulated eons before it appeared in the Bible, and similarly defined by thousands of cultures throughout the existence of Homo sapiens. Perhaps the only rational conclusion one can draw from this is that the development of moral principles has less to do with God, real or invented, and more to do with rational human beings developing methods to ensure order in the species, thereby ensuring the survival of the species.

Oh, and lest you think the application of human morality is so complex that something as simple as the Golden Rule cannot rule all of moral behavior, try to think of an instance in human intercourse where its application would not apply or where it would fail. The Golden Rule; so simple, so elegant, so true, so moral, and so human.

BUSH AND MORALS

The pundits, analyzing the presidential election nearly to the point of nausea, have reached a myriad of conclusions. But one thread that seems to run inexorably through the analysis is that the moral right was largely responsible for electing George W. Bush in November because they believe Mr. Bush shares their moral values. Mr. Bush proudly and publically pronounces his faith in God and his deep religious convictions, and from these pronouncements naturally flows the perception that he is a man of high moral values. We have had other presidents so perceived, and when that perception reflects reality, it is a noble thing indeed. But if we're going to talk about morality, we have to define moral. I'm not sure there is an absolute definition of moral, the extreme right notwithstanding. There's also no absolute definition of pornography. But like pornography, we know moral when we see it, and we see Mr. Bush as a moral man.

But there's a disturbing aroma swirling around Mr. Bush's morality. When we scratch the surface, and we don't have to scratch very hard, we find a dark side to Mr. Bush's moral underpinning, and the examples are numerous. He sat silently as a high-level official in the Justice Department, Roberto Gonzales, wrote questionable memos sanctioning the use of torture on Islamic detainees. And Mr. Bush sanctioned detainees' indefinite detention without due process. Mr. Gonzales characterized the Geneva Conventions as "quaint and outdated." Now Mr. Gonzales is about to become Mr. Bush's attorney general. Last fall, Senators John McCain and Joe Lieberman wrote an unambiguous statement regarding torture and interrogation: "No prisoner shall be subject to torture or cruel, inhumane or degrading treatment or punishment that is prohibited by the Constitution, laws or treaties of the United States." That language was included in an intelligence bill. However, the language was dropped from the bill after Condoleezza Rice wrote a letter saying, "it (the language) provides legal protections to foreign prisoners to which they are not now entitled." She is now Mr. Bush's secretary of state. If, by strict legal definition, foreign detainees who represent no established government aren't entitled to legal protections or due process as Rice and Gonzales claim, does that make it moral to torture them or detain them indefinitely without hearings? Is anything you do that's legal automatically moral? Is God's law superseded by Caesar's law?

Mr. Bush has eased smokestack emission standards for industry. He has eased clean water standards. He has eased logging restrictions in our national forests. He has run up the largest deficit in the history of our nation. He promoted and pushed through Congress a questionable drug program for senior citizens shortly before the election but failed to provide the funds to implement it. He vigorously pushed for No Child Left Behind legislation but failed to push for funds to implement it. Is all of this moral? Doesn't Mr. Bush have a moral obligation to be a good steward of this nation?

Mr. Bush told the American people that Saddam Hussein was an immediate threat and linked to the 9/11 terrorist attack, when it was patently untrue (Mr. Cheney still won't concede). Is that moral? Is it moral to declare war on another nation for reasons other than self-defense or the defense of another and, as commander in chief, to squander the lives of nearly 1,500 American servicemen and women as well as many thousands more noncombatant Iraqis?

One has to ask oneself, what is George W. Bush's definition of moral? Does Mr. Bush have a special definition? Does he know moral when he sees it? And when you and I see torture, degradation of the environment and the economy, and the war in Iraq, do we see that as moral?

I have a question for those of you who are good, decent, religious people who voted to give George W. Bush a second term. When you worship in your church, or temple, or mosque, and pray to God for the guidance to understand what is right, and the grit to do the right and moral thing, does any of Mr. Bush's behavior bother you, and if not, have you asked yourself why?

I make no pretense at being religious, but I know moral when I see it, and when I see Mr. Bush's morals, it troubles me.

SHIP'S LOG
SAILING VESSEL *BOLERO*
FT. LAUDERDALE TO ST. CROIX

January 13, 1996

0725 - Leave the bulkhead at Ft. Lauderdale. It's clear and cool with a northwest wind at 8 knots. We've slipped the lines on a beautiful morning. Mel had to leave us, so we're down to five hearty souls, eager for wind and warmth.

0823 - At sea buoy PL to meet the photographer who is on his way.

1023 - It's blowing up to 35 knots and we're blasting along from 9.5 to 12 knots—what a ride. Flying the main and staysail.

1400 - We're nearly abeam Great Isaac Light. It was a spirited ride for a while—winds to 45 knots and large, lumpy seas. Things have calmed down a lot, but we are still doing 9+ knots. A fine blue water vessel. The crew is holding up rather well. A touch of seasickness, but that will soon pass. By this time tomorrow we will all be well settled in.

We passed Great Isaac Light at 1410 and bore off for Great Stirrup Cay, then Bridge Pt., Eleuthera, and a final heading change for Puerto Rico.

January 14, 1996

We've fallen into a rather natural and relaxed watch. All hands are well and up to speed, unlike the weatherfax and compass light. Such is life at sea, a constant contest between people and things. If you do it right, people win.

We passed Bridge Pt., Eleuthera, at 0406. The seas are down, wind fresh, and sailing is beautiful at around 9 knots.

Vernie fixed a proper breakfast this morning, which raised spirits, renewed hopes, and infused the crew with energy and optimism. The weather is perfect. We're beam reaching on port at 8.5+ knots, 15–20 knots apparent wind, yankee, staysail, and main flying—wonderful.

At 1030 we have about 675 miles to Puerto Rico. Our first day's run was 227 miles.

1200 - Noon to noon distance 221 miles.

January 15, 1996

1340 - Dipped engine tank, 2/3 full. Pumped fuel from lower tank until dry—filled engine tank. Transfer fuel from upper tank to lower.

It was a spirited night last night, lots of air, close hauled with yankee, staysail, and main. A tack around 2300 set us back a bit, but no real harm done.

Noon to noon 225 miles.

Vernie fixed a lovely roast duck dinner, the skipper had a wee touch of cough syrup, and all was well with the world.

Today we're still close hauled with main and staysail only. 25–30 knots of wind and close hauled, *Bolero* is riding very well.

January 16, 1996

Since 0430 it's been blowing stink, 35–47 knots. We're beating. The crew is not so sure sailing is all that much fun. The seas are very lumpy, and *Bolero* is being pounded hard. She seems up to it, except every port leaks, and it is a condition of constant wet below. We passed Grand Turk Island a little before noon. Our noon to noon today was 181 miles.

We will, of course, get there eventually; it's just that time hangs slow living under these conditions.

Gunther has been on the helm for hours; the consummate master taking care of his vessel.

January 17, 1996

This is our fifth day at sea and a lot more pleasant than the last. Yesterday was one of those days that make you think you will never go to sea again, but you know you will and today confirms it.

We blew out the staysail around 0400 this morning. The leach line somehow caught on the starboard spreader and wouldn't come loose. We winched the sail down as much as possible then cut the leach. The line still flies from the spreader like a giant telltale.

We are now about 70 miles off the coast of the Dominican Republic headed for Mona Passage between the Dominican Republic and Puerto Rico. Our first landfall will be St. Croix. We're beating pleasantly in 20-knot trade winds under sunny, warm skies. The crew feels much refreshed and more lively than yesterday.

January 18, 1996

Our trip through the Mona Passage was wonderful. We had clear skies, a good breeze, and a quiet passage. The Southern Cross was our companion, a new one for some of us. Lights from villages on the Puerto Rican coast and the sight of an occasional freighter reminded us we are still part of this world and not characters in some wild sailor's dream.

Since we turned the corner off the SW coast of Puerto Rico, things have deteriorated significantly. Our heading to St. Croix puts the wind square on the nose, 20–35+ knots. The seas are uncomfortable and it looks like it's going to take a long time. We have decided to motorsail with the main only (a batten came adrift this afternoon) on a shallow tack angle, hoping things ease and/or shift by this evening.

January 19, 1996

We motorsailed all night, beating our way to St. Croix against 20–30 knots of wind. A little wet and a little bumpy, but not bad. One more tack and we will fetch Christiansted sometime this evening.

Saw five porpoise this morning—a good sign.

January 20, 1996

Here we are at last, snug in Christiansted Harbor. King Neptune didn't give us up easily though. We ran aground in the harbor entrance, and despite efforts to be towed off and to kedge off, we remained firmly attached to the bottom until around 0400 when Gunther wiggled and wormed us off with the engine. A few minutes later we went aground again while trying to fetch a mooring in front of the marina. Here we remain. We'll get a tow a little later, anchor, and get our lives back together.

This is a beautiful place, and the weather couldn't be more ideal.

It was a grueling passage, but we had a sound vessel and an able crew. The destination is the reward, but so is the passage.

This ends the log of a passage from Ft. Lauderdale, FL, to Christiansted, St. Croix, USVI aboard the American yawl Bolero, *Gunther Sunkler owner and master. Log recorded by Harry Sarazin, navigator.*

NOTES MADE BEFORE DEPARTURE:

January 12, 1996

1635 - We arrived yesterday - 13 bags, crates, boxes and all, including new windows for the dog house and a crystal chandelier. No, I don't know why.

We met Vernie, a young Austrian paid hand and cook, and Mel a laid-back, easy going, religious Antiguan who acts as engineer.

Part of yesterday and today were spent getting the boat ready. Gunther pays attention to detail and seems to be very safety conscious. He is gruff, straightforward, and a bit picky, but in a somewhat charming way. He loves to tell stories and can be rather entertaining.

Vernie (Werner) is energetic, a hard worker, polite, and ever ready to pitch in. He is also an accomplished cook.

Bob is his usual charming self and anxious to get going. Ty is quiet and clearly doesn't want to make a fool of himself—he won't.

I have been appointed navigator or co-navigator, I'm not sure. Co-navigator, no doubt.

We set sail at 0600 tomorrow, fetch the sea buoy off Ft. Lauderdale, and rendezvous with a photographer who is doing a photo spread of *Bolero* for *Sailing* or some such magazine.

This is going to be an interesting trip.

A cold front is passing now. The temperature has dropped as has the barometer to 29.95. It's blowing 15–20 out of the W, and there is an occasional sprinkle. Tomorrow should be clear with 15K winds out of the NW—that's good.

Among the rules on board:

> 1. No deck shoes worn below.

> 2. Only the cook can get food or drink—the crew must ask him.

> 3. Nothing left adrift.

> 4. Sit down when using the head—both numbers.

Gunther is insistent that *Bolero* be a show piece, and I guess with what he's spent he has the right.

FIRST SNOW

Snow and cold and dark invade
On winter's footsteps not delayed.

My private world of placid bliss
Is rent by winter's evil kiss.

What right to crash this quiet place
With snow and ice and frigid face,

And sweep through here like Caesar's ghost,
Not caring twit for that which most

I held, but now for which I dearly long,
The sweet, sweet warmth of summer's song.

WORK ETHIC

My first job was selling newspapers on the street in Superior. I tried for a paper route, but was told there were none available, so selling papers on the street seemed a logical second choice. I guess I was around ten or twelve, and I had never sold anything before except candy bars from an orange crate on the sidewalk next my house. I ate a lot of candy bars. On my first day, I stood on the corner of Tower and Twelfth Street with a pack of papers under my arm and a pocket full of change. I considered shouting "Telegram! Get your Telegram here" like I had seen in the movies, but embarrassment prevented that.

After standing for a while at that busy corner, and not selling a single paper, I figured I needed another marketing approach. I noticed earlier that a couple of other boys selling newspapers, more experienced than I (all boys on earth were more experienced than I), disappeared into the bowels of nearby saloons with loads of papers under their arms, only to emerge paperless. Obviously that's the secret, I thought, so gritting my teeth (my mother would have experienced the vapors if she knew I was sliding into the saloons of Superior), I went into the nearest bar—the one from which one of the urchin newspaper boys had just emerged. I didn't sell a newspaper; everyone in the bar already had one. This event was a clear preview of my business acumen. I threw the unsold papers away and didn't go back the next day for more. That bothered me, because

I had been taught things like responsibility, hard work, dependability, and all the other Midwest ethic models.

I had a lot of summer jobs when I was a kid, including grocery truck driver, fairground worker, railroad roundhouse worker, railroad section gang, and, the best of all, railroad fireman, and I did them all to the best of my ability. When I got my first real job, a commission in the US Navy, I worked very hard at it. My annual leave days piled up because I was reluctant to take leave. What kind of message would it send if I went off cavorting somewhere with an umbrellaed drink in hand, bare feet, and cool shades, instead of showing up for work and putting in long hours? The very thought of that made me shudder. I was successful in the navy, and was told shortly before I resigned my commission to go into the FBI, that if I stayed, I would almost certainly make admiral.

I worked hard in the Bureau, often putting in fourteen- or sixteen-hour days and working lots of weekends. Again, I was reluctant to take leave, but my family revolted, hinting that I was bordering on psychotic, so I used my annual leave, awash in guilt each time.

Then I retired. I was now master of my destiny; I was the king of all I surveyed, and I could do whatever I wanted. The government paid me handsomely to do nothing, but nothing is not what I could do, so I went to work. I was a prisoner of that damn Midwest work ethic, and no parole was in sight.

I retired twenty-two years ago, and I stopped working about six years ago, the final effort being a failed business venture; I should have remembered my newspaper days. Since then I have been totally and gloriously unemployed. I haven't, as they say in the South, hit a lick at a snake, and guess what? I love it. Not only do I love being unemployed, I find I have developed a visceral aversion to commitment. When I have a scheduled appointment, when I have to be somewhere at a specific time, I break out in a sweat; I'm sure hives will be next. How dare life dictate to me what I have to do? I'm retired, and I'll do as I please, when I please. And if it pleases me to do nothing, I'll do that too. So put that in your cranky, rigid Midwestern pipe and smoke it. I want to have, as Thoreau said, "a broad margin to my life."

You'll have to excuse me now; I think I'll shower—no, not because I have to, but because it is my decision to do so. Let's see, it's about twelve thirty; my gosh, where has the morning gone? Actually, it hasn't gone anywhere; I used it—wisely.

THE SKIPPER

I once made a five-day passage on a ketch owned and skippered by a bright young man whose dedication to sailing and the intensity with which he ran his boat would do credit to Captain Bligh. I don't wish to imply that he was cruel or merciless, or even that the captain's masts he held each morning were unfair. Not at all. Everyone on board was equally a son-of-a-bitch in his view; thus, none of us felt slighted.

Helmsmanship was his forte. From deep in the bowels of the boat, while seated on the head, he could sense the slightest alteration of course.

"Can't you steer this goddamn boat? If you can't I'll find someone who can," he would roar. We wondered where the next helmsman would come from, since all on board had, at one time or other, received the same constructive criticism.

While he was asleep on the afternoon of the second day out, I carefully searched the entire boat, chain locker to engine compartment, bilge to headliner, for a repeater compass or other instrument that warned him of the helmsman's incompetence, but found none. I could only conclude that he must have had a micro-miniature gyro-sensing device surgically implanted somewhere in an unused portion of his body.

Unfortunately, the precision with which he insisted that his boat be steered was not transferred to the navigation table, where I observed that the proper use of parallel rulers was to line them on the compass rose, then slide, not walk, them over to the plot. I assume this guaranteed a directional accuracy of at least plus or minus seven degrees. Once the course line or track was properly laid down, distances were measured to the nearest few miles. No wonder helmsmanship had to be so accurate.

During all of this, our skipper maintained the magnificent air of a fellow just coroneted—a truly superior person, worthy of awe.

On the other hand, I have sailed with skippers who let their boats sort of run themselves, secure in the belief that anything so pure as sailing will automatically turn out all right if left alone.

Somewhere between affected superiority and casual abandon lies the sort of skipper who runs his craft efficiently, fairly, and to the mutual benefit of all on board. There are indeed such skippers—many of them.

What is there about the good skipper that makes him good? Let's understand from the outset that trying to psychologically dissect such an individual is difficult for the professional and impossible for the layman. However, some observations might form a catalyst for further thought.

Captaining a 40-foot sailboat or a large corporation has more elements in common than at variance. Many of the same ingredients of character are necessary for either endeavor. But perhaps the single most important ingredient which the captain or chairman of the board must have to be successful is leadership. Sure, the fellow who sails with his wife and next door neighbor as crew doesn't apply precisely the same type of leadership as the corporate head, but the inescapable fact is that, big or little, afloat or ashore, the guy in charge must be a leader to be effective.

Aboard naval vessels orders are given and obeyed in a precise, formalized way. The seaman apprentice obeys the chief, who obeys the lieutenant, who obeys the captain because the rank structure and the law say they must. But they are in for an added treat of high morale and contentment if they also obey because the man above them displays leadership. In other words, because he exudes that quality that makes others want to follow because of the person, not the position.

But you don't sail in the United States Navy; you sail on your own boat, and usually with family or friends. However, it goes without saying that, no matter how casual the afternoon is, and no matter how good the friends are, the thing will not run properly, or indeed at all, unless someone is in charge. Someone has to decide what sails to put up, when to reef, what constitutes danger, etc. This is best accomplished not by popular vote, but by one person making the decisions.

Realistically, on a cruise with five or six people aboard, all good friends, there are no "Ai Ai, Sirs," and there shouldn't be. No one is required by law to do as the skipper says, and no punishment will be meted out to the rebellious crew member, although he probably will never sail on that boat again. It follows then that the skipper's entire success must be based on leadership and, certainly, the good sense of the crew. In other words, the skipper must get accomplished what he feels must be accomplished for the safe and efficient running of the boat, purely through friendly persuasion. This is what leadership is all about.

There have been volumes written on leadership. The military sends its officers to school to learn it, and industry sends its executives to seminars discussing it. Lists of traits have been drawn, which include every good quality but virginity. Some say leaders are made, and others say they are born. But learned or inherited, leadership has its component parts. There are four that I believe to be basic. Each skipper, in order to be a competent leader, must possess at least a measure of these traits. The greater the share, the better the skipper; it's as simple as that.

First is charisma. The dictionary defines charisma as "a special quality of leadership that captures the popular imagination and inspires unwavering allegiance and devotion." This special quality, unfortunately, is the one characteristic of leadership over which we have the least control; either you have it or you don't. If you have it, you can culture it; if you don't you may never be able to develop it. It's the inward glow that's a reflection of the total personality. All great leaders have it in rather large measure, even the not-so-nice ones. It's truly the quality that inspires. A lack of charisma does not mean that one cannot be a good leader, and thus a good skipper; it just means that to do so is a little more difficult.

Second, and perhaps most important, is maturity—not in years, but in attitude. Maturity is the calm, careful consideration of all aspects of a problem and includes the ability to seek and heed good advice. Maturity is the guts to be the guy up front making the decisions, positively and with authority. Maturity is patience and tact in dealing with others when they are wrong or not-so-knowledgeable. It is a complex characteristic, not learned, but helped by learning—not inborn, but helped by the genes. It is difficult to describe, but each of us knows it when he sees it.

Third is competence. The skipper must know his boat and how to handle it; every aspect of it. He must know the sea and the wind and be able to stand his vessel safely out of danger under all circumstances. And, he must be organized. A shoddy, haphazard plan of action does little to instill confidence in the crew. Study and patience are the architects of competence. Natural ability may play a part, but it's amazing how much natural ability can be honed to a fine edge with diligent effort.

Lastly is fairness. It is difficult to distinguish fairness from maturity, for surely fairness is part of maturity. A truly fair skipper does not treat each crew member equally, simply because each crew member is different. A fair skipper recognizes these differences and utilizes the strengths of each to the advantage of all. Although the skipper may have his favorite, if he is skilled, the crew will never know who it is. Fairness will soothe ruffled feathers on a long, confining passage and will allow each crew member to know precisely what is expected of him. Fairness will never demand of any crew member more than he is capable, but will expect from each his maximum effort. Fairness will publically commend good work and will quickly and privately admonish careless action.

Some of these four components of leadership may be viewed as basic personality characteristics; thus, to suddenly acquire them would involve a radical personality change. I don't propose that this piece be a "cookbook" solution to character transformation. I do suggest, however, that if we are aware of the traits that make a good leader, and are concerned about our own role as skipper, then perhaps we might build on those strengths we already have. At any rate, it's not a bad place to start.

HANCOCK
A Short Story

I was four years old when my dad built a small cabin on about two acres of land on an isolated lake in northwestWisconsin. In fact, my first memory in life was walking across the subfloor of the cabin one warm summer afternoon as it was being built—not a full, detailed memory, just a few seconds of childlike bliss, but enough to stay fixed in my mind through the years.

The idea was to have a little place where my mother, dad, and I could escape on summer weekends to help ease the pressures of business that weighed on dad constantly. Why this particular spot was chosen was because Earl Carpenter had a place adjoining ours to the north. Earl, at the time, was engaged to my Aunt Frances, and it was Fran who encouraged dad to buy the property next to Earl's. Earl and Fran's relationship eventually ended, and just how that came about was the subject of a family myth (she dumped him) until I learned more than sixty years later that it was he who dumped her. I can understand that. Fran could be a very difficult woman. The end of their engagement didn't sour the relationship between Earl and my parents, probably because it was clear to everyone, despite the family lie, that beautiful, charming, intelligent Fran had behaved badly once again.

Our land was low and flat with only a four-foot rise from the lake to the cabin. To the north, Earl's land rose sharply so that his place was easily thirty feet above water. Partway up the hill, between our two cabins, nestled in the pine, poplars, and scrub oak, and barely visible from our place was a small dark brown cabin, which was the home of Earl's caretaker and general handyman about town, Hancock.

Hancock. No one, even Earl, ever knew if that was his given name or surname, or even his real name, but it was generally agreed it was probably his surname. Hancock had suddenly appeared in Barnes (Barnes Township, Wisconsin, 126 square miles, about twenty-five permanent residences) three or four years before Earl hired him to be his caretaker. Hancock said little and never anything about himself, but he soon gained a reputation as a competent handyman, able to handle carpentry, plumbing, or electrical problems with a fair degree of expertise. He was a tall, lean man with a long, sad, well-weathered face and thick black hair always a little longer than was the fashion at the time. I had only seen Hancock at close range a few times, but it was his hands that I recall. They were hard and usually dirty with calluses and cuts just healing, but they were at the same time graceful. His fingers were long and slender, and when he did things with his hands, they moved with a grace and economy of motion that impressed me, even though I was just a kid.

One hot summer afternoon when I was about eight or nine, Earl and my dad sat on our porch sipping a beer and the conversation eventually got around to Hancock. I liked listening to my dad talking to other men. I learned much and harbored the hope that someday I could talk with men the easy way my dad did. Earl admitted he knew nothing about Hancock—where he came from, his family, or what he had done before alighting in Barnes. Earl had tried, even telling him he couldn't hire him unless he knew something about him, but it did no good, and Hancock made it clear that if Earl didn't want to hire him that was just fine. He was hired. That was six years ago, and he has proven himself to be honest and reliable. Then after a few moments' thought Earl said, "You know, there's something about him that's different. It's not his quietness and intense privacy. It's something else. There's something in the way he carries himself and the way he looks at you when you're talking with him that almost makes you think he might have once been something far different than he is now, maybe something dark like the stories about him." Then Earl laughed and said, "I'm being melodramatic. Maybe it's the musician in me." Earl, a highly successful physician, was in his heart a passionate musician who wrote music and played the piano with extraordinary competence and style.

The stories about Hancock, all fueled by imagination devoid of fact, ran the gamut of improbability, but that hardly lessened their credibility among those eager to know the "truth" about him. One story was that he was a deposed prince from some unnamed Baltic state, forced to flee his home after the unexplained violent death of his older brother, and the authorities were still looking for him. Another was that he had been married to an unfaithful woman somewhere in Illinois, or Indiana, and when he caught her in his bed with her lover one afternoon, he killed them both with a double-edged axe. How he escaped the law for that one was never fully explained, but then it didn't have to be. The story was its own verification. The stories were an especially fitting topic for older children to tell younger around a campfire at night, and they generally had the desired effect of terrorizing. So as time passed, the stories became ever more embellished and varied, and the common thread through them all was a generous portion of horror.

It was in the summer of my twelfth year when, on a cool, rainy, late Sunday afternoon in August at the cabin, the water pipe leading from the pressure tank burst. It was a mess, particularly since it wasn't discovered immediately. Dad got the pump shut down, and he and my mother began mopping up the water. The nearest plumber was twenty-two miles away, and the prospect of getting him out on Sunday afternoon when there were fish to be caught was slim. "Michael, go up and see if Hancock can come down and take a look at this pipe," my dad said. A chill immediately ran up my spine to the base of my skull. I had never been to Hancock's cabin, and I wasn't particularly interested in going there, especially after hearing the stories about him. "It's OK, Mike. Just run up, knock on his door, and see if he can come down," said dad with a little smile that let me know he knew what I was thinking.

"OK," I said with the enthusiasm of someone about to undergo open heart surgery.

There was a deer trail leading up the hill, and it went directly past Hancock's cabin, which made walking up there relatively easy with little underbrush to fight. I made my way up the trail, and as I approached the cabin, I could hear violin music. It was classical music, just a violin, no other instruments, no orchestra, just the violin, and it was beautiful. Obviously Hancock was listening to the radio or playing a phonograph. It surprised me because people who do the things Hancock is supposed to have done don't listen to classical violin music—they don't listen to music at all, but instead just sit around dreaming up evil things to do, I was pretty sure of that. I knocked on the door and the music stopped. I could hear shuffling inside, and I could hear my heart beating faster and faster. I didn't like this, but my dad had sent me and I had to do it. The door opened and there he stood. Very tall, lean, and hard, dressed in a long sleeve work shirt and bib overalls. His face was expressionless as he looked down at me. "Yes?" he said softly.

"Ah, Mr. Hancock, my dad wanted to know if you could come down," I said, pointing in the direction of our cabin, "and take a look at our water pipe. It busted."

He said nothing for a moment, and then said, "You run along and tell your dad I'll be down in a bit." And with that he closed the door.

He came as promised, and I watched him work, being careful not to get in the way. He was quick and thorough and totally silent throughout the process. When he finished he talked briefly to my dad who gave him some money—I don't know how much—then they shook hands and Hancock disappeared up the deer trail.

Watching him work fascinated me. There was something about the way he did it that was gentle. I wasn't sure how work could be gentle, but it was when he did it, and it made me wonder if all those stories about Hancock were really true.

What happened after that baffles me to this day because what I did was totally out of character. My fear of Hancock turned to curiosity, and I decided to talk to him if he would let me, even though the thought of it made me shudder. I had never sought out an adult whom I didn't know to talk to. But I had to do it, I didn't understand why, but I had to.

I decided to make a visit to Hancock's cabin the following weekend, and I wasn't going to tell my parents. I rehearsed what I was going to say over and over in my mind all week, and each time I flinched a little. We went to the lake Friday evening, and by late Saturday afternoon I hadn't carried out my plan. Sunday was my last chance, so early Sunday afternoon as my mother was inside reading and my dad was occupied with something in the tool shed, I crept up the deer trail to Hancock's cabin. This time there was no violin music coming from his place. I knocked and waited. Nothing happened. I knocked again, and the door instantly opened. There he stood, expressionless, looking down at me, like the last time I knocked on his door. It was impossible to tell what he was thinking. "I, ahh, ahh, Mr. Hancock, can I talk to you?" He stood silently, his gaze still riveted on me, and I began to tremble.

He must have noticed because a barely perceptible smile crossed his face, and after a long moment he said, "Come in," and turned from the door, leaving it open.

The cabin was small—a tiny living room with a wood stove, one small bedroom, a kitchen area with a table off the living room, no bathroom, but an outhouse nearby. His place was neat and clean, but old. The furniture and carpets and lamps were old; everything was old and muted.

Because the cabin was nestled deep in the woods, there was little natural light filtering through the tiny windows, and that bit of light was largely blocked by heavy linen curtains, giving the place a cloistered feel. He sat in an enormous overstuffed chair and motioned me to sit on a couch nearby. "What is it you want to talk to me about, son?" he said softly.

"Well sir, you ah, I guess maybe you know about all the stories people tell about you. I mean, people say some pretty awful things, and I don't think they're true. Oh, my name is Michael Connolly." I figured if I told him I didn't believe the stories he might like me better, but I did believe them, at least some of them.

He never took his eyes from me, but slowly a smile formed on his sad face and he said, "Yes, Michael Connolly, I know of the stories. But why don't you think they're true?"

"I don't know," I said nervously. "I guess it's because, I mean, I think, I mean, I don't think you're the kind of man that's done that stuff," I said awkwardly.

"Just what kind of man do you think I am?"

I now realized I was nervous not because of the mysterious stranger I was with, but because for the first time in my life I had initiated an adult conversation with a stranger, and I was in a bit over my head. "I just don't think you're a mean person," I blurted out, feeling a little silly. I didn't like the questioning, and I thought if this went on I would become hopelessly tongue-tied. "Where did you come from, Mr. Hancock?" I asked, hoping to change the course of the conversation.

"Why is that important for you to know, Michael Connolly?" he asked gently.

"I guess it's none of my business, but I just wanted to know the truth about you," I said, feeling slightly more confident now.

He took his eyes from me and thought for a long moment, then, turning back to me, he said, "And if I tell you about myself, what will you do with the information?"

I felt a chill go through me. I had no idea how to respond to this. What did he mean? Is this some kind of test, and if it is, what's the right answer? "Gosh, I don't know. I just want to know the truth. I mean, I don't think people should say things about you that aren't true." I instantly realized this didn't answer the question, but I didn't know what else to say.

"Were you afraid to come up here, Michael?"

"Yes, sir, I was."

"Are you afraid now?"

"No, sir. I don't think so," I stammered.

We sat silently as he stared at me, measuring me, then he said, "All right, Michael Connolly, I'll tell you about myself, but only on one condition."

"Yes, sir?"

"You must promise you will never tell another person what I tell you, not your mother, not your father, not your friends, not Dr. Carpenter, no one. Can you promise that?"

What awful thing was he going to tell me that it must be kept secret? I suddenly wasn't so sure I had done the right thing by coming up here, but I wanted now more than ever to know, so I said, "Yes, sir, I promise."

He said nothing, but continued looking at me. Then he got up and walked into the bedroom. I could see him open a kind of trunk at the foot of his bed and take out a case of some sort. Then he reached in the trunk and withdrew what looked like a scrapbook. He returned to the living room and laid the case and scrapbook on the table, opened the case, and took out a beautiful violin and a bow. He put the violin between his shoulder and chin and plucked the strings as he adjusted the tuning pegs. He paused for a moment, closing his eyes, then he began to play. Music exploded into that small room, and it startled me. It was music like I had never heard before. His long, slender fingers flew over the fingerboard so fast they were a blur, and the music, the beautiful, complicated music, poured from the violin and from Hancock, because it was clear they were one.

I don't know how long he played, but it wasn't long enough. I was transfixed by the music and by the sight of this handyman making it with such skill and love. When he was finished, he placed the violin carefully back in its case and closed it. "Wow," I said almost in a whisper. He turned to me and smiled, then he picked up the scrapbook and sat next to me on the couch.

"Michael," he said, "I was a concert violinist once with a promising career. I appeared in concert halls all over the world and won much acclaim." With that he opened the scrapbook and placed it on my lap. It was full of newspaper clippings, some in foreign languages. One of the first I read was from the *New York Times* about a young violinist who had appeared with the New York Philharmonic and how he had dazzled the audience with his brilliant performance of Sibelius' violin concerto. The reviewer wrote, "He attacks the music and makes it his own while ever remaining respectful of it. His tones are as clear as gin, and his intonations quite as intoxicating, as the thrill of his dramatic ending compels the listener to leap up with shouts of bravo." But there was something odd about this clipping, and all the clippings. Wherever the performer's name was mentioned, it was carefully blacked out. Some of the clippings had pictures of the violinist, and there was no doubt it was Hancock, but any reference to his name was obliterated. Some of the clippings referred to his being accompanied on tour by his wife, and her name was also blacked out. I took a long time going through the scrapbook, reading most of the clippings that were in English, and when I finished I looked up at him and said, "What happ...I mean, why are you here?"

"That's a story of tragedy and weakness, Michael. Perhaps someday I'll tell you, but for now this is enough. You'd better run along."

"Is it OK if I come up again sometime?" I asked hopefully.

"Yes, Michael, it's all right."

Each summer I visited Hancock several times, and we talked, and he played for me. As I grew older, our conversations became more adult. I came to understand that he was a brilliant, gentle, man, not the man of the stories. Despite his apparent isolation, he had an astonishing grasp of the world about him and a view of that world that was refreshingly empirical. He told me of his performing days. Stories about the fame and glitter and stories about the darker side of fame—the charlatans and leeches and liars and frauds. I genuinely liked and respected him. I respected his intense privacy. I never asked him again what the tragedy and weakness was that caused his life to change so drastically and brought him to this place, and he never told me. I also kept my promise to never reveal what he told me that day when I was twelve years old.

One spring day I got a call from my dad. By this time I was married with two kids and living in the east. "Our old friend Hancock died," Dad said. "Earl found him on the floor of his cabin earlier this week. Apparently it was a heart attack." I was saddened by the news, but not surprised. Hancock, by this time, was an old man.

Later that summer, when we were at the lake on vacation, I saw Earl. "What happened to old Hancock?" I asked.

"Well, Mike, he suffered a heart attack last winter and was hospitalized for a while. His heart was in pretty bad shape, and I think he knew he didn't have long to live. He came back to his cabin. You know, a few years ago he told me he didn't think he was any longer physically able to be my caretaker and that he would be moving out of the cabin. I asked him where he would go, and he said he didn't know. I told him he wasn't going anywhere, that I wanted him to stay in the cabin as long as he wanted and it didn't matter if he couldn't work anymore, so he stayed. Well, late last spring I hadn't seen him for a few days so I went to check, and I found him dead on the floor. At least the poor old fellow didn't suffer."

"Earl, did he have any family that you know of?" I asked.

"No, no one to notify and no one to give his stuff to."

"I don't suppose he had much stuff. Did you find anything?" I still felt bound by my promise.

"I thought it was kind of odd; all I found were some clothes and a few books. He had an old trunk in his bedroom, but that was mostly empty. I didn't find anything that was really personal."

"Not even a scrapbook?"

"Not even a scrapbook."

ON BEING A BOY

I listened carefully today to some women of my era (a bygone time) describe, in exquisite detail, the travails of young schoolgirls in the old days as they struggled with ill-fitting cotton stockings, garter belts, long pants under skirts, and long underwear. I listened, but I had little sympathy. No, not little sympathy—no sympathy. Not a twit, nary a scintilla, not even a smidgen. Cruel, heartless, unfeeling, wretchedly self-absorbed? No, none of these. I lack sympathy for your sorry plight only because my story is even more plight-ridden. My story will, when you hear it, evoke a gush of sympathy, a waterfall of empathetic sorrow, an ocean of concern.

Telling this story is delicate business, because the subject is delicate. That is to say, it's not something readily discussed in polite circles. But I'm going to tell it anyway, because as I look around, I see a circle of sorts, but I'm not fully persuaded it's polite. In other words, ladies, you can take it.

This tale begins with a chemistry lesson. At some point in a boy's life, Bobby and Billy, the Ball Brothers, awaken to fulfill their destiny and start manufacturing testosterone. Ahhh, testosterone, a simple chemical, just nineteen parts carbon, twenty-eight parts hydrogen, and two parts oxygen—three simple elements forming an exotic cocktail, powerful enough to make rational men do irrational things. About the same time the Ball Brothers get into the testosterone manufacturing business, they expand their product line to include sperm. While all of this is going on, Pierre, the prostate, begins manufacturing seminal fluid. Thus, the orchestra is assembled, ready for the signal to play the reproductive symphony, and our little boy doesn't have a clue what's going on. As testosterone courses through the body, it affects certain parts of the brain, causing results that we'll get to in a moment.

OK, so much for the chemistry lesson; now let's get practical. Those of you who have raised boys may be somewhat familiar with what I'm about to say, but even if you are I suspect there are a few gaps in your understanding. The reason is no boy would ever share with his mother what's going on. Any real boy would rather be stripped naked and eaten alive by fire ants than share with his mother what I'm about to tell you.

Something very strange happens to a boy about the time testosterone kicks in, and it happens deep in the night. Like a cat burglar, it sneaks into the boy's room when he's fast asleep, and into his dream-ready mind, causing what we euphemistically refer to as a wet dream. It is a well-known fact that seminal fluid is one of nature's most perfect starches, and it's also a pretty good glue. The result is that when the boy wakes up, he discovers that not only are the front of his pajamas starched stiff as board, but Mr. Happy, the Ball Brothers' ever faithful and constant companion, is likely glued to the inside of said pajamas. Peeling Mr. Happy off is often a painful exercise. Our young hero isn't sure what happened during the night, but whatever it was, he loved it. So, those of you who have raised boys may have experienced the stiff pajama fronts on laundry day, and you may even know why, but now you know the whole story.

The wet dream experience is far too embarrassing for any boy to discuss with his mother, and should an insensitive mother bring the subject up, she is likely to see her precious little boy die, right there on the spot, right before her very eyes.

But there's more. There's the issue of those girls who finally struggled to get their long pants off in the cloak room and roll down their cotton stockings, exposing their bare legs, as their garters flutter in the updrafts. What those little girls unwittingly do to little boys is well understood by all boys, but not so by girls, who generally giggle and think it's disgusting.

Testosterone, besides doing its work at night, also causes Mr. Happy to stand at attention. This is not an idle freak of nature; it has far deeper meanings. It is a profound and welcome symbol of manhood and a requirement for the continuation of the human race.

But this manly symbol, this reproductive imperative, comes with a price. When you're a boy, you quickly discover that Mr. Happy will stand up at the swish of a skirt, or the flash of a leg, and usually at a most inappropriate time. It is not unusual for a young boy to stand in the front of the room in Mrs. Snodgrass' English class, about to read his assignment, when he glances at that cute little blond in the front row, with her bare, beautiful legs folded ever so gracefully, one over the other, and her skirt hiked just a trifle up. POW! With the speed of light, Mr. Happy responds, and there, for all to see, stands the hapless boy with a huge bulge in his pants. In utter despair and total humiliation, the young lad thinks, "Death, be my companion."

School dances are also an occasion of substantial embarrassment. When you're slow dancing with Bambi, in subdued light, Mr. Happy will often respond as if the national anthem is being played. This causes the boy to bend at the waist so the lower part of his torso is moved away from the girl, lest she feel his predicament. Dancing at this time takes on a sort of awkward, geriatric appearance, as the poor youth begins to sweat profusely and babble unintelligibly.

So you see, ladies, I have little sympathy for baggy stockings, long underwear, garters, and the rest. You think you had it hard. HA—you don't know what hard is.

MENTOR

We met a long time ago. There was a big disparity in our ages; he was older, but that didn't seem to matter. We clicked immediately. As time passed, he became my mentor and teacher and remained so until he died.

He wasn't a large man, even small I suppose by today's standards, only about five-foot-seven, but he was well-built and strong. I never knew him when he didn't have white hair. It turned before his thirtieth birthday. His face was slightly round, with pale blue eyes and a wide smile.

He was a quiet man who listened more than he talked. But he had a razor-sharp wit and could, with disarming speed, interject a hilarious and pointed comment into nearly any conversation. He smoked a pipe and was rarely without one. After college he opened a car dealership which, after a couple of years, he turned into a truck and farm equipment dealership that he ran for over thirty years.

He had only a few close friends, probably because he was so private. But he had a huge pool of acquaintances, all of whom respected and liked him. I don't think he had any enemies.

One of the reasons we were so close is because, despite the difference in our ages, he listened. My thoughts, feelings, hurts, joys, accomplishments, and failures always mattered to him. He made me feel I had real worth and wasn't just some goofy kid or a clueless teenager tripping blindly through life trying to understand where I fit in.

The most important result of our relationship was the lessons he taught me, and he taught them in a most powerful way—not by edict, or threat, or force, but by quiet instruction and example. Nothing was more important to him than integrity and the value of his word. He was honorable. In the cutthroat world of business, he was a rare beacon of veracity.

Compassion was part of his being. Every month, thousands of dollars were owed to him, mostly by poor farmers whom he knew were struggling, trying with hard work to drag a living out of the land. He never threatened, never took legal action, and never charged interest; he simply said, "They'll pay me when they can." And more often than not, they did. He earned their respect and admiration. For him, the Golden Rule was the rule of his life. It was from him that I learned honesty, honor, and compassion are not options; they are imperatives. He was a gentle man and a gentleman.

He's gone now. He died thirty-four years ago, and I still miss him. He was my friend and my teacher. He was my dad.

LETTER TO SHINGLEDECKER

I belong to the St. Croix Writer's Group, which meets weekly. One of our group is Chuck Shingledecker, a young man who is a faithful, practicing member of the Greek Orthodox Church and somewhat of a religious scholar. But Chuck does not blindly follow; he thinks. He recently wrote the below referenced book, which examines Canon Law in all its peculiarity and contradictory aspects. Since the book came out, he has received a lot of vicious hate mail, much of it from the clergy. I wrote the following, read it at one of our regular meetings, and presented him a copy.

January 23, 2012

Dear Mr. Shingledecker:

A friend bought your book, *The Crazy Side of Orthodoxy* (actually he's my former friend; we parted company when he bought the book). He showed it to me, and I can't remember when I've been so disgusted. I had difficulty even touching it.

As one who purports to be a man of faith, I can't imagine how you could, in good conscience, write such a salacious, scandalous, heretical work of blasphemy. Every page of your terrible tome drips with Satanic toxin designed only to poison the minds of the unsuspecting. Have you somehow become possessed, or are you just an evil man to your core?

In the acknowledgements you cynically cite the guidance of God in the writing of your ghastly work. I have no doubt that act alone will ensure you an eternity in hell, a fate you richly deserve.

You have desecrated the holy Canon which, as we all know, is the sacred word of God, delivered to His people personally by Him. I think it was right after the Ten Commandments thing, but I'm a little fuzzy on that. At any rate, you have no right to question even one word of the Canon, much less dismiss any of it as unnecessary.

As a man of deep faith, I talk to God on a regular basis. I mentioned your book to Him recently and he said, "Oy vey (God is Jewish, you know), such a book that young man writes." Surely you can see that is a clear condemnation of your work.

Finally, I have not read your book, nor do I intend to. To do so would undoubtedly condemn my immortal soul to the fires of hell for eternity. I do not have to read it to know how evil it is; the title itself tells me all I need to know.

Repent before it's too late.

Yours in Christ,

Rick Santorum

P.S. If you'll donate to my campaign, I'll put in a good word for you with God.

INTROVERT

I don't like cocktail parties. For that matter, I don't like large gatherings of any sort where I am expected to interact with others I don't know. It's not them; it's me; I'm somewhat introverted. The psychologist Carl Jung coined the words "introvert" and "extrovert" in the early part of the twentieth century. People who are completely introverted or extroverted are, he said, whacko (not his exact word, but that's what he meant). Most of us fall somewhere on a spectrum between total introvert and total extrovert, and if you're right in the middle, you're an omnivert, as the author Susan Cain, herself an introvert, put it.

Don't confuse introversion with shyness. Shy people are uncomfortable with any sort of interaction that draws attention to them. Introverted people like interaction, but only on a small scale, and they prefer to occupy the cathedral of their own minds rather than the amphitheater of the sweaty masses. I like small gatherings, say four to six people who I know and respect and can talk to. Conversation is the key here. Spirited, meaningful conversation, not the latest bargains at Macy's, or the fact that Tom Cruise and Katie Holmes broke up, or that your granddaughter won a medal in the third grade for eating all her vegetables at lunchtime. I find meaningful conversation is hard at cocktail parties where most there are strangers to me but usually not to each other. Some good friends, who are extroverts and love this sort of thing, hold a large cocktail party each Christmas season. Almost everyone there are members of their church. Obviously that lets me out because I don't go to church. I accept their invitation because they are good friends and nice people, but I would rather not. My palms start sweating; my sphincter snaps shut with a sound that for a terrifying moment makes me think it may never open again. I get the uneasy feeling everyone at the party is looking at me and simultaneously thinking, "Where did they find this jerk, at some rescue mission?" I'm uncomfortable walking up to someone, putting my hand out, and saying, "Hi, I'm Harry." Somewhere in the back of my cerebral cortex I imagine them replying, "So what?" and walking away. I'm not good at banal chitchat. "Lot of rain we got yesterday," says the guy with the hair growing out of his nose. No kidding. He continues, "Did you hear Fred slipped off a ladder and broke his leg?"

"No I didn't. Who's Fred?" Even a few cocktails don't do much for my antisocial (at least as perceived by the extroverts) behavior; they only make my attempt at small talk less intelligible, and I realize right after I say something how stupid it was. There's no way out. It's a social supermax, and the only parole is the end of the party.

My wife died a couple of years ago, and I am sometimes asked if I'm lonely. That's a hard question to answer. I don't think I am. I would prefer not to be alone, but I'm not lonely. We introverts have lots of inner resources that keep us company. I am quite content to curl up with a good book or a good movie. Being able to discuss it with someone would be nice, but it's not a necessity.

Society rewards the extrovert. We encourage our kids to be outgoing and extroverted; they're the ones who succeed, who get to the top of the heap. Perhaps, but we introverts are the ones who tend to be deep thinkers, the ones who invent and innovate, the ones who write the really insightful books that even the extroverts notice, the ones who (as studies have shown) make better decisions as CEOs. Charles Darwin was an introvert who took long walks alone so he could think. Steve Wozniak, who, with Steve Jobs, founded Apple, is an introvert, as is Philip Roth. Donald Trump is an extrovert. Who would you rather have dinner with?

No, I'm not lonely. I like being on the introverted side of the continuum. I'm comfortable in my own skin, and my best friend is me. I don't get bored with me; in fact, I never get bored. There's too much going on in my mind for that to ever happen.

Next time you're at a cocktail party and you see someone who's squirming with discomfort, it may not be gas; it may be they are introverts, and what you don't know is they're watching you and the rest of the extroverts and softly chuckling.

A NICE DAY

I'm going to describe to you a culinary experience the Mrs. and I had today in Fells Point. For those of you who haven't been there, Fells Point is a funky waterfront section of Baltimore. We were to have met Ann and Bill at Bertha's, but they couldn't make it, so we drove to Baltimore anyway and went to John Steven. First, I must describe John Steven. It's a bar that's been around for, well, I don't know how long, but decades at least. The bar area is in front and a dining area (a little more upscale) resides in the rear. A full menu is available in the bar. The bar, ahhh, the bar. *Esquire* magazine rated John Steven's back bar as one of the ten best in the nation a few years ago. The bar is just the right combination of old, musty, slightly beat-up, and Fells Pointey, which is to say a bit artsy, a bit offbeat, and comfortable as an old slipper. Besides the food, two things make John Steven unique: the clientele and the music. I have been there when at one end of the bar was a hooker a bit juiced up on vodka martinis and at the other end a couple in formal attire on their way to the BSO (Baltimore Symphony Orchestra). Lawyers, doctors, drunks, retired FBI agents (same thing), scam artists, artists, musicians, bums, and high society coexist quite nicely at John Steven. The music plays constantly from a library of hundreds of CDs. Today, as is true most days, it was rich with traditional jazz—I mean the Gerry Mulligan, Thelonious Monk, Cannonball Adderley, Miles Davis, John Coltrane, Oscar Peterson kind of jazz—the good stuff.

We ordered three things: Maryland crab soup, steamed mussels, and Guinness. The soup, oh my, the soup. It's a tomato-based broth with corn, peas, celery, onion, some other stuff, and plenty of crab meat, spiced with Old Bay seasoning, salt and pepper, and probably some more things. It is soup to transport the soul to levels undreamed of. It is nirvana without having to be a Buddhist. The mind fairly floats in a state of sublime bliss with each sip. The mussels were steamed in their own juices with a touch of white wine and served with drawn butter infused with sautéed garlic. They were farm-raised mussels, but that's OK. They were not only succulent and flavorful, but the dipping butter elevated them to perfection. It's beyond my literary skills to accurately describe the taste of a steamed mussel dipped in garlic butter, so I'll use an analogy—orgasm. Finally, there was the Guinness; enough said.

She-Who-Will-Not-Be-Denied and I decided we're going to buy some canned crab meat this winter and try to replicate John Steven's crab soup. If we can, watch out Barnes—here we come. We're gonna blow your socks off next summer.

We also visited a newly opened Irish pub in Fells Point where, as luck would have it, they also serve Guinness.

As you may have guessed, we had a wonderful first day back in the eastern digs, and we can't wait until April when we head back to Wisconsin. The two faces of happy.

LOON

Along my hurried way
To some meaningless encounter,
I paused by waterside
Still with fall's cool touch,
And saw a loon today.

Noble bird with feathers black and white.
Master in his lonely world.
He dove as I approached,
To tell me I may watch,
But have no business in his life.

Then reappearing, nearer still,
He looked with fiery eye, and I understood.
He is more than a mournful tremolo.
He is for me, forevermore,
Memory of a Choptank day.

DEEP CONCERN

Three years ago I had some concern, as the Bush administration launched a massive initiative to start a war in Iraq. The decision to go to war was made before Bush was elected to his first term, and it was made by those whom he later gathered around him, who represented The Project for the New American Century, and who became powerful beyond any who had occupied their positions before them: Donald Rumsfeld, Dick Cheney, Paul Wolfowitz, Richard Perle, and others. Making the intelligence fit the decision to go to war, instead of letting the intelligence inform that decision, was arrogant, deceitful, and ultimately disastrous. Diverting from the real war on terror (Osama bin Laden is still free) to prosecute a war in Iraq caused me not only concern but curiosity. Why would Bush do that? Hussein never posed a threat to the US. He was a despotic secular saber rattler who was hated by those who are our real enemies, the Islamic extremists. So why would Bush do that? Why would he sacrifice so much? Why didn't he listen to his own father and to James Baker, both of whom warned that a war in Iraq could ignite the entire Middle East? My concern grew.

Then it happened, just as the elder Bush and Baker had predicted, just as a State Department estimate made well before the war, and ignored by the White House, had predicted, and just as the CIA station chief in Iraq predicted in a cable to Langley soon after the invasion (he was replaced shortly thereafter); the insurgency began. Iraq became a nursery for terrorism, and the blood of our sons and daughters began to flow in the sands as our coffers began to be drained at the rate of $7.4 million per hour. The focus on terrorism shifted still further away from the target. My concern grew deeper.

Then came Guantanamo, Abu Ghraib, and "extraordinary rendition," a euphemism for delivering persons in US custody to third-world countries to be tortured. All of this as the White House and the attorney general declared the Geneva Conventions "outdated." And of course there is the matter of warrantless wiretaps. That one's easy. Bush won his second term on fear, and he has managed to skirt around the law on the warrantless wiretaps, again using the fear card. After all, he is protecting the homeland. What loyal American doesn't buy into that?

My concern has now become despair. I deeply love this country, and I am profoundly proud of what it stands for: freedom, equal justice, due process, and the rule of law. Mr. Bush, who says God speaks to him, has abandoned the rule of law. He has abandoned the rule of international law, including treaties in which the US is a party. He has abandoned the rule of civility and fair play. He has diminished the reputation of the United States throughout the world, and he has isolated the US to a degree beyond any in my memory. We are becoming a pariah among nations.

I am immensely proud of our military. They are well-trained, brave young men and women who are doing a job they are ordered to do by their civilian leaders. And those leaders, Mr. Bush at their head, have shamefully squandered the lives of nearly 2,300 American servicemen and women in Iraq and left almost16,700 wounded and maimed. Our national debt is $8.3 trillion. And what do we have to show for all this? An Iraq near-civil war, terrorism on the move worldwide, a military stretched so thin we couldn't possibly fight on another front, the largest national debt in history, and a sullied reputation; we are a nation in a nearly catatonic state of isolation.

The first job of government is to protect its citizens. November will mark the fifth anniversary of 9/11, yet our airspaces are still vulnerable, and less than 5 percent of containers coming into US ports are adequately inspected. For the terrorist, that means a 95 percent chance he can slip a nuclear device into this country undetected. The Bush administration has reacted with cool enthusiasm to the recommendations of the 9/11 Commission, which were crafted to protect our citizens. Why, Mr. Bush? When Hurricane Katrina hit, the government stood fixed, immobile, frozen, like a fly caught in amber, as thousands of its citizens died or lost everything? And this was an event for which the administration had plenty of warning, unlike the next terrorist attack.

I am deeply concerned for the welfare of my country, as this hubristic little man, who justifies his incompetence with bumper sticker-like slogans and fear rhetoric, drags us down still further, unwilling or unable to rethink a failed policy, and unwilling or unable to seek council divergent from his precast ideology.

There have been a few calls for Mr. Bush's impeachment. That's foolish. Gross incompetence and raging hubris don't rise to the level of high crimes and misdemeanors. But there will be a reckoning. After he leaves office, and fades into obscurity, he will eventually see the judgment of early history declare his administration one of the worst in our history.

FIRST IMPRESSIONS

I visited the ophthalmologist the other day, a fairly routine event for me. I got there a bit early and found the waiting room unusually crowded, then I settled in with my book, not particularly caring when they called me; it was a good book.

Bringing a book was, perhaps, not a good idea, because in places where there are a lot of people I don't get much reading done. I am an addicted people-watcher. Crowded airports are my Disneyland, and I can sit for hours watching every sort of humanity drift by, as I imagine what their personal stories might be and what tragedies or good fortunes have befallen them. Even when I'm engrossed in a good book, I can't resist looking up and watching when I sense someone entering the room or sense some other movement nearby. So it was that not long after I arrived at the doctor's office that a young woman with a very young child and a large bag full of diapers, bottles, snacks, and toys, I assumed, came in and sat diagonally across from me to the left. She was wearing jean shorts, sandals, and a sleeveless nondescript shirt, a bit tattered around the edges. Both of her legs and arms were adorned with rather large tattoos— designs mainly, not verbiage. I couldn't quite make out what they were—reproductions of ancient Mayan fertility symbols, perhaps. The tattoos, her somewhat beat-up clothing, and what I perceived to be a lack of gentleness on her face gave her a sort of hard, scrabble look.

I peg people when I see them. I know, that doesn't make a lot of sense, and I'm often wrong, but I peg them anyway. I'm convinced it's a genetic defect. Well, let me tell you, I had this gal pegged all right—a tough broad, probably with a drinking problem and not adverse to a joint or a little crystal meth from time to time. It was obvious why she was there. Her little boy wore glasses thick enough to resist a bullet, and his eyes seemed to wander in different directions at the same time. "Poor kid," I thought. "He's not going to get much TLC from this babe. Probably the only reason she's here is because child welfare made her take the kid."

I continued watching her as she organized her gear and got herself settled. Then suddenly she broke into a radiant smile and began talking to the baby as she gently nuzzled him with her face. He started to giggle, and as he did she became even more animated. She was totally focused on her little guy, and the concern and love she had for him radiated from her like a light. So much for pegging. With a smooth and seamless movement, she brought the baby up to her breast, and without exposing herself the little guy latched on and began to suckle. David Copperfield couldn't have performed that maneuver any more smoothly. As the baby drank his lunch, she looked down at him with a look only a mother can generate.

Earlier, I had pegged another woman in the room. She sat diagonally to my right, fifteen or so feet from the mother and baby. She was a heavy-set woman in her sixties with a large, flat face—a face that demanded attention. It bore, I was sure, a permanent snarl—the look of someone eating a rotten egg while stumbling over a decomposed body. Actually, what occupied the front of her head was more of a gargoyle than a face. "This," I thought, "is a sour, gnarly old woman. I hope she's not married."

When the little boy was finished, the mother removed him from her breast with the same easy, fluid motion that began it all, as she reached under her shirt and adjusted her bra. Then she laid the baby on her thighs, feet pointing toward her, unbuttoned his pants and checked his diaper. It was wet. She quickly removed it, rolled it up, and put it in a plastic bag. She retrieved a clean diaper from her bag, and she raised the baby's bottom, lifting him by the ankles.

Gargoyle, who now looked even nastier than before, said in a loud voice, "There's a bathroom out there, you know." All eyes turned to her, and I'm fairly certain everyone in the room gave her a look as disapproving as I did. Meanwhile the mother, who didn't glance at the old witch, said nothing. In a moment she was finished diapering her son, and held him up to burp him as she sang gently to him. He's a lucky little guy.

Shortly, mother and son were called into the examining room. A few minutes later, a bent old man came into the waiting room and joined gargoyle, who snarled something at him as he bent still further in a well-practiced supplicant posture. They left, she in the lead, a human T-Rex, ready to devour any creature that got in her way.

"Well," I thought, "fifty percent isn't so bad. One serious mis-peg and one dead-on."

FRESH FLOUNDER

I n June of 1961 my squadron (VP-26 from the US Naval Air Station, Brunswick, Maine) deployed for six months to Iceland, more specifically the US Air Force facility at the Keflavik International Airport.

For those of you who have never been to Iceland, describing it is a little difficult because it is a land of many faces. Baron, rocky, mountainous, glacierous; full of icy cold lakes, hot springs and volcanoes. But mostly baron—a starkness like the other side of the moon that chills the soul. Then there's the weather, almost constantly overcast and gray. The whole thing is quite enough to drive one to drink, and it's a very short trip.

Among our responsibilities as a Navy patrol squadron was to patrol the North Atlantic between Iceland and Europe looking for Soviet submarines and Soviet fishing fleets. Imbedded in the fishing fleets were ELINT (electronics intelligence) trawlers, which were not fishing trawlers at all, but sophisticated electronic listening platforms run by the Soviet Navy and crudely disguised as fishing trawlers. It's a little hard to pretend your vessel is a fishing trawler when it has dozens of antennas, no nets, and no sign that a fish has ever been on board. When we found them, we would note the position and time, and we would make a number of low passes over the vessel from all directions, photographing it with particular attention to the antenna array. We called it photography, and the Soviets called it harassment—the

Soviets were partly right and we loved it. Every now and then, some of the trawlers' crews would break out a rifle or handgun and take a few shots at us. My response was to fly toward them, very low, on a collision course with their wheelhouse. As we approached the vessel, I would open the bombay doors, just to see if they were paying attention. When we got very close, I would pull up to avoid a collision, as I said over the intercom, "Stand by, stand by, drop," and the ordnance man would, through a rear hatch, drop a large bag of garbage we saved for the purpose. I actually got quite good at judging the time to drop, taking into consideration the speed of the plane, altitude, wind speed, velocity, etc. That we didn't start World War III is somewhat of a miracle.

Another one of our duties was to exercise (use) various NATO bases—bases in such remote places as London, Copenhagen, and Stavanger. There was also a Norwegian Air Force base in Bodo, Norway, which we flew into regularly. Bodo is a small community located on Norway's rocky Atlantic coast roughly forty-five miles north of the Arctic Circle. Flying into Bodo was always a pleasure because we got an opportunity to spend time with our Norwegian Air Force counterparts. Pay in the Norwegian Air Force was dismal, just a fraction of ours for both officers and men, and certain items they needed to buy were very expensive at their equivalent of the PX. The two things they wanted most were canned vegetables and fruit for their kids, and booze. Every crew that flew into Bodo took up a collection and bought as much of these things as we could to bring to our friends in the frozen north.

I became acquainted with a young Norwegian captain, whose name I have unfortunately forgotten, and we hit it off famously, probably because of the flounder incident.

The first time I flew into Bodo he showed me around the Officers' Club and the BOQ where I would be staying for the night. He showed me the laundry room in the basement of the BOQ in case I had anything I wanted to wash. I noted that the washing machines looked entirely different from ours—much more bulky. My new friend explained that in Norway the water is heated by the machine rather than using hot water run into it from the tap.

Before long we settled in at the Officers' Club and began to sample some of the fine spirits we brought. We sampled, and sampled, and sampled, well into the early morning hours, at which point, neither of us being in full control of our faculties, my friend said in his nearly impeccable English, "You wanna go fishing?"

"Sure," I replied, and off we went. The details of the fishing adventure are a little spotty in my mind, rendered vague, no doubt, by the passage of time. Or vague, perhaps, by the ingestion of whiskey. But I do recall we walked about a half mile or less in the otherworldly half-light of the midnight sun to get to the rocky coast and the North Atlantic Ocean. We had one rod and one lure. He handed it to me and instructed that I toss the lure in and let it sink to the bottom. Almost instantly I had a strike—a huge strike. I fought that monster for a long time while simultaneously fighting to keep my balance, largely as a result of the previously mentioned sampling. At last I landed the creature, a huge flounder—flat, with two eyes on the same side, staring up at me with unmistakable malice.

"We have to eat this," I said to my friend. "Is there a kitchen where we can cook it?"

"There is a kitchen in the BOQ, but it's locked at this time of night," he replied.

We stood for a while in the half-dark, with the fish flopping at our feet. Then I said, "Let's clean it. I've got an idea." We cleaned the fish; actually, he cleaned the fish. I'd never seen a live flounder before. "Follow me," I said. We retraced our steps to the basement of the BOQ and into the laundry room. "Let's put some water in one of the washers, turn the thermostat all the way up, and poach the fish," I said.

"What? We can't..." my friend replied in shocked protest.

"Sure we can. Let's give it a try," I said. Reluctantly he agreed.

Before long the water was hot, not boiling, but hot. I slipped the firm, white flesh of my second new friend into the washing machine, and we waited. It didn't take long and the flounder was done. We scooped it out, laid the pieces on a laundry folding table, and began to eat the best fish dinner I have ever had.

My friend and I agreed we would never reveal our secret, at least until those who could reprimand us were transferred, retired, or dead. I can only imagine the look on the face of the next person to use that washing machine when he took his underwear out, thinking it was clean and fresh, only to discover it smelled like flounder.

HANK
A Short Story

My name is Hank. My father's name was Hank, and his father before him. It's a proud German name, and I come from proud German stock. I want to tell you, very briefly, the story of my life, because it may help you to understand why I did what I did. I have no illusion that my life is noteworthy enough for a real biography, so just think of this as a sort of thimble biography.

I was born in rural eastern Pennsylvania in 1898. My father farmed a small plot of land he homesteaded. He worked very hard on that small patch of land, but we never had much. My parents and brother and I lived a simple, essentially peasant life. I suppose we were happy, but it was hard, and it took a toll on my parents.

There wasn't much time for education. My brother and I quit school after the eighth grade because dad needed help on the farm. "A man doesn't need to learn a lot of things from books to be a good farmer," he would say in his thick German accent, and I suppose he was right. Speaking of accents, I didn't learn English until I started school, and after I learned it, I taught it to my parents and younger brother. They say I speak with a little bit of a German accent, but I don't hear it, so I guess it doesn't matter.

When I was sixteen, my mother died of the influenza, and a few months later so did my dad. I really think he died of a broken heart and despair at having worked so hard all his life yet resulting in so little. My uncle, from northwest Wisconsin, came out and sold the farm, then took my brother and me back to live with him and my aunt in a little place called Barnes. They were nice people, and they were good to me and my brother, and I was grateful for what they did for us.

In April of 1917, America entered the Great War, and a few months later I enlisted in the army. I eventually wound up in France and saw some heavy fighting. On November 1, 1918, we had broken through the German lines at the River Meuse, during the Meuse-Argonne Offensive, when I got shot in the gut. That was just a few days before the armistice. Some luck. I don't remember much about the next week or two; everything is kind of hazy. They patched me up pretty good and sent me home to be discharged. They said my gut was torn up kind of bad and that I would get disability pay every month after I was discharged.

I went back to Barnes to live with my aunt and uncle until I could find work and get my own place. I didn't know it, but my aunt had died while I was overseas, and my uncle had turned bitter and quiet. My brother had moved to Milwaukee where he got a job in one of the breweries. I could have gone there, I guess, but I kind of liked it in Barnes. I like the openness, and the woods, and the lakes. I'm not much of a city person. Cities make you feel too, I'm not sure how to put it, too tiny, and I don't like feeling tiny. I'm a very big man, tall and broad-shouldered, with big arms, big hands, and big fingers. No, I was perfectly content to live in Barnes where I felt my size.

I got a job logging. It was hard work, and it was outdoors, and at the end of the day you were sore and sometimes cut and bruised, but you felt good all over; you had accomplished something, and you just felt good.

I saved my money, including my disability checks, and before long I bought a plot of land on Bony Lake. I'm pretty good with my hands, so I put up a small log house that was as tight and as solid as a fort. I had a well with a pump in the kitchen sink, an outhouse, and an old potbellied stove I bought at an auction. It was a good house—cool enough in summer and warm enough in winter. I settled in and was fairly content, but I didn't much like being alone all the time.

I like to drink beer, and I like people, and I like to dance. Most every evening I made my way to any one or more of several taverns in Barnes where I drank beer with the other locals and danced with any girl that would let me, if there was music, and there usually was music. I became a kind of fixture in the local taverns, and I liked that. I liked walking in and hearing everyone greet me. One year folded into another. I knew most of the people in town (Barnes isn't very big), and everyone seemed to like me well enough. It was a pretty good life, but still I had a gnawing feeling in my stomach that life could be even better with someone. I was now thirty-two and anxious to meet a girl.

Then it happened. A friend, Michael Fitzpatrick, told me his sister, who wasn't quite thirty, had just come to Barnes from Chicago for an extended visit, and he wanted me to meet her, so he invited me to dinner one Sunday. I learned later that she had been jilted by a guy she was engaged to, and she wanted a fresh start. I guess Michael had told her about me so she wouldn't be taken by surprise, and she agreed to meet me. Her name was Kathleen, and when I saw her something happened inside me. She was tall and slender with long, wavy hair the color of a sunrise. She had deep blue eyes and a smile that made you smile and let you know in an instant that her heart was warm. We talked easily that evening, and when dinner was done, we went for a long walk and talked some more. I guess this is kind of silly, but I fell in love with Kathleen Fitzpatrick that night, and I knew in my bones that one day she would be my wife.

Kathleen and I began seeing each other, and as the days and weeks and months went by, we discovered we were very much alike. We professed our love for each other, and although it wasn't exactly discussed, there was a sort of mutual understanding that we would get married. I was happy, happier than I had ever been, and I knew Kathleen was happy too.

I came home from work one day, and when I went in the house I saw an envelope with my name on it on the dining room table. I opened it and began reading:

My Dearest Hank:

By the time you get this I will be on my way back to Chicago. There is no way I can tell you this easily. I know it will hurt you, and I'm sorry for that, but it just has to be.

I've been thinking about this for a long time. I can't marry you. I don't want to spend the rest of my life in Barnes. I love you, but not enough to overcome the terror I feel thinking of a lonely life here in the woods.

I hope you understand. It just wouldn't work between us, and we would both be miserable. Forgive me; I don't mean to hurt you, but I have to do this.

Please don't come after me. It's over between us and nothing will change that.

Kathleen

Well, you can pretty well imagine how I felt about that. I thought my life had ended, and I had all kinds of emotions swirling around in me for a long time—some I wasn't even sure I understood.

That happened forty years ago. I still have Kathleen's letter. The hurt has faded, but I still think about her, and no one knows this, but I still love her. I never married. I guess I never met anyone that was, well, I just never married. But I'm getting ahead of my story.

I quit logging and began doing odd jobs for people around Barnes, mostly summer people who hired me to do plumbing jobs, carpentry jobs, electrical jobs, even stone work. I was pretty good at it, and people seemed to trust me. I liked the idea of setting my own hours and not having a boss to answer to. Besides, I was doing all right financially. I don't need much, and what I made, along with my disability pension, was plenty.

I eventually tore down the log house and built a larger home out of poured concrete and cinder block, and I sided it with half logs. This was a solid house. I was very pleased with it, and I've got to admit, a little proud of what I had done.

One day, when I was around forty or so, I finished a job for a fellow who I knew didn't have much money. When it was done, he asked me what he owed me, and I told him. "Hank," he said, "I have a violin that belonged to my father. I'm not sure what it's worth, but would you take it in payment?" *What the hell am I going to do with a violin?* I thought. But I knew he was kind of up against it, and I didn't want to embarrass him, so I took the violin and went home.

I had never held a violin, but I had seen enough of them played, so I brought it up to my chin and drew the bow slowly across the strings. It didn't sound like violins I'd heard, but it fascinated me, so I decided I would learn how to play it.

I won't bore you with the details, but after a few lessons bartered from a music teacher I did some work for, and a lot of hard work practicing, I learned how to read music and how to play the violin. People say I was kind of good at it.

I brought that violin with me everywhere. I played in all the taverns around Barnes, and I had a wonderful time doing it. I didn't play for money, although people often bought me beer; I played because I liked it, and I liked the smiles on my friends' faces when I played. I even learned to play some classical music, but I kept that pretty much to myself.

A few years ago, I turned seventy-four. I had stopped working for the most part because my legs and hips were kind of giving out, and I had arthritis in my fingers. I had to stop playing the violin because I couldn't finger the strings any more. That hurt. The violin was my good friend, and the music I made was my pleasure.

Last year I had an attack and passed out on my living room floor. A friend found me and called an ambulance. They took me to Duluth and operated on my gut. It had something to do with my old war wound, and they had to take out part of my intestine. Things weren't the same after that. I had to wear one of those bags. My eyes started to get worse so that I could no longer see well enough to drive. I had to rely on others to take me around. The whole thing was humiliating. Here I am, a huge, strong ox of a man, wearing a bag, fingers and legs so bad I can barely function, and forced to rely on the charity of others even to go out for a beer. That was no way to live. It wasn't living at all.

This morning I got up, took a bath, and shaved. I put on my best bib overalls and a fresh, clean shirt. I sat down at the dining room table and wrote a long note—the same table where Kathleen had left the note for me so many years ago. It was a beautiful summer day today—sunny, warm, and still. The flowers in my garden leapt out with their brilliance, and the grass smelled fresh and clean. I took my favorite deer rifle and went outside. I lay down on that sweet, soft grass for a while with my eyes closed as the sun spread over me like an old familiar quilt. I thought about the life I'd lived, and you know, it was pretty good. Sure, I've had some disappointments, but I've had more good times than bad, and I have a lot of friends who care about me. I smiled as the thoughts of my life swirled about in my head.

Some of you will not approve of what I did, but I hope you will understand. I am now at peace.

ODE TO A FELLOW ANCIENT MARINER

From over the sea, from a distant land,
He came to my office one sunny day.
With Ed by his side to lend a hand,
He announced to all that his name was Ray.
      I wasn't sure.

COS and SRA; the posturing began in the usual mode.
But soon I learned that this Chief so new
Was a stand-up guy with a heart of gold,
And as time passed by our friendship grew.
      To my delight.

By sea we assaulted the lamb-like foe.
Off sailing we went on a sloop so proud,
With Chinese, African, or whoever would go,
Through quiet and calm and Halloween crowd.
      With Bushmills too.

Yemen will never quite be the same.
The poor lad was awed, and lost all his gall,
As Ray was there to guide the game,
While Dominic's taxi answered our call.
        More Bushmills.

"Do you want a job?" he said one day.
Now being retired and advancing in age,
I accepted with glee and got back in the fray,
Grateful to serve with such an old sage.
        His hair is gray.

Comes now the time to move ahead,
To venues anew with paint and brush.
But hear me all; now let it be said,
This guy named Ray is a royal flush.
        Good luck my friend.

CALLISTA'S HAIR

I am fascinated by Callista Gingrich's hair. Ariel Levy, in a recent *New Yorker* article said, "Her hair is platinum blond and very stiff, with one remarkable lock styled into an immobile, upward swoosh."

It has been said that hair expresses the personality. I suppose that's true, and if it is, perhaps Callista's bold sweep to the left (not politically, directionally) denotes an intelligent (she graduated cum laude), open-minded, forward-thinking person. On the other hand, her hair never changes. It looks precisely the same day after day, week after week, and month after month. There is never a hair out of place. It looks as if it could withstand the wind tunnel test. It's as hard, immobile, and unchanging as Michelangelo's *David*. The leading edge of her sweep looks sharp enough to cut meat. So, does this monotonous rigidity denote someone who is intellectually deprived, close-minded, and small-thinking? Perhaps; she is a Republican, after all.

I worry about Newt. In those tender moments with Callista, how does he run his fingers through her hair? Does he break his nails and fracture his phalanges when he tries? Is it like running your fingers through a wire brush? What about in bed at night? I can picture poor Newt, dog tired after a long day of spinning the truth, wanting only to get some sleep. He finally doses off and Callista rolls over. As she does her hair crackles and breaks like peanut brittle, and Newt is once again awake.

I wonder how she gets her hair that way. The left sweep sort of hangs there suspended, like a whore—no visible means of support. But hair doesn't do that naturally, so she has to help it along with shellac, or varnish, or bear grease, or something. Perhaps she has a special formulation of Elmer's Glue, packaged in a spray can, especially for her. But you can't get the hair to suspend itself then spray it, and once sprayed it becomes immobile, so she must use some sort of frame or jig. My God, but that seems like a lot of work.

There is another possibility. Maybe it's not hair at all. Maybe she's completely bald, shaving her head each morning right alongside Newt as he shaves. That's kind of a tender picture. What we think of as her hair might really be a carefully crafted fiberglass or carbon fiber helmet. This makes sense. It's a lot easier to put a helmet on than to go through the ritual of fixing the hair. And, it has some wonderful possibilities. She may have a GPS receiver embedded in the top of the helmet with a heads-up display inside the sweep that hangs just off her left eye. She could have a whole array of electronics imbedded in the helmet, all displaying their information on the inside of her sweep. All she has to do is glance left to see the display, and no one would know.

If it is a helmet with electronics, and I'm now convinced it is, I wonder if she's shared it with DOD. I can picture soldiers and Marines all over the world wearing Callistas. She'll make a fortune. I wonder if she's hired Newt as a lobbyist, I mean, historian.

CONTRACEPTION LUNACY

The Catholic Church is in a snit because the Obama administration wants to make birth control available to everyone, by all health care providers, including those who oppose contraception on moral grounds.

The Church's prohibition against birth control goes back to the Bible. Although the Bible doesn't specifically prohibit contraception, Catholic apologists cite Genesis 38:9, which says Oman "spilled his seed upon the ground." Then in the next paragraph, Genesis 38:10, God whacks poor Oman "because he did a despicable thing." Of course this has serious implications for all those little Catholic boys who flog the log, but that's another subject. The point is that in ancient times no one, including the Church, knew about human reproduction. It was thought that sperm contained the entire essence of a human being, and the woman's womb was merely an incubator. Then around 1875 it was demonstrated that women's eggs are fertilized by sperm, resulting in life; thus, sperm was only half of the equation. But alas, the Church, which has an abysmal record of recognizing science (ask Galileo), didn't change its stand. So, when Oman spilled his seed upon the ground, he really didn't spill a viable human being for which God got so pissed off. I don't know if God apologized to Oman for murdering him.

In 1962 Pope John XXIII convened the Second Vatican Council. When he did, he set up a commission of one hundred people, including clergy, laymen, scientists, sociologists, and historians. They were asked to determine whether or not the Church should continue its ban on contraception. John died before the Council was finished, and Pope Paul VI took his place. He kept the commission in existence. In their final meeting, they voted on the issue. It was ninety-eight to two to do away with the ban on contraception. They reported this to Pope Paul, and he ignored it.

Now it's the twenty-first century, and, in an attempt to catch up to the rest of the civilized world, the Obama administration wants all health care providers to provide contraceptives, a legitimate health care issue. But, the Catholic Church, living in a century long past, is apoplectic over this, far more so than they ever were over pedophilic priests. They want an exemption for Catholic health care providers. This is, in a way, almost humorous. What they want is for the administration to do that which they can't do themselves, and that is to force women not to use contraceptives. Estimates are that 89 percent (some estimates put it at 98 percent) of Catholic women of child-bearing age use contraceptives. So, if those angry old bishops can't get the flock to follow the rules, let's get the government to help out.

Of course, the uber-Catholic Rick Santorum, who obsesses over contraception and said in a January 22 interview on CNN that if a woman gets pregnant as the result of rape that she should consider it a gift, is jumping all over this saying the administration is attacking the Catholic Church, and indeed all religions. By the way, if you're a woman, I think I know how you feel about Santorum's "gift." If you're a guy, ask your wife and daughter how they feel.

The Obama administration isn't attacking religion at all. It is not unusual for secular law to trump religious rights when the common good is at stake. Indians of the Southwest who use peyote buttons as part of their religious ritual can't do so because peyote is a controlled substance and it's against the law. A Sikh, whose religion commands him to not cut his hair and to tie it up in a turban, can be fired from a construction site if he can't put a hard hat over his turban. Parents who refuse medical help for their sick child on religious grounds are prosecuted when the child dies, unless a judge takes the child away from them first and orders treatment.

Making contraceptives available to women is good public policy when you consider that contraceptives are often used to treat a variety of medical disorders. For example, oral contraceptives can reduce the incidence of endometrial and ovarian cancer by as much as 70 percent. The pill provides for lighter and less painful periods, PMS relief, endometriosis relief, and more. But even if they were used solely for contraception, it's still good public policy because it's a woman's right to make her own reproductive decisions, despite the Catholic Church's misogynistic view. Also, a healthy sex life is part of the glue that holds a relationship between a man and a woman together, so it would seem that birth control, which assures worry-free sex, is indeed good public policy. In a June 2002 piece, ABC News reported that over half of the Viagra prescriptions written are covered by health insurance—a double standard?

Now the Republican Party is weighing in because they see a juicy issue to rally the ultraconservatives among them. Senator Roy Blunt (R-MO) recently introduced a bill in the Senate that would allow employers and insurance companies to choose which health care benefits they will provide based solely on their so-called moral beliefs. In other words, they can withhold benefits for maternity care or diabetes screening or any other health care benefit, and all they have to say is that it violates their moral principles—no further explanation required. Thus, if the bill passes, the Affordable Health Care Act will likely be gutted.

I hope we are a more compassionate and enlightened society than that, but hope may not be enough.

COUNTERTOP CONFRONTATION

A Very Short Play in One Act and One Scene

Dramatis Personae
She
Glass
Toaster

Act 1, Scene 1

The scene is a kitchen. It is evening. She has just placed a glass on the kitchen counter—a heavy-bottomed highball glass, placed close to a high-end, burnished metal two-slot toaster with particularly long slots to accommodate artisanal bread from boutique bakeries.

Toaster, condescendingly

I haven't seen you here before glass. Where did you come from?

Glass, annoyed

From the cupboard above you. Where the hell do you think I came from?

Toaster

Well, I thought she kept her cheaper pieces in a box somewhere. But that's all right. You're here so I guess we'll just have to make the best of it. Do you think you'll be here long?

Glass, still annoyed

Make the best of it. What's your problem, toaster? I'm not good enough for you? I don't live up to your expectations? I'm...

Toaster, interrupting

It's not that. It's just that I have to be careful. I don't know if you realize it or not, but 47 percent of glasses are useless. They take, but don't give. They are a drag on kitchen equipment everywhere.

Glass, confidently

And what do you give, toaster?

Toaster, with condescending bravado

That should be obvious. She puts bread in me, and after I work on it for a short time, I return it to her golden brown, slightly crusty, and smelling delicious. In other words, I make something valuable, and I ask nothing from her except that she clean me from time to time.

Glass

That's wonderful, toaster, and I can see that you are perfectly content in your little world, undisturbed by anything you see, or don't see, around you. Your world view is one of privilege and entitlement because of who you are. You're an expensive piece of equipment, and you produce something pleasant and aromatic for her; thus, you have value.

Toaster, feigning humility

I'm not sure I would put it exactly that way, but you do seem to understand our relative positions.

Glass

Indeed I do, and I'm sorry you don't. To you I am merely a vessel; I change nothing nor do I produce anything. But, and this may surprise you, I too have value. In the morning she pours her orange juice in me and sips as she reads her e-mails. During the day she fills me with water, and it quenches her thirst. In the evening she pours wine into me, which she enjoys with her dinner, or perhaps after dinner as she reads. In doing what I do, she takes me to various places in the house; I get around. You may not be able to see it, but I have value, because what I do gives her pleasure. And by the way, I'm transparent.

Toaster, angry

You're all the same. You think because you're mass produced by Libby and sell cheap in discount stores, you can tell us sophisticated appliances what to do. I've never had to associate with your kind, and I don't intend to now.

Glass, as he's being filled with an expensive wine

Sorry, toaster, I have to go. She's filling me with a 2000 Chateauneuf-du-Pape, and I'll be carried to the fireside where I'll hear wonderful music as she puts her beautiful lips to me and sips slowly. Don't get too lonely until the next piece of bread is dropped in your slot tomorrow morning. That is, unless she decides to have cereal.

[Exit glass, with a smile on his rim].

DYING WELL

I updated my obituary the other day. Perhaps I should explain. I wrote my own obituary some time ago because, out of a sense of shameless bravura, I didn't trust anyone else to write it. I do, after all, want to be the hero of my own obit. As I was updating it, I began thinking about death, since I'm far closer to the end than the beginning. I'm not afraid of dying, but I'm a bit concerned about the method. I suppose lethal injection wouldn't be so bad, but beheading, hanging, or being burned at the stake don't strike me as particularly appealing. It would be nice to go out with something of a flair, with a "Give me liberty or give me death" kind of exit, but with the fervent hope it's liberty over death.

Edmund Rostand's wonderful play, *Cyrano de Bergerac* has a final scene worthy of one who strives for a grand exit. You will recall that Cyrano, who considers himself ugly and unappealing to any woman because of his enormous nose, has secretly loved Roxane for years. But she loved Christian, who spoke beautiful words to her under her balcony at night, and who wrote her a tender love letter before he was killed in battle. What Roxane doesn't know is that all of Christian's words were Cyrano's. He told Christian what to say under the balcony, and he wrote the letter. Cyrano has been visiting Roxane weekly at a monastery where she secluded herself after Christian's death. Now, on his final visit, mortally wounded, he, as is his custom, recites to her the news of the week from the *Gazette*, and as he does so, he momentarily faints. Then he continues:

Ah, yes! The moment that so rudely interrupted the *Gazette*. As I was saying, on Saturday, the twenty-sixth, at dinner-time, Monsieur de Bergerac was murdered.

It is now clear to Roxane that Cyrano is gravely injured. He goes on:

To be struck down by a sword in the heart, from a worthy opponent's hand! That's what I had dreamed of! Oh, how Fate mocks me! I, of all men, killed in an ambush! Struck from behind and by a lackey's hand! 'Ts very fitting. I've failed in everything, even in death.

Finally as death is near, Cyrano struggles to his feet, and drawing his sword says, I see him. He, the noseless one, dares to mock my nose. How insolent! You say it's useless. That I know. But who fights believing that every battle will be a success? I fought for lost causes and fruitless quests. You there! I see you. Thousands of you. All enemies of mine. I know you now. Ah! There's falsehood! [*He strikes the air with his sword*] And Compromise! Prejudice! Treachery! Will I surrender? Never! And there you are, Folly! I know you'll be the one to take me down at last. Yet I'll fall fighting, fighting still! You've stripped me of the laurel and the rose! Of glory and love! Take it all! But there is still one thing I hold against you, and when I enter God's house tonight, I shall wave one thing in salutation across heaven's blue threshold. For there is one thing I have left, void of smear or stain, and I take it with me despite you. My white plume.

He doffs his hat with the white plume and falls to the ground, dead.

Now that's an exit. Unfortunately I don't own a sword or a hat with a white plume. And the odds are I'll exit sitting in my favorite chair with drool coming out of my mouth. Or in a fleabag diner with a piece of cheap beef stuck in my throat and no one around who's ever heard of Dr. Heimlich.

But maybe not. Perhaps I'll be walking down a quiet street some night when, from the darkness, a crazed fiend attacks a sweet young thing walking ahead of me. I rush to her defense, and as I break him away from her, he pulls a knife and stabs me in the chest and stomach. As I am about to fall, I land one last blow on the attacker, knuckles to the throat, collapsing his trachea and leaving him in a heap, gasping for breath. The girl escapes. I fall to the cold pavement, withering in pain. As life drains from my body, I hear the distant sound of sirens; then fade to black.

On second thought, I'll take the chair and drool.

DOES GOD EXIST?

Does God exist? To the believer this is a silly question, because the answer is obvious—of course God exists. He knows God exists, and if you don't know it, shame on you, and you'll probably go to hell. But the believer makes a mistake when he confuses belief with fact. The existence of God, any God, is a function of faith, not fact, and if the faith is strong enough, it becomes fact in the mind of the faithful, but the fact is, it is faith.

People come to God through different paths, and like the "fact" of God's existence, each belief system "knows" and teaches that it is the only true system to the exclusion of all others. Some even go so far as to declare that if you don't believe in their system you will go to hell. Since there is more than one belief system that espouses this teaching, it follows that all mankind will go to hell. So who's right? No one can ever really know, and that's why it's a mistake of arrogance to ever assume there is only one true belief or religion—you may find out, postmortem, that you're wrong.

Consider this. One of the arguments for the existence of God is the complexity, magnitude, and order of nature. How could anything so complex, huge, and orderly simply come into being? There must be an all-powerful force behind it. So, we believe in God, a force so magnificent and orderly that He created the heavens and the earth and all that are in them. The Unmoved Mover—a being that had no beginning and will have no end. A being so powerful there is no power beyond Him and there never can be. But wait a minute. Isn't that substituting one mystery for another? We can't understand how nature came into being, so we attribute it to a God the existence of whom we don't understand either. Could it be that "nature" is God? That in some form or other nature has always existed and always will, and that the complexity and orderliness we see around us has occurred as a result of a sort of natural selection? What if there existed a universe before the Big Bang quite unlike the one we live in now or maybe just like it—it doesn't matter? And what if in millions or billions of years our universe collapses and another Big Bang occurs, resulting in a form of nature perhaps with the same rules of physics, perhaps no? And what if this has always occurred and always will? Is that scenario any less logical or more difficult to accept than the existence of God?

MISS KATHERINE
A Short Story

Something happened today. Something that made me think back—twelve, fourteen years, perhaps; that's when I met her. I had forgotten—it's been so long—until today when something happened. I am, by avocation (and spirit), a sailor, and I have had a not-so-secret love affair with the Chesapeake Bay for over twenty years. I have sailed its length and found safe harbor countless times in quiet coves, busy harbors, river bends, and behind tree-walled points of land. I have discovered secret places I was sure no other human had visited, only to wake the next morning and find other boats swinging nearby on their hooks. But never mind, when you're a dreamer, those sorts of things scarcely diminish the thrill of discovery.

Much of the sailing I have done has been single-handed. I have a family, and we sail regularly, but I slip off by myself from time to time, because I find that single-handing refreshes the soul and realigns priorities, and I discover once again just where I fit in the order of things.

Today something happened that made me think of a cruise I took many years ago to Saulk. I had never been there, but looking at it on the chart intrigued me—nestled in a small cove (a perfect anchorage, I thought) on the Ounce River, just a few miles off the bay. It's been so long that details are a bit hazy, but I recall the day was stormy and cold. It was fall, when sailing is best, but a time when chill winds and cold spray crawl into every pore of your body no matter how many layers of woolies you wear, and you swear you'll never do it again. But you know you will, and you only swear you won't because it somehow eases the cold.

The cove was as I had pictured it, small but deep enough for my little sloop. Nearby, in an arc following the natural line of the shore, was Saulk's downtown—some stores, a bank, a diner, and Tim's Tap. Between the water and the street, lining the shore, were elms, sycamores, beeches, oaks, and other trees I'm not sure of, all in their fall colors. And such colors were made even more brilliant by the setting sun, which had broken through the black clouds in one final golden sigh before going to rest. Herring gulls and sandpipers guarded the beach in an uneasy coexistence, endlessly searching for another meal, as Canada geese honked their way through the darkening sky.

I ate on board. Something hot after the chill of the day. The clouds soon closed in again as the sun slipped behind the trees on the far shore, and a starless darkness shrouded us all—town, trees, birds, and me.

I have long had an irresistible fondness for bars. Not modern upscale downtown hotel bars, full of phony wood and phony people, but neighborhood bars in ethnic pockets of big cities, or country bars far away from big cities, or little bars in little towns near the water—like Tim's Tap in Saulk.

I sat on the boat looking at Tim's, a narrow two-story building with paint-peeled front and an old Budweiser neon in the window. There seemed nothing special about it, but all bars have personalities. They're like people—each an individual. Some are good, some bad. Some fascinate, and some are so boring you can't imagine how they exist, or what right they have to. I have sat in bars in small fishing towns on the Eastern Shore of Maryland and Virginia listening to watermen talk after a day searching for crabs or oysters in the Chesapeake and have tried to understand their unique dialect, rich in Old English. I have frequented the Cat's Eye Pub on the waterfront in Baltimore, with its cast of characters straight out of a Damon Runyon short story. I have sat in little log bars in the north woods of Wisconsin, listening to men in flannel shirts and wool trousers talk of deer hunting, with the ever-present Scandinavian tonality in their voices. And I have sat in little country bars in Georgia, Mississippi, and Louisiana, listening to the good-ol'-boy farmers talk of soybeans and rain with a richness of sound that rushes magnolia trees and cotton into the imagination. Each experience has taught me a little about the people and customs and language of the area. I have met people I would be proud to call friend, and some I wouldn't, but I have rarely been disappointed, and I have always come away richer than I went in.

So I sat looking across the now quiet water at Tim's, and it didn't take a lot of personal debate to decide. In a few minutes I was in the inflatable heading toward shore.

Tim's Tap was all I hoped it would be. It had been built sometime around the beginning of the nineteenth century and had changed little since. It wasn't always a saloon. It had been a general store and later a funeral parlor, but it had always involved people—for better or worse—and it had been Tim's since not long after the repeal of the Eighteenth Amendment—and probably before. The bar, on the left, ran almost the entire length of the building, ending just in time to accommodate two small bathrooms and a storage room in back. Although the victim of neglect for some time, it was solid oak with what appeared to be the original brass foot rail, tarnished but still in good condition. But the back bar was the treasure of the place. A large beveled mirror topped by hand-carved oak in the Georgian style and flanked by iconic columns dominated a large area of the back wall. On each side of the smoke-clouded mirror, cluttered with stickers, labels, and last year's Little League schedule, were shelved cabinets with cut glass doors. The entire thing might have fetched a fortune at Sotheby's, but here, in this little place, is where it belonged.

It was Saturday night, and I thought Tim's would be crowded with locals and perhaps a few wanderers like myself. But Tim's was empty— not a customer. In fact, there was no one in the place at all, not even a bartender. I found a stool near the back on the chance a crowd might materialize and I would be in a good position to observe and listen. Soon, from the rear storeroom, I heard a door open and close and the sound of soft footsteps approaching. In a moment, rounding the corner of the short hallway, came an older woman in a tan blouse, mid-calf brown pleated skirt, and penny loafers. Her hair was mostly gray, thick and cut short. She was not a large woman, and in spite of her years, she retained a remarkably youthful build. Her face was classic. She had clearly been a beautiful young woman, and although lines now caressed the sparkling blue eyes and full mouth, there was a liveliness in her face and an under-standing in her look that made you feel she might be able to see into your soul and understand.

"Hi," I said, with as much casual friendliness as I could muster, a result of my long-held belief that it's the outsider who needs to set the tone—palms up—no weapons.

She stopped, and her face became thoughtful for an instant as she studied me. Then, apparently having passed inspection, the expression changed to a warm and reassuring smile as she said, "What can I get you, young man?"

There's something about being called "young man" when you're not by someone old enough to call you that and get away with it that is dis-arming. Now I was not only the outsider, but I had been gently nudged in the ego by this little lady with the engaging blue eyes and the look of a philosopher.

I ordered a beer and settled back to survey my new surroundings. Tim's Tap had seen better days. The wooden floor had long since yielded any trace of varnish, and the walls, mostly covered with beer signs, dime store prints, and posters of local events long since passed, were dingy, dark brown, and looked like they hadn't been attended to since the end of the last great war. The ceiling, like ceilings in many great old eastern bars, was an orderly pattern of hand-tooled tin squares with ornate scrolls and lines, painted chocolate brown in a later time, in an effort to cover the fifteen-cents-an-hour work of immigrant Southern European craftsmen—a not-so-subtle comment on misplaced values. This was clearly a beer-and-shot place. No extra dry martinis with a twist here. The stock on the shelves of that lovely old back bar lacked any trace of expensive scotches, imported vodka, and vintage wine. Just good, solid American whiskey. And in the coolers, no doubt, rested not a bottle of Carlsberg or Erdinger Weiss—no need. This was Tim's Tap, and if you didn't like the fare here, then folks here probably wouldn't like you much either.

But most fascinating was the woman, now busying herself filling a cooler with Bud and Miller Light. She somehow doesn't belong here, I thought. There was something about her that's different. I watched her move, wrestling armloads of beer, but with the ease and style of a dancer, with that certain carriage that defines words like grace.

"Kind of quiet tonight," I said at last, feeling instantly silly at such a moronic attempt to start a conversation. I might as well have said, "It's dark out" or "That's a brown skirt you're wearing," but then I was never very good at starting these things. She didn't reply, nor did she give any indication she had even heard as she put the last of the beer into the cooler. Then she straightened up, gave a little sigh, turned to me, and smiled.

"Yes, it is quiet. The young people don't come around as much on Saturday night as they used to, probably because I don't have live music here. Young people seem to need so much stimulation these days. But then I'm showing my age, aren't I?" And she chuckled quietly.

"I don't think you're showing your age at all; I think you're right," I said. We talked, interrupted only occasionally by customers who never stayed long. I learned her name was Kathryn Donlan, although I soon found that whenever anyone addressed her it was always as "Miss Kathryn." She was warm and friendly, and called everyone by name, but there was a reserve in her presence, and she was treated with the respect one might bestow on the village priest.

"Good evening, Miss Kathryn," someone would say. "Kinda quiet tonight, ain't it?"

"Good evening, Sam. Yes, yes it is quiet."

Kathryn Donlan moved to Saulk years before with her husband who was ill. They bought Tim's Tap since there was little else available in such a small town, and they needed the income. Mr. Donlan died not long after they arrived, and Miss Kathryn had been running the place by herself since. There was a lot of sadness in Kathryn Donlan. Sadness at the loss of a husband and the need to carry on alone, and another sadness that was evident, but which she didn't speak of. Kathryn Donlan's conversation was never down or self-pitying—she was too elegant for that—but this little woman carried a hidden burden.

Saulk became a frequent stop on my solo sailing ventures, and as the years went by, Miss Kathryn and I became friends. We shared a love of the Chesapeake Bay, good books, and good ideas. She had a facile mind, and I was enriched by my contacts with her.

She had been born Kathryn Glick in Boston; how long ago was never offered, and I never asked. Her family had been prominent, and young Kathryn Glick grew up wanting for nothing. After graduation from Radcliffe, she met and fell in love with Charles Donlan, a struggling young Irish lawyer from an immigrant family who had recently graduated from Boston College. Her family objected to the relationship, so strongly that her father threatened to disown her if she married Donlan. But Kathryn Glick was not one to be intimidated, and although the prospect of alienation from her parents hurt her, her love for Charles was more powerful, and they married. Her family never spoke to her again.

Charles Donlan was bright and had an insatiable capacity for work. He prospered and became a respected member of the Boston Bar. Miss Kathryn revealed little else about her earlier life, but in speaking of her dead husband, the love on her face was unmistakable. It was clear there was more to her story, but she was not a woman you questioned. You listened, and discussed, and even disagreed from time to time, but you never questioned. Miss Kathryn told what she wanted to tell, and to press further would not have been proper.

Something happened in their life. Something that caused the Donlans' existence to unravel. Perhaps it had to do with a child, or failed business venture, or a scandal, but whatever it was tore Charles Donlan apart, and in time his health and fortune were in ruins. It was then that they moved Saulk and bought the bar: a strange twist to a productive and predictable life.

Now her husband was dead, and she was left alone with little money and a difficult business for an old woman to run by herself. But Kathryn Donlan was made of tough stuff, and carry on she did, asking no sympathy and always radiating the grace and courage that caused all who met her to call her Miss Kathryn.

My last visit to Saulk was a month ago, the first solo cruise of the season. Tim's Tap was closed and a realtor's sign hung in the window.

Miss Kathryn died, the waitress at the diner said. She didn't open one day, and when concerned neighbors went to check, they found her slumped in a living room chair. A stroke, said her doctor. She was buried in the small cemetery just outside town, next to her husband. People from all over came to say good-bye to the gentle woman from Boston who had entered the hearts of so many. No, the waitress didn't know of any relatives; in fact, as far as anyone knew, Miss Kathryn had no living relatives.

That was a month ago. Today I received a small box in the mail. It contained a letter from some attorney saying it had been Kathryn Donlan's wish that I have it and explaining he had some difficulty tracking me down. Also in the box was a large brown envelope, nearly an inch thick, and well-sealed with tape. My name was written across the front in a neat, even hand. When I opened it I found on top a letter dated September 12, 1985.

"Dear Michael:

"Several years ago you came into my place one cold stormy night, just another one of the boat people that stop in occasionally, and frankly I didn't pay much attention to you. But as time went by, you came back again and again and I got to know you. I appreciate those visits Michael. You have been kind and understanding, but most of all you remind me so much of my son Michael—a son I could never enjoy watch grow into a man. If he had, I think he might have been a man something like you.

"I hope this doesn't embarrass you, but I want you to know how grateful I am for your kindness and how much I treasure our conversations. I have little to give, but I want you to have these because they are so much a part of me. I know you will understand."

/s/ Kathryn Donlan

When I took the rest of the papers from the envelope, I discovered pages of poetry written in her own hand, lovingly and carefully. Poetry of pain, and happiness, and introspection, all set down over the years. A pouring out of her heart and soul. Poems about her husband, some written before his death, and a tearful, anguished poem written shortly after he died. And there were poems celebrating the beauty of nature and the people and things that surrounded this lovely lady always. But the most gripping were poems of love and grieving for her dead son, who had been taken so early in his exuberant life, and how this loss had changed the Donlans' lives forever.

I sat, this afternoon, reading and rereading those beautiful, personal expressions. And as I did, I experienced emotions I find difficult to describe. How grateful I am for this precious gift—the gift from a beautiful soul—Miss Kathryn.

Author's Note:

You'll not find Saulk or the Ounce River on your Chesapeake Bay charts. Celebration of the human spirit doesn't need a place.

SONNET

Ere we parted when thou saith thou loved me not
My heart was victim of mortal love's plunder.
My soul wandered as if lost in barren desert hot,
And in my tortured mind I could not but wonder
If I had wisely loved.
But then my thoughts of thee, tho filled with longing as thee I miss,
Reminded that loving thee had gloved
My heart in rare and wondrous bliss
Which helped to ease the loss of part of me with its toll.
My thoughts turned back through full score time,
And in them I beheld the flower of thy soul
And all my time with thee sublime.
Now, sweet thief, thou hast again stolen my heart,
And in the taking thou hast made whole of me, no more apart.

WINTER

I haven't spent a winter in northern Wisconsin since my youth, and my youth was a very long time ago indeed. Part, or all, of my summers were spent here, and the lushness of the forest in full bloom, the beauty of the lake in front of our place, with its face in constant motion, the tremolo of the loon and the kaw, kaw, kaw of the crow in early morning, all galvanized me to the richness, diversity, and beauty of this place. Soon, all too soon, fall would come with chill winds and a color palette that would bring a tear to Rembrandt's eye. Then I would leave, anticipating my return the following spring.

Now I am here permanently. My summer cabin, nestled in the woods, has been transformed into a home. I am experiencing my first winter in northern Wisconsin in fifty years, and I am in awe. The lush foliage is gone, replaced by leafless trees, except for the conifers. A thousand shades of green have morphed into a largely monochromatic theme based on a melody of gray and black with an occasional high note of green lichen. The dancing, ever-changing lake is frozen—a sleeping beauty awaiting the kiss of spring to awaken her. Added to all this, somewhat to my consternation, but perhaps even more to my sense of beauty, is the snow. Everything is covered with snow—a thick lush covering, a velvet blanket of tiny ice particles. All the sharp edges have been rounded. Every branch and pine needle wears a shawl of white. And the color—the pure white contrasting with the otherwise dark dullness of the woods—creates a new and vibrant scene, a scene of shadow and light and variation and utter beauty.

Today, as I sit in my study writing this, it is snowing. As I glance out the window, the air is filled with thousands of white specks floating gently to the ground. I can't see the other side of the lake. My flag is motionless; a feeling of total stillness and peace pervades. The only movement other than the falling snow is an occasional black-capped chickadee foraging for food, or a squirrel nervously skirting across the top of the snow, perhaps on his way to his stash of nuts carefully put away in the fall.

I am in awe, and I am at peace. But above all, I know I am where I belong.

THE RACE

I have never thought it a good idea to go on an extended sailing trip with people I don't know. It's easy to get in trouble out there, and I want to be sure my shipmates know enough to handle most situations. So, when Pete told me his friend Shelly had asked him to crew in the Annapolis - Newport race, and asked Pete if he knew a navigator, and he suggested me, I was a bit skeptical.

I'd known Pete for a number of years, and in fact I had taught him to sail. Pete was the state's attorney in our county—a very bright and capable guy. But Shelly? I didn't know Shelly from Adam's house cat. Pete described him as a surgeon from a small town in Maine who Pete had met at the University of Maryland. Shelly had purchased a 42-foot bare hull sloop and finished the interior himself. Now Shelly wanted to do the Annapolis - Newport race, about 495 nautical miles, or three to four days at sea.

No, Pete had never been sailing with Shelly, he had never seen Shelly's boat, and he hadn't talked to Shelly for a number of years, but what the hell? It might be fun. Yeah, it might be, I thought, and then the adventure of the thing overcame my long-standing rule, so I agreed to go.

We were to meet at City Dock in Annapolis at 0800 the day of the race. Our class, Class C, was to start at 1100. A little odd, I thought. If I was skipper, I would want to get everyone together at least the day before to get acquainted, set up the watch system, and attend to all the other prerace details.

The day was warm and clear. My wife drove Pete and me to Annapolis, dropped us with our sea bags and other gear at City Dock, and after a kiss and "Good luck," she was gone.

It wasn't long before Shelly and the rest of the crew arrived in an overloaded Blazer driven by Shelly's wife. She only stayed long enough to drop the crew and their gear, but that few moments in time remain carved on my brain. She was a sour, frozen-faced woman, but I found it hard to take my eyes off of her. It was her luxurious black mustache that so intrigued, one that would make a Berber drool with envy.

Then we met the crew. First was Shelly, a little, abrasive, humorless man with an inner nervousness that kept him in perpetual motion. Shelly's nephew Bill, a cheerful, young college student from Colorado had flown in the day before to help crew. Next was Mark, a large, bearded OB/GYN from a small town in northern Maine. Mark was a friendly, intelligent fellow whose wife had recently left him. He was going on this trip, he said, to clear his mind and to try to decide what to do next. He had two options: either continue his practice or return to Harvard Medical School, which had offered him a teaching position. Oscar was a huge gorilla of a man who was an auto mechanic. He idolized Shelly, and it became clear early on that he considered himself Shelly's protector and bodyguard. It wasn't until I got to know Shelly a little better that I understood why he might need a bodyguard. The last member of the crew was Joe, a tall, lanky, slightly stooped potato farmer from Maine who owed Shelly money for surgery Shelly had done. Joe was crewing to help pay the bill. It was his first time on a sailboat.

It would be difficult to assemble a more disparate crew. I wasn't sure about Shelly's sailing experience, but I knew Pete had no ocean time, Bill had only sailed Sunfish on inland lakes, Mark had limited experience, Oscar was a regular on Shelly's boat, and of course Joe had no sailing experience at all.

My trepidation on meeting this kaleidoscopic assemblage of humanity was palpable, but I had agreed to go, so I wasn't going to back out.

Then Shelly dropped the bombshell. In a casual, oh-by-the-way sort of delivery, he announced that he hadn't actually entered the race because they wanted a fifty-dollar entry fee. Add cheap to Shelly's many attributes. This might be the deal-breaker. I had taken vacation time to go on this race, and now, at the last minute, I'm told we're out of the race because this cheap little creep couldn't spring for fifty bucks. I turned to Pete and said, "I'm outa here." Pete agreed. Then we talked it over and decided since we were here we might as well take a casual, laid-back sail to Newport.

We boarded *Blazer*, Shelly's boat, stowed our gear, and slipped the lines. It was about 1000 and Shelly was motoring out of Annapolis Harbor and straight for the starting line. "What are you doing, Shelly?" I asked, fearing the answer I thought was coming.

"Our start time is 1100, and we're running a little late," was the irritated reply.

"We don't have a start time," I said. "We're not in the race." He ignored me.

Now, with the mainsail and genoa set and Shelly shouting orders frantically, we began maneuvering near the starting line with the other boats in Class C. This little twit is going to start with the fleet, I thought. "Shelly, we better get the hell out of here before we interfere with someone who's actually racing," I said. He ignored me again. Then OB/GYN and Pete joined the chorus urging Shelly to sail out of the area. Gorilla and potato farmer didn't have a clue what was happening, and nephew didn't want to offend his uncle. With teeth clenched in anger, Shelly sailed clear, and we hung out near the east end of the starting line waiting for the 1100 start canon.

The sail down the bay in relatively light air was uneventful. Shelly had calmed down, and the crew began to fall into the routine of sailing. What Shelly hadn't announced was what watch system he intended to use and who would be on each watch. Risking the wrath of this disagreeable little man, I asked him how he intended to set up the watch. This seemed to irritate him, and after a pause he said, without shame, "I hadn't thought about it."

"Well," I said, "how about the Swedish watch system?"

"What's that?" he asked.

"There are two watches," I replied. "Port and starboard. Starting at midnight the watches are 4 - 4 - 6 - 6 - 4 hours each. This gives you short night watches and it's self-dogging. It's a good system with a small crew like ours."

Shelly, who was at the helm, never looked at me as I talked. He was silent for a few moments, then told OB/GYN to take the helm, and he disappeared below. After fifteen minutes Shelly reappeared on deck with a piece of paper in his hand, which he later posted on the bulkhead near the nav station. "Here's how we'll run the watch," he said, and began to explain a system he had devised that would take a Cray computer three hours of crunch time to straighten out. My watchmate was potato farmer, because, Shelly explained, I had considerable experience and potato farmer had none.

It was warm and clear, but progress was slow because of light air. It was late, I was tired, and potato farmer and I were off watch, so I crawled into my berth. Pete and nephew were on watch, and all was well. Suddenly, at around 0330, there was a lurch that immediately awakened me. We had run aground. As I began to roll out of my berth, Shelly went by me in a dead run in his T-shirt and blue boxers. His voice had risen to contralto level as he screamed expletives at Pete and nephew. Soon the entire crew was on deck as Shelly continued to scream. "Goddamn it! You're going to cause us to lose the goddamn race!" he shouted, as he jumped straight up and down repeatedly like a tiny Zulu dancer. Pete, ever-stoic Pete, didn't reply, and nephew was too terrified to speak. Everyone else was silent.

Finally I said angrily, "Shelly, there's no race to lose. You didn't enter the goddamn thing." I don't think he was accustomed to being spoken to like that. For the first time since we started, he actually looked at me—well, more of a glare than a look—and said in a much calmer voice, "Give me a heading to get out of here." I took the deck log, went below, and in a few minutes determined where we were, what the state of the tide was, and the best heading to free ourselves.

I went topside and said, "Your best heading is 124°."

"You're wrong," Shelly said emphatically.

"Suit yourself," I said, thinking I've had it with this jerk.

After several failed attempts which drove us further aground, Shelly reluctantly got the boat turned, using the engine and heeling the boat by putting the entire crew on one rail. He came to a heading of 124°, and we inched our way free.

Pete confided to me later that the reason he and nephew had run aground was because Pete has very poor night vision, and nephew had sat on and broken his glasses on the plane, and he couldn't see much without them. He was afraid to tell Shelly.

Over the course of the next few days, I got to know the crew, and they were an interesting bunch. Shelly, of course, was a complete ass. Gorilla was a dour man with anger seething just below the surface. Nephew was a bright, young guy with a casual upbeat manor. OB/GYN was an interesting, humble man with a marvelous disposition and sense of humor. Potato Farmer, my watchmate, was a quiet, pragmatic man with a gentle soul. I genuinely liked him. Despite his poverty, he never whined, and he had a sort of New England pride that made him endearing.

Shelly never stopped racing and nearly drove the crew crazy with his yelling, berating, and demonstrations of ill-deserved and self-anointed superiority.

We rounded Montauk Point and entered Block Island Sound in the early afternoon, reaching slowly in light air. As night fell the wind collapsed, and we entered a heavy fog bank abeam Block Island. The crew was restless, just wanting the nightmare to be over. Finally, someone suggested to Shelly that we should strike the sails and motor into Newport. Shelly would have none of it; after all, we were racing. The crew grew even more sullen. Finally, apparently realizing that mutiny might be eminent and he could be set adrift in the dingy like Captain Bligh, Shelly ordered the sails struck and tried to start the engine. It wouldn't start. It turned over, but wouldn't start. Now morale, which was already at rock bottom, fell completely through the floor. Shelly ordered me to call the Coast Guard. "What do you want me to tell them?" I asked.

"Tell them we have no air and can't start our engine. Tell them to stand by."

"Shelly, that's what the Coast Guard does. It stands by," I protested.

"Call them."

I went below and keyed the VHF mic. "Coast Guard station Point Judith this is the sailing vessel *Blazer*." There was no response. Repeated attempts yielded no response. Attempts to raise any vessel yielded no response. Our VHF was out of order. I started to trace the antenna cable only to discover that Shelly, who had finished the boat himself, had run the cable and most of the electrical wires through the bilge where they resided more or less permanently in saltwater. What an idiot.

We finally got the engine started and motored into the Goat Island Marina in Newport. All hands were eager to get off the vessel from hell, so moments after tying up, we were on the dock. All hands except Joe, the potato farmer.

"Come on, Joe, we'll get a few drinks and a good meal," I said.

"No, I think I'll just stay on the boat," he said softly. It was obvious. Joe had no money.

I took Shelly aside and said, "Shelly, Joe isn't going ashore, and I think it's because he's broke. Can't you give him some money?"

"He'll be all right," said Shelly, and with that he turned and was gone.

Pete and I gave Joe some money and convinced him to come ashore with us. We had a wonderful time.

A couple of weeks ago I checked the entry list for the Marion, MA - Bermuda race, which went off in June of this year, and which I've done four times. One entry jumped out. It was *Whisper*, a 48-foot boat owned and skippered by Shelly. That's odd; he didn't ask me to navigate.

SURVIVING FLIGHT TRAINING

The trilogy of airfields naval aviation trainees go through are Saufley Field in Pensacola, Florida, for basic training; Whiting Field, about twenty-five miles northeast of Pensacola for intermediate training; and Naval Air Station, Corpus Christi, Texas, for advanced training. At least that's the way it was fifty-four years ago when I went through navy flight training.

The first airplane the student encounters is the T-34, a prop-driven (it's jets now) small two-seater (tandem front and rear seats with the instructor always in the rear), which is a variation of the Beechcraft Bonanza. It is here that you're first introduced to a stick, rudder pedals, pitch, roll, inverted flight, and barf bags. After about eleven hours of instruction, and if your instructor thinks you're ready, you solo, which is the highlight of the entire eighteen months of training. Shortly before I soloed, a more advanced student told me that when you lift off that first time by yourself, be sure to turn around and look at the backseat, and when you see it's empty, the full impact of soloing sets in.

It's a beautiful, warm, sunny day. My instructor and I have been flying for about an hour, and now he directs me to land at an outlying grass field. I do, and when I roll to a stop, he gets out and says, with the traditional pat on my helmet, "You got it. Pick me up when you're through." Wow—solo. I taxi to the end of the runway, push the throttle all the way forward, and in a few moments I'm airborne. Up with the gear and then the look in the backseat. Yup, it's empty, and I'm thrilled. When I turn back, I discover that, as a result of twisting in my seat, I've pushed the stick forward; my ascent is now a dive, and I'm headed directly for the trees—very nearly an abrupt end to a promising career. Damn, if my instructor saw that, I'm toast.

If he did, he didn't say anything, and I moved on to Whiting Field. At Whiting we graduated to the T-28, a bear of an airplane compared to the puny little T-34. It was as powerful or more so than most of the WW II navy fighter aircraft, with a 1,425 hp radial engine, top speed of 343 mph, service ceiling of 39,000 feet, and a 4,000 foot-per-minute rate of clime. Wow—this is big time.

Whiting Field is actually two airfields about a mile apart, Whiting North and Whiting South, with a total of four runways, which means there are eight possible landing approaches. For reasons I can only attribute to sadism, the administration devised devilishly complicated approaches to each runway, far more complicated than any I ever encountered later in the real world. To make matters worse, we were not allowed to have with us approach plates, small diagrams showing the prescribed approach, as pilots routinely do. Instead we had to memorize the eight approaches. Good luck with that exercise.

It's another typical warm, sunny day in north Florida. I'm just finishing a solo hop during which I practiced aerobatics, such as spins, rolls, loops, hammerhead stalls, half Cuban eights, etc., and I did a few simulated strafing runs on houses and cars. The latter is prohibited, of course, but if you don't get too close, they can't get your tail number. I'm confident I have the approach to the duty runway down cold. Now, ten minutes before returning to Whiting, the tower announces that the active runway has changed. Oh God, now what? I'm screwed. Let's see, fly the upwind leg at 800 feet until abeam the white house, turn cross wind, then fly the downwind leg, descending to 600 feet—no, that's wrong; that's for runway 14 at the South Field. Okay Sarazin, stay calm, you can wing it. And wing it I do. A perfect landing. Oh, oh, damn, I'm on the wrong runway. Stick forward, flaps up, throttle balls to the wall. Get as much speed as possible, lift off, then climb out of sight in case an instructor decides to chase me. As I approach an intersection halfway down the runway, I'm gathering speed. I see another plane about to taxi across my path, but he suddenly stops, and as I whizz by, he's a blur. OK, 95 mph, pop it off the deck, suck up the gear, but keep it low and level to gather as much airspeed as possible. Take it all the way to the tree line. Closer, closer; now, haul back on the stick; climb, climb, climb.

A half hour or so later, I make it back and somehow get down on the right runway. The tower didn't tell me to report to the duty officer, so maybe I'm home free. I go into the ready room, and I see a friend who can hardly wait to tell me his story. "I was on a hop with my instructor," he says. "We were taxiing to the intersection of the inactive runway when this idiot lands on the inactive. He rolls out a little, then I guess he realized his mistake, gives it balls to the wall, passed right in front of us, lifts off, but keeps it level, just above the runway. Then he headed for the clouds. Man, did he climb."

"Did you get his tail number?" I ask with a slight crack in my voice.

"No, he was going too damn fast."

"Too bad. What a jerk," I say, and with a quiet sigh of relief, I turn away, as my stomach slowly unknots.

My last hop at Whiting was just before the Christmas break. If I successfully completed that, I would be on my way to Corpus Christi for advanced flight training. If not, I would have to wait until well after the new year, setting me back several weeks. The hop was a nighttime solo round-robin from Whiting to a designated point a hundred or so miles away, then to another point, and back to Whiting.

Every pilot, whether flying a 747 or a Piper Cub, has a checklist he uses prior to takeoff and a similar checklist prior to landing. It is a rule, as firmly engrained as "thou shalt not kill," that you never, under any circumstances, memorize the checklist, because if you do, you will surely, at some point, miss something, and that might kill you. We had kneeboards, which were small clipboards with a semicircular back to fit on the thigh, and a strap going around the thigh to keep the board in place. This is where we kept our checklist.

It's a crystal clear, moonless, but star-filled night. I climb aboard the T-28 that has been assigned to me, and start the checklist: fuel shut-off—on, supercharger—low, mixture—idle cutoff, prop—full increase rpm, etc., then I start the engine. The checklist continues. Something's wrong. The engine isn't acting properly. I'm going to down this plane and get another. I call the tower for another assignment, and they give me one. I hurry to the second plane. If I'm late, they won't let me go, and I'll be stuck here until well after Christmas. I've got time, but I'll have to hustle. There's something wrong with the second plane, and I down it. Now I'm panicked. I may not make it in time. I'm on a dead run to the third plane, and panting from the run with the weight of a parachute on my back, while sweat trickles down my face. I get in. I strap in then look down at my checklist. It's gone. It has somehow become dislodged from the kneeboard in the second plane or between the second and the third. If I go to look for it, there is no way I'll make the cutoff time for the hop. Oh well, I've done this so many times, I shouldn't have any trouble remembering it. The plane is all right. I mentally run through the checklist then taxi to the end of the runway with less than three minutes to spare. I'm cleared to go. Run up the engine, release the brakes, and a few moments later I'm airborne in the smooth, cool night air. I made it. A sense of relief and tranquility comes over me. Up comes the gear, then as I begin to ease the flaps up, the engine quits. There is terrifying silence—deafening, deadly silence. Aw shit. I'm going to crash and burn. Then, with a sweet roar, the engine comes back to life. I finish my round robin without further incident.

I don't know how long the engine was off or why it quit. It seemed like forever, but in reality was probably no more than a couple of seconds. Don't ever think you know the checklist.

POWER

The memory of 9/11 is still fresh in our minds, as are the horrors of Al Qaeda-inspired atrocities that have continued throughout the world since 9/11. We can't take lightly the warnings of Bin Laden and al-Zawahiri that their sworn mission is to annihilate the US and that more attacks on our soil are coming. They mean what they say.

So, given that, our natural tendency is to demand our government do what governments are supposed to do, protect and defend its citizens. There is a stirring in all of our souls, mine included, to say to our government, "Do whatever is necessary, but keep us safe."

It is in this frenzied atmosphere of anger and self-defense that the administration has ceded to itself powers to eavesdrop without warrants. Many legal experts say this is in violation of the Fourth Amendment and the Foreign Intelligence Surveillance Act (FISA) of 1978. The administration says the president has the authority to order warrantless eavesdropping based on the power granted to him in Article II of the Constitution; a reading of the Federalist Papers; a resolution passed by Congress three days after 9/11 that authorizes the president to use "all necessary and appropriate force" against those responsible for the attack; and a three-pronged test of presidential authority established by the Supreme Court in Youngstown Steel and Tube v. Sawyer (1952), which struck down President Truman's authority to seize the country's steel mills in the name of national security.

Who's right? I don't know; no one knows. A plausible argument can be made on both sides. I do, however, have that uncomfortable feeling in the back of my mind that history proves power tends to seek power for its own sake, always to the detriment of the governed. Lord Acton, the British historian, on commenting that a person's sense of morality lessens as his or her power increases, said, "Power tends to corrupt; absolute power corrupts absolutely." We've all heard that quote before, and it's frighteningly true.

Congressional hearings won't determine if the president exceeded his authority: they will likely be a partisan farce like the Alito hearings. This is clearly a constitutional issue, and the final arbiter of constitutional issues is the Supreme Court. The problem is, how will a case get to the Supreme Court, since none of the "victims" of warrantless surveillance are aware of it, and the government isn't about to reveal who they are. Some lawyers representing Guantanamo detainees have filed suit, but they're on shaky ground since they can't prove they were electronically surveilled.

This is not only fascinating stuff; it's deadly serious. Benjamin Franklin said, "Any society that would give up a little liberty to gain a little security, will deserve neither and lose both." Think about the wisdom of that remark by a founding father who was an active participant at the Constitutional Convention.

SAME-SEX MARRIAGE

I like Joe Biden. He is a bright, articulate, decent man who speaks his mind, and therein lies the problem; he speaks his mind. Memo to Joe: Joe, support the boss, expand on what the boss says, but don't get out in front of the boss. That's just what Joe did recently when he said he supports gay marriage, while the boss waffled, saying his position was "evolving"—whatever that means. Then Obama, having been pushed into a corner by Biden and several cabinet members, came out with a somewhat lame endorsement of same-sex marriage by injecting the caveat that it should be up to the states. Let's talk about same-sex marriage.

There are three things at work here. One is moral, another religious, and finally one is human. When I refer to moral, I mean the immorality of denying basic rights to any group because of race, gender, ethnicity, national origin, or sexual orientation. There is, I think, a legal aspect also. Denying two adults who are in love and want to commit to each other the opportunity to do so in a way that has profound social and legal consequences is a violation of the due process clause of the Fourteenth Amendment, which states in part, "No State shall…deny to any person within its jurisdiction the equal protection of the laws."

Marriage is, and historically was until the church intervened, a civil contract. Listen to the words of the minister, priest, rabbi, or whatever religious person is officiating at a wedding. At the end he or she says something like, "By the power invested in me by the state of _____,

I now pronounce you husband and wife." It's the state that sanctions marriage and decides who can get married. It's the state that decides how marital property should be divided, who should have custody of the children, how one spouse can make medical decisions for the other in times of crisis, how inheritances should flow, and so on. If you live in New York and your church says you can't marry someone of the same sex, you can get married by the state, and it is a completely valid, legally binding contract. Your church may not be too happy with you, but at least you have all the legal rights and protections that marriage brings, and that, from a practical point of view, is what's important.

People get married for a variety of reasons, but in our culture the most predominant reason is because they love each other and have mutually decided that they want to devote the rest of their lives to each other, and in doing so they want to enter into a public and legally binding contract—marriage. Who of us can say that the love of two men or two women is less valid than the love of a man and woman? What legal grounds does the state have for denying the gay segment of our population the same rights the rest of us have? How does that denial benefit the state?

Now let's tackle the so-called religious argument against same-sex marriage and, by extension, homosexuality, which I find to be particularly irksome and hypocritical. Many of you remember when it was immoral and against God's natural law for people of different races to marry. And it was immoral and against God's natural law for the races to integrate. Christian fundamentalists, including the KKK, punched the air with the fist of righteousness with one hand, while holding the Bible in the other, declaring that interracial marriage and integration are sins against God. Now it's de rigueur. Did God change his mind, or did we?

The fundamentalists argue several points regarding same-sex marriage. One is that it destroys the institution of marriage. Really, what does a 50 percent divorce rate do to the institution of marriage? I saw in the Sunday *New York Times* not long ago, under the wedding announcements, two middle-aged guys who had just married after a twenty-seven year committed relationship. Does that sound like it destroys the institution of marriage, or honors it? The opponents also argue that the purpose of marriage is to have and raise children. Really? By that logic, anyone who is beyond the childbearing years, or who otherwise can't have children, or decides not to, should be prohibited from marrying.

The core objection to same-sex marriage is that homosexuality is a choice and is unnatural and a sin. Think about this for a moment. Who in his or her right mind would, in this homophobic climate, choose to be gay? Scientists have found genetic traits specific to homosexuals. It's well settled in the scientific community that you don't choose your eye color, and you don't choose your sexual orientation. As for it being a sin, refer to the Bible. Leviticus 20:13 says, "If a man lies with a male as with a woman, both of them shall be put to death for their abominable deed." I guess lesbians get a pass. Here's where the hypocrisy comes in. When you hear the Religious Right quote that part of Leviticus, they leave out the part about putting gays to death. On the one hand, they claim the Bible is the indisputable and immutable word of God and should be taken literally, but on the other hand, they are selective about God's word because they're a little squeamish about murder, even if God commands it. Can't have it both ways, folks. Either you accept all of God's word, or not. Of course there are some who think murdering gays is just fine.

The Bible (word of God) also says that if your son is stubborn and rebellious, he should be put to death by stoning, Deuteronomy 21:18-21. Again, girls get a pass. Any of you killed your male children for being stubborn and rebellious? The book of Exodus gives explicit instructions on buying, selling, owning, and treating slaves, but most of us consider slavery to be immoral. Deuteronomy 22:22 says that if a married woman is raped by a man in a city, they shall both be put to death by stoning. The reasoning here is that if it happens in a city, she could have cried for help, but didn't, so she's guilty too. Is that the way we treat rape victims? Perhaps we can all agree that murdering your son, or a rape victim, or keeping slaves are immoral acts. And most of us probably agree that murdering homosexuals is an immoral act. If these are all immoral acts, then it's hard to escape the obvious; the Bible promotes immorality. To get around this uncomfortable little fact, the Religious Right hypocritically picks out of the Bible what it wants, while ignoring many of its demands and directives, which are discomforting, immoral, and, in our society, illegal. It seems to me, then, the biblical argument against homosexuality, and by extension, the uniting of homosexuals in marriage, falls flat on its face.

Finally, let's reduce the question of same-sex marriage to the individual human level—down to us. If you oppose same-sex marriage, there is probably nothing I or anyone can say to change your mind. As Kathryn Schulz point out in her wonderfully insightful book, *Being Wrong*, we humans have a very difficult time admitting we are wrong, and will usually reject our wrongness even in the face of evidence that we are. But consider this. If you and your opposite-sex spouse are living happily on Shady Lane and Bill and Tom or Laura and Jane get married at the court house, how does that affect you really? Is your marriage less valid? Are your kids less yours, or less legal? Does your mortgage payment change? Do your taxes change? Does anything in your life change? And, unless you read the nuptials in the paper, do you even know these folks got married? So what's the fuss all about? Is it really any of your business? I suspect what it's all about is a seething, just under the surface, loathing of homosexuals and homosexuality. Hating people who are different from us is not part of our DNA. Remember the wonderful song from *South Pacific*, about how you have to be taught to hate. Little children don't hate people of different races or different sexual orientation. We loath homosexuals because we learn to hate from our parents, relatives, friends, our churches, and the homophobic society in which we live. It's a loathing accompanied by fear—fear because they are different from us. That difference makes them unknown, and we have little inclination to get to know them. I think the odds are that all of us know, work with, or are related to gay people, but we don't know they are gay because they are afraid to come out—afraid of people like us. We judge them and like them because of their character and personality. If we find out they're gay, would their character and personality change, or would our view of them change? In other words, would they become different people or would we? Step outside your prejudice for a moment and think about that. And please, don't teach your kids to hate.

HOW AMERICA WORKS

Most of us hate the penny. Many, or most, of us leave them behind when we get change. I try to never have more than four in my pocket at any time. Most industrialized nations, including Canada, recently have done away with their equivalent of the penny. Why? Because it's essentially useless.

It costs 2.41 cents to make each penny; therefore, the government loses 1.41 cents for each penny minted. In 2011 the Treasury minted 4,938,540,000 pennies for a loss of $69,633,414. That seems pretty foolish doesn't it? Eliminate the penny and no one would complain. That's not quite true. The zinc lobby would, and does complain whenever there is a movement to do away with the penny, which is 97.5 percent zinc. It took 15,047,144 pounds of zinc to make all those pennies in 2011, so it's clear the zinc industry is heavily invested in seeing to it the penny stays.

Bottom line: The public doesn't want the penny; the government (taxpayers) loses money making the penny; but it stays anyway because of an industry lobby.

By the way, speaking of lobbies, you probably think your tax laws are written by Congress. Think again. They are passed by Congress, but written by the lobbyists on K Street. If you're wealthy, or part of a major industry, rest easy. The tax laws are written just for you. If you're not in those two groups, and you can't afford one of the expensive lobbyists on K Street to represent you, you're out of luck. That's why Warren Buffett's tax rate was 17.4 percent in 2010, and his staff's was, on average, 34 percent. And that's why a number of giant corporations, like Bank of America, Boeing, Citigroup, Exxon/Mobil, General Electric, and more than a dozen others, paid no taxes in 2010.

John Boehner, Speaker of the House, used to pass out envelopes bulging with money from the tobacco lobby to House members on the floor of the House while it was in session. That doesn't happen anymore; the House voted to do away with that practice—not the practice of accepting money from lobbyists, but the practice of passing it out publically while the House is in session. Just a little too tacky even for them.

Will Rogers was right when he said, "We have the best Congress money can buy."

Ain't it wonderful how America works?

GOOD-BYE

I take my wife, Marilyn, to physical therapy once a week. We see many of the same people there each week and have chatted with some of them. The staff is particularly caring and competent, so the weekly events are rather pleasant.

Last week, Marilyn was into her session as I waited outside the unisex bathroom in a situation that, had it lasted much longer, would have escalated from simple need to embarrassing emergency. There were two women, in their early seventies, I guessed, chatting nearby. Since I am a compulsive eavesdropper, I listened to their conversation. Most of it was the usual woman-chat: "I love your hair." "Oh, thank you. I had it done yesterday." "Did you hear that Barbara fell last week?" "Oh my, did she hurt herself?" "I don't think so, but it's scary." "It certainly is." I'm rarely bored, but occasionally my automatic bore switch shuts out that which might trigger boredom, and it was about to do so with this conversation when I heard one of the women, the one with the dark curly hair, wearing the beige blouse and dark slacks, say, "This is the worst day of my life." That got my attention. She paused for a moment as her friend awkwardly looked away and said nothing. Then she went to the chair, which signals the staff to check blood pressure and pulse. She sat, gave a sigh, and looked down at the floor. Someone said, "Margaret, is this your last day?" Margaret looked up, and as her face slowly twisted in anguish, she said very quietly, "Yes, yes it is." Then she began to cry quietly, softly, personally.

Why is this woman so disturbed by ending her physical therapy sessions? I thought. Then it occurred to me that here, in this place of healing, Margaret had found a family. Why, I wondered, is that so important? Is she alone? Was she abandoned by a no-good husband, or was she abandoned by death? Does she have any kids, and if so, do they pay any attention to her; after all, she's old and, well, you know, kind of disposable in the modern world of iPods and Blackberries? Does she have any friends outside of the family she has established here at the PT center? Is this really her family now?

The senior citizens shuttle bus came, and Margaret left, walking slowly and slightly bent, not looking back, as if to do so would cause a catastrophe, as befell Lot's wife. Shortly thereafter, Marilyn and I left. I couldn't shake the image of that agonized woman publically displaying her pain, and I couldn't escape the thought of how terrifying the silence of loneliness must be, like a night that never ends.

Margaret, they won't lock you out of the PT center; your family is still there, and I suspect they love you just for who you are—no baggage allowed or recognized.

MEMORIAL FOR RUSS
AUGUST 5, 2000

The graveside memorial service for Russ was at one p.m. Russ, who was only forty-six, was tragically killed in an industrial accident in Texas in May, and today his ashes were interred while his common-law wife Theresa and friends looked on.

Theresa is Marilyn's niece. Marilyn felt she had to go because Theresa's mother, Marilyn's sister, would have been there had she not died four years ago, so Marilyn went for her sister, and I went out of curiosity. Theresa, you see, didn't turn out too well. She is one of three of Marilyn's nieces whom I collectively refer to as the felonious bunch. The other two are Kathy and Billie. Billie couldn't make it because they wouldn't let her out of the halfway house, but Kathy was there today, somehow sausaged into a floor-length black dress and stiletto heels. If she was trying to make a fashion statement, it was in a language I didn't understand. Theresa, who is short and thin as a reed, was similarly dressed along with high-heeled black boots and what was clearly her very best black leather biker jacket. But I'm getting ahead of myself.

We pulled into the cemetery promptly at 12:50. The only living human we saw was a man in his early fifties standing forlornly by his pickup next to the chapel. I asked if he knew anything about a graveside service scheduled for one o'clock, and indeed he did. He was cemetery staff, and he said the service would take place right over there, pointing to a small hole in the ground covered by a green cloth. Just out of the hole's grip and on solid ground was a black box about eighteen inches on a side. "Since it's raining, I expect they might move the service into the chapel," he said, pointing to the gray nondescript building nearby. Then he told us the group had been there earlier, but they decided to repair to the Beacon Saloon just down the road for a little refreshment. "Can't miss it," he said, "if you want to join 'em." We declined. Actually Marilyn declined—it sounded pretty good to me.

Just after one p.m. the group arrived. Besides those I've mentioned, there was the preacher, Big Daddy something-or-other, tall and muscular with a magnificent huge mustache, red bandanna, a black Harley-Davidson T-shirt that said "Only the Best," faded jeans slit at each knee, and work boots. The others were similarly attired as befits a biker memorial service. The cemetery guy was right; the service began in the chapel where we were soon joined by a dog who was the faithful companion of one of the attendees. I think it might have been the skinny fellow who sat reverently in his pew smoking a cigarette as the dog lay at his feet.

Theresa and Kathy carried several items, which they placed carefully on the nondenominational alter. Most prominent was the urn containing poor Russ, I presume. I couldn't quite make out what its shape represented, but at the very top, probably where they poured Russ in, was a miniature motorcycle helmet. To the left of the urn was a picture of Russ with his biblically full beard, dew rag, and leather vest, seated atop his Harley hog. To the right of the urn was a Harley-Davidson beer can holder containing a can of Budweiser. I assumed that was Russ' beverage of choice.

Big Daddy began the service with a rather touching remembrance of Russ, which he had written on several pieces of tablet paper. This was followed by a beautiful poem (without attribution) whose theme was I'm not in that grave, I'm in the air, and water, and sky, and in your heart and memory. Finally he read the Twenty-Third Psalm. Then Theresa got up and emotionally told those there assembled that Russ was a wonderful man who got more wonderful each day. She said they had some hard times (he beat her up from time to time), but they weathered the bad spells and she would miss him greatly.

Now, having been bonded by our common loss, we moved outside to the grave as a cool, soft mist hung in the air. It was at this point that I saw what was written on the lid of the black box—"Harley-Davidson." Big Daddy lifted the lid, and Theresa placed the urn inside. Then she popped the tab on the Bud and poured it around the grave. When she was done, she gently placed the empty can in the box, and Big Daddy replaced the lid. Then, choking back the tears, he said, "Let us pray," and delivered a touching little prayer.

We declined the invitation to go to Kathy's house where the group was to solemnly gather for refreshments. I tried to get Marilyn to go to the Beacon Saloon, but no luck, so we had lunch and drove back to the lake.

INVASIVE SPECIES

Florida is besieged by dangerous invasive species like the giant African land snail, the wild hog, and the Asian swamp eel. But the most dangerous of all, a slithering, slimy, hog-like species, dangerous to humans, found in the Palm Beach area, is called the Rush of the genus Limbaugh, and commonly referred to as Rush Limbaugh.

I guess you have to be brain-dead to not have heard about the Rush Limbaugh debacle involving thirty-year-old Georgetown Law School student Sandra Fluke. It all began on February 16 when Rep. Darrell Issa (R-Calif.) rejected a request to let Fluke testify at a congressional hearing on government rules requiring employers to offer insurance coverage for contraception. Issa's loaded panel of "expert" witnesses consisted of only men, most of them representing far-right religious groups.

On February 23 Fluke testified before an unofficial congressional hearing in which she said that Georgetown, a Jesuit school, unfairly denied women contraceptives saying, correctly, that the pill isn't just for contraception. It is often prescribed for medical reasons. For example, oral contraceptives can reduce the incidence of endometrial and ovarian cancer by as much as 70 percent. The pill provides for lighter and less painful periods, PMS relief, endometriosis relief, and more. Of course, an unwanted pregnancy, in addition to causing an enormous emotional burden, frequently results in a financial drain on public resources, and may result in abortion, which the Religious Right says they are against.

The formula seems simple—no pregnancy, no abortion. But being against both contraception and abortion as the Religious Right is, is a little like being against eating and starvation—a bit difficult to have it both ways.

It is not unusual for secular law to trump religious rights when the common good is at stake. Indians of the Southwest who use peyote buttons as part of their religious ritual can't do so because peyote is a controlled substance, and it's against the law. A Sikh, whose religion commands him to not cut his hair and to tie it up in a turban, can be fired from a construction job if he can't put a hard hat over his turban. Parents who refuse medical help for their sick child on religious grounds are prosecuted when the child dies, unless a judge takes the child away from them first and orders treatment. It seems to me that making contraceptives available is simply good public policy.

On February 27 the conservative blogosphere began attacking Fluke. A CNN headline read, "Sex-crazed coeds going broke buying birth control..."

Then on February 29 Limbaugh, that Svengali-like Republican puppeteer, attacked Fluke personally, not her testimony, but her personally. He said that she "goes before a congressional committee and essentially says that she must be paid to have sex, what does that make her? It makes her a slut, right? It makes her a prostitute. She wants to be paid to have sex. She's having so much sex she can't afford contraception. She wants you and me and the taxpayers to pay her to have sex. What does that make us? We're the pimps. The Johns." Of course the taxpayers don't pay for contraceptives; the employers and health insurance companies do. But Limbaugh, that paragon of conservative moral rectitude, never lets the truth stop him from a vicious attack when he smells blood. The next day, in a statement that should warm the heart of every sexual deviant in the country, Limbaugh said, "If we are going to pay for your contraceptives, thus pay for you to have sex, we want something for it, and I'll tell you what it is: We want you to post the videos online so we can all watch." Perhaps Rick Santorum could use the videos as teaching tools for his home-schooled kids who are, no doubt, learning that evolution is an evil left-wing conspiracy, global warming is a farce, and the separation of church and state makes one throw up.

What kind of a man is this Limbaugh? I think his own words clearly set him down as an insensitive, vicious, misogynistic lunatic, probably suffering from narcissistic personality disorder. By the way, Limbaugh is on his fourth wife and has no kids. I wonder if someone is using birth control.

Limbaugh issued an apology to Ms. Fluke, which was no apology at all. He said, "Against my own instincts, against my own knowledge, against everything I know to be right and wrong, I descended to their level (the political left) when I used those two words to describe Sandra Fluke." Even in his so-called apology there is an attack.

Limbaugh has lost dozens of sponsors, and rightly so. Any sponsor who stays with him sends a message that they agree with him. Limbaugh has put the Republican Party, already in disarray, squarely between a rock and a hard place; he is, after all, the voice of the Republican Party. On March 2 Speaker John Boehner said Limbaugh's comments were "inappropriate." That's like saying the genocide in Darfur was "inappropriate." On March 3 Mitt Romney said, "It's not language I would have used." Really, Mitt? In other words you agree with Limbaugh, but would have used different language?

Sandra Fluke is an intelligent, articulate, young law student who stuck her neck out to champion women's reproductive rights and women's health issues. What she did reminds me of a bumper sticker I saw recently: "Well Behaved Women Seldom Make History."

THE DINNER
A Short Story

It wasn't always like this. There was a time, in the beginning, when it was all right. No, more than that, it was wonderful. But those days faded, then, with time, twisted into something ugly and evil. She looked in the mirror and saw the bruises she would once again have to explain away. How many times do you run into a wall at night? Or trip over a throw rug? She supposed no one believed her any longer, but her pride wouldn't allow her to publically admit the truth.

She met George through a mutual friend, thirty-two years ago. She was twenty-one and just finishing nursing school; he was twenty-three and working in a butcher shop, learning the trade. He seemed nice—very polite, and actually kind of handsome in a crude sort of way. He wasn't tall, just a couple of inches taller than she, but he was well-built, muscular, and athletic, with thick, dark hair and a broad smile that was at once reassuring and warm. Their mutual friends had invited the two of them to dinner. It was no accident, she learned later; it was a setup so they could meet. It worked. They began to date, and as she got to know him better, she began to like him. He was kind, and thoughtful, sort of funny, and sometimes just silly. But that was all right. Better silly than rigid and cold. His dream was to have his own butcher shop—maybe even a chain of them. He was ambitious, and that was good. She fell in love.

"Hey Abby," he would say on a typical call. "Let's go to the Eastern Shore Saturday. It's going to be a beautiful day, and we can bring a picnic lunch and eat it in that little park in Oxford on the Tred Avon. What do you think?"

"That's wonderful, George. I'll pack the lunch. Pick me up around nine so we can have a nice, long day."

"OK. Love you. Bye."

Abigail graduated from nursing school and became a scrub nurse at Greater Baltimore Medical Center. George saved his money and bought a small butcher shop in Catonsville, just a few miles west of downtown Baltimore. Then they were married. They bought a small, three-bedroom house in Catonsville and settled down to married life.

In a year and a half, Jennifer was born, and two years later Mark. George expanded his store and hired another butcher, Max, along with a clerk, Irene, but his dream of a chain of butcher shops eluded him. He was a first-class butcher, but not a good businessman. Abby kept his books and helped out in the store from time to time. George taught her the basics of butchering. They were doing all right financially, and the kids were well-adjusted and getting good grades. It was a lot of work, but Abby was happy and felt settled and secure.

Now, looking in the mirror at her bruised face and arms, these thoughts washed over her. She couldn't say exactly when things began to change, but they did. George became withdrawn and subject to fits of anger, often over nothing at all. By now the kids were in college and nearly ready to leave the nest. Eventually both left, but stayed in Maryland where they found good jobs—Jennifer as a graphic designer and Mark as a stock broker for Legg Mason. Both later married wonderful spouses.

George's dark moods became darker. He and Abigail fought constantly. He was verbally and emotionally abusive. Then one day, at the height of a violent argument, he backhanded her in the face knocking her down. He seemed almost as shocked as she, but said nothing, and never apologized.

The physical violence continued. The kids quickly became aware and tried to talk to George, but that always ended in a fight, very nearly becoming physical. They suggested that Abby file a complaint with the police, or get a restraining order, or better yet, move out. They each offered to let her live with them. She turned all these suggestions down. She wasn't really sure why; perhaps it was in the dim, irrational hope that things would change, but they didn't. The kids distanced themselves from their father, and he distanced himself from everyone. Even his loyal customers began to whisper that he had become surly and rude.

Now, today, looking in the mirror, she knew she couldn't take it anymore.

She left the same message on both kids' voice mails. "Come over to the house after work this evening. We need to talk about something."

They came, with their spouses. Abby began. "Guys, dad left three days ago. He packed up and left. He wouldn't tell me where he was going, but he said he wouldn't be back."

Jenny blurted out, "Is there another wo...?"

"No. No, I don't think so. I think he was very unhappy and just left," said Abby.

"Maybe he'll change his mind and come back," said Jenny. "He loved the store. I can't believe he would just disappear."

"He won't be back," said Abby with a curious certainty.

"What are you going to do, Mom?" asked Mark.

"I've been thinking about it. I've decided to quit my job at the hospital and take over the store. I think Max and Irene and I can make it work. I'm a fairly good butcher, and what I don't know Max can teach me. I think I can make this a very prosperous shop." They sat in silence for a while. When the talk resumed, the kids were supportive, and it was decided that Abigail's plan might just work. Another common ground was that none of them was sorry to see George go.

Three months later, on George and Abigail's thirtieth wedding anniversary, Abby invited the kids and their spouses over for dinner. She prepared a feast, the centerpiece of which was a huge, succulent roast. "Wow Mom, this is delicious," said Mark. "I don't think I've ever tasted a roast like this. What is it?"

"Yes, it's fabulous," said Jenny, "But it does taste different." And the two spouses chimed in with their approval.

"Well, it's a special cut," said Abby. "The taste comes from the feed it got before it was butchered. Not the usual stockyard feed."

The meal continued with light, happy conversation, then following a lull, Jennifer said, "This is kind of creepy, but I have a weird sense that dad is with us." A chill caused her to shake for a second.

"God, I've got the same feeling." said Mark. "This really is creepy. Do you feel it Mom?"

Abby smiled softly, the smile of a woman with a secret. "More roast anyone?"

THE POOR CLICHÉ

Pity, you should, the poor cliché,
Maligned with rancor in every way.

Editors, scholars; all men of the word,
Flush with rage when a cliché is heard.

Why do they act like their ox has been gored?
Do they fear the cliché to be mightier than the sword?

Do not these men of literary good manners
Understand clichés are but tiny banners

Flying against all odds not to be uncouth,
But to deliver succinctly a tiny truth?

Shame on you who would damn the cliché.
You have closed your souls to the light of day.

Your spirit will fade as old grapes on the vine,
While we of the cliché will sup life's wine.

MUSHROOM WORLD

I live in the woods of northern Wisconsin, hard by a beautiful lake. This is not Walden and I'm not Thoreau, but I sometimes fancy that I could be. There is a road, sparsely traveled, going by my place. The area around the house has been cleared of underbrush, but most of the trees remain, and they regularly clothe the ground with pine needles and cones. The grass, what little there is, struggles to grow in the sandy soil, heavily shaded by the trees. That's just fine with me; I'm not a yard person, and my joy is not in planting, mowing, trimming, or puttering. I'm far more inclined to indolence, and I say that without the slightest trace of shame.

Each spring the various grasses grow tall in the yard, and even I have to admit it doesn't look very good, so I have it cut. The grass grows so slowly after the spring cutting that it only needs two more cuttings until the chill of fall sets in and all growth stops. I consider myself fortunate that I don't have a pristine, brilliant green, well-manicured lawn that I have to cut every few days, or more if it rains. I am quite content.

I was sitting on my porch one evening this past summer, looking out over the lake, listening to music drifting down from the outdoor speakers, sipping a sundowner (a nautical term referring to the result of the distiller's art) and thinking, as I often do, how very lucky I am to live in such a beautiful place, as four deer walked slowly across the lawn a few feet in front of me, searching for morsels of green. When they had disappeared into the woods, I noticed off to my right, about thirty or so feet away, a beautiful mushroom that had birthed itself from the ground. It had a domed pale yellowish cap with white scales. It was only a few inches high and no more than two or three inches across. Its shape and color were quite beautiful.

I have a mushroom book, and occasionally I try to identify mushrooms I see, but I don't trust myself. Mushrooms tend to often look alike, so I don't eat any mushroom I haven't paid for. I narrowed this one down to two possibilitiesagaricus augustus, commonly called the prince, and very edible, or amanita muscaria, commonly called American fly agaric, and very poisonous.

I got my camera and took several shots, none of which turned out particularly well. The next evening (better light then) I got my camera again, but this time I used a tripod, and the shots turned out rather well; at least one of them was a keeper. I was quite satisfied with myself. I have a folder of pictures on my hard drive captioned "Fungus and Lichens," None of them are positively identified, but they're all beautiful, so I added this one to the folder.

The third evening as I sat on the porch, I glanced over at my delicious or deadly little friend, but it was gone. I walked to where I was sure it had been, but there was no trace, not a scrap, not a morsel, not a crumb. Even the ground which it had pushed up to spring into life, showed no evidence of a scar. It was as if it had never existed. It came forth into the world, lived long enough to display its beauty, then disappeared—no trace, nothing—just gone, surely to be forgotten.

It occurred to me that mushrooms are a metaphor for human existence. We enter the world very much alike, yet all different. Some of us are beautiful, some ugly, some plain. Some of us are deliciously wonderful and some toxic. Some of us, like mushrooms, serve a useful purpose by making life richer for everyone, and some of us contribute nothing or still worse, cause pain, grief, and even death. And after our time in the sunlight, we all go the way of the mushroom. We disappear into dust and leave no trace of where we have been, or even that we existed. Of course that's not strictly true. We humans do have loved ones who hopefully remember us, and we leave some record that we were here, even if it's only an official file. But you understand my point. Lest we get too puffed up about our importance in this world as a species, we need to understand that we are more like the mushroom than we are not, although I doubt mushrooms have loved ones.

OBSCENE

I have a couple of friends, both women, who are hypersensitive about what they view as dirty or obscene words. I don't say this critically; they're both good friends and good women; it's just a fact. One of them took me to task recently because of my sometimes salty language. Fair enough. I have a lot of other women friends who aren't bothered by any words, and of course, most of my male friends aren't particularly sensitive.

I find this dichotomy interesting, so I began thinking about it, and finally decided to write an essay about obscene words. I thought it would be a rather straightforward project. I was wrong. Writing about obscenity is like trying to corral fog; it's virtually impossible to get your hands or head around it. The problem, or course, is determining what is obscene and what is not. One of the ladies mentioned above finds the word "boob" offensive, although the *Oxford English Dictionary* classifies it, when referring to a woman's breast, as simply informal, not obscene or vulgar. So you can see that defining obscene is a daunting task. Justice Potter Stewart of the Supreme Court artfully dodged the question when he wrote, "I shall not today attempt further to define the kinds of material I understand to be embraced within that shorthand description [hard core pornography], and perhaps I could never succeed in intelligibly doing so. But I know it when I see it…"

I have a reverent respect for words—all words. I love their sound, their texture, their meaning, and their etymology. Words are jewels that enrich our species and allow us to express ourselves as only our species can. I find very few words objectionable, and most of those deal with intolerance, bigotry, and hate. So, the stage is set. Some words offend some people, but not others, and even a Supreme Court justice can't define what makes them objectionable.

In 1972 George Carlin did a hilarious monologue he called "The Seven Words You Can Never Say on Television." It's been on the Internet for years, and I assume most of you have heard or seen it. The seven words he listed are "shit," "piss," "cunt," "fuck," "cocksucker," "motherfucker," and "tits." In 1973 Carlin released an album, *Occupation: Foole* in which his seven words monologue was included. In October of that year a Pacifica radio station, WBAL-FM, broadcast the album in the afternoon. John Douglas, an active member of Morality in Media heard it on his car radio and filed a complaint with the FCC asking that it exercise its regulatory authority to restrain the broadcast of Carlin's album. In other words, Douglas wanted Carlin's album censored.

The FCC agreed, and the case bounced around in court until, in 1977, the Supreme Court, in a five-to-four decision, ruled in favor of the FCC, but the decision was very narrow. It said the routine was indecent but not obscene. It ruled the FCC can prohibit such broadcasts during hours when children are likely to be listening, saying "Words that are commonplace in one setting are shocking in another." To paraphrase Justice Holmes, "One occasion's lyric is another's vulgarity." The court further said, in what I think was a well-reasoned statement: "The Commission's decision rested entirely on a nuisance rational under which context is all important. The concept requires consideration of a host of variables." In other words, it's all about context. The court essentially upheld Carlin's right to perform his monologue, but in the context of a suitable setting. Obviously the court was sensitive to the overarching authority of the First Amendment.

Obscenity and pornography, or what some think is so, have existed in many cultures for millennia. Even the Bible is replete with obscenities—not the words we are familiar with, since they were quite different thousands of years ago, but behaviors. Lott's two daughters get him drunk, sleep with him, and each gets pregnant, Genesis 19: 30-38. Tamar plays the role of a harlot, seduces her father-in-law, gets pregnant, and has twins, Genesis 38: 13-19.

Various attempts have been made to curb obscenity, but the problem has always been defining it, and sometimes the attempts have been ludicrous. A New York crusading moralist named Anthony Comstock petitioned Congress to enact a "decency" bill. The result was the Comstock Act of 1873, which banned any publication of information about family planning, abortion, venereal disease, contraceptives, etc. Even a printed discussion of birth control was deemed obscene and therefore not protected by the First Amendment. Comstock even saw the woman's suffrage movement (to give women the right to vote) as undermining American morality.

Religion has routinely defined obscenity, usually insisting its definitions are inspired by God, then, in an attempt to control thought, taken actions to ensure the faithful (sheep) are sheltered from evil. Book burning was common in the early Christian church, followed in more recent times by lists of banned books, ominously declaring that if you dared read them you would suffer the fires of hell for eternity. Reason and the First Amendment be damned.

Back to the Supreme Court. In a landmark 1973 case, Miller v. California, one of the country's largest purveyors of adult (pornographic) material, Marvin "Ass Man" Miller, sent out a mass mailing describing some of his books and magazines. There was a complaint, and the case wound up in court, eventually making its way to the Supreme Court. Chief Justice Warren Burger, writing for the majority, said, "Obscene material is not protected by the First Amendment." But the court acknowledged the inherent dangers "in undertaking to regulate any form of expression," and said, "State statutes designed to regulate obscene materials must be carefully limited." The court decided to tackle the definition of obscene, saying, "The basic guidelines for the tier of fact must be: (a) whether the average person, applying contemporary community standards would find that the work, taken as a whole, appeals to the prurient interest, (b) whether the work depicts or describes, in a patently offensive way, sexual conduct specifically defined by the applicable state law, and (c) whether the work, taken as a whole, lacks serious literary, artistic, political, or scientific value." The three-part Miller test stands today.

Justice William O. Douglass wrote an eloquent dissenting opinion in which he leaned heavily on his fealty to the First Amendment. He said,

"The idea that the First Amendment permits government to ban publications that are 'offensive' to some people puts an ominous gloss on freedom of the press. That test would make it possible to ban any paper or any journal or magazine in some benighted place. The First Amendment was designed 'to invite dispute,' to induce 'a condition of unrest,' to 'create dissatisfaction with conditions as they are,' and even to 'stir people to anger.' The idea that the First Amendment permits punishment for ideas that are 'offensive' to the particular judge or jury sitting in judgment is astounding. No greater leveler of speech or literature has ever been designed. To give the power to the censor, as we do today, is to make a sharp and radical break with the traditions of a free society. The First Amendment was not fashioned as a vehicle for dispensing tranquilizers to the people. Its prime function was to keep debate open to 'offensive' as well as to 'staid' people. The tendency throughout history has been to subdue the individual and to exalt the power of government. The use of the standard 'offensive' gives authority to government that cuts the very vitals out of the First amendment. As is intimated by the Court's opinion, the materials before us may be garbage. But so is much of what is said in political campaigns, in the daily press, on TV, or over the radio. By reason of the First Amendment—and solely because of it—speakers and publishers have not been threatened or subdued because their thoughts and ideas may be 'offensive' to some."

Justice Douglas' dissent should be framed and put in every classroom, every school administrator's office, every library, and every congressperson's office.

"Contemporary community standards," as set out in Miller, change over time, and a good example of that is in literature, which has long been the target of the Religious Right who strive to save us, usually against our will, from evil. Three examples are particularly interesting.

Fanny Hill, Memoirs of a Woman of Pleasure, written in 1749 by John Cleland about a prostitute, was declared obscene in 1821, a ruling that was not overturned until the Supreme Court did so in 1966.

Ulysses, by James Joyce, was finished in 1922, but serialized in a 1920 literary magazine. The New York Society for the Suppression of Vice was shocked by it and got it banned by a trial court in 1921. The ruling was overturned by the Supreme Court in 1933, and it now stands as one of the giant works of English literature.

Tropic of Cancer, by Henry Miller, written in 1934, was widely denounced as an obscene work of outrageous smut. In 1964 the Supreme Court ruled that it is not obscene. It is now considered by many critics to be one of the greatest novels ever written in the English language.

We still have not answered the big question. What is it that's obscene about an obscene word? Is it the word itself, or what the word represents? Does my good friend who finds "boob" offensive find the same word offensive when it is intended to mean a stupid or foolish person? Is the word "shit" obscene, or is it the feces it describes? Is the word "fuck" obscene, or is it the act of sexual intercourse it describes? Is this acceptable? "Bill tried to fix his car, but he sexual intercoursed it all up." If it's the word "shit" that's obscene, then is it all right to say, "I don't give a feces?" If the things these words represent are obscene, does that limit the timid from effectively communicating? "Doctor, the you-know-what that comes out of my you-know-where has been bloody. I'm concerned." OK, that's a little silly, but it illustrates a point, and the point is that what is obscene is not only fuzzy, but can degenerate into the ridiculous. Perhaps the question of what's obscene about an obscene word has no answer.

Where does this leave us? Still confused, I'm afraid. But two truths emerge from the confusion. First, the First Amendment is sacred, and any attempt to impinge on it, or censor what is said, is an assault on our democracy, our constitution, and our freedom. We need to be ever mindful that although we may recoil at some language, even hateful, bigoted language, we must vigorously defend its right to be said. Second, there is no universal definition of obscene. It is essentially in the eye of the beholder. Your obscene may well not be mine, so I will acknowledge your right to be offended, so long as you acknowledge my right not to be.

ONLY CHILD

Let's get one thing out of the way right off. Many of you probably wonder why I'm so (how shall I say this and remain humble) perfect. There, I said it, and I have no regrets because as a writer, it is my Aristotelian duty to tell the truth. The answer is it's because I'm an only child. I'll expand on that shortly, but first some parental background might be helpful.

My father was one of seven children, a son of one of Superior's most prominent families. My mother was one of three children, the daughter of a coal dock worker. Dad was a quiet, introspective, kind of Victorian sort of guy, but with a good sense of humor. Mother had illusions of grandeur and sought desperately to climb the social ladder to the top rung. Both were secretive. Certain things were never discussed in our house: money, cousin Jim's schizophrenia, Uncle Tom's odd behavior, or the fact that Aunt Fran got dumped by Earl. The family story was that she was the dumper and he the dumpee. I only learned the truth about fifteen years ago. Mother always fancied herself the belle of the ball; Dad would rather not go to the ball.

I'm not sure how they met. It was never explained to me and, in fairness, I guess I never pressed the issue. Dad was going with Mable, but she wasn't Catholic, and in those days that sort of thing mattered, so they broke up. Mother and Dad got married in the church rectory; only Earl (of the aforementioned dumping) and my Aunt Myrtle were in attendance. I thought this odd because the marriage of Dr. Sarazin's son should have been the occasion of a Romanesque celebration. Neither of my parents ever came clean. I asked, but the answers were as nebulous as a hooker's tax return; the truth was never forthcoming. I strongly suspect my father's side of the equation vehemently objected to the blessed union. They didn't have a quickie marriage because my mother got knocked up, of this I'm certain, because I wasn't born until five years after that quiet little marriage.

We all have trouble visualizing our parents "doing it." Yuk. But in my case it's more than yuk; it borders on profound disbelief. My father never discussed sex, and even the word "sex" sent Mother into fits of Catholic guilt, certain she was awash with the devil's filth at the mention of the word. Of course as a teen and even young adult, I brought the subject up frequently, just for the reaction. But I'm jumping ahead.

When I was born, my father told me, he had to hire a live-in nurse, as they were called then, to take care of me. After the birth, my mother repaired to her bed with the vapors or something. I got him to admit years later that the real reason he hired Mrs. Brieland (I think that was her name) was because mother was terrified of taking care of a new baby. As for breast-feeding, I doubt she could imagine anything so disgusting. I don't know if Mrs. Brieland was a wet nurse, but if she was, I'm walking around with a stranger's immune system. At any rate she took care of me for at least two years, possibly longer. I, of course, have no memory. So, you ask, why have a baby at all? Simple. What would people think if Mr. and Mrs. Sarazin remained childless? That might be a broken rung on the way up the ladder.

So, for reasons that should now be obvious, I'm an only child. I grew up in a near-normal household. I never considered my mother odd, any more than I would have considered his hump peculiar had Quasimodo been my father. To my parents' credit, they loved me, took care of me, and, most important, gave me an enormous amount of freedom. They, particularly my mother, praised me. I never felt inferior, quite the contrary. (It occurred to me years later that had I been, I probably would have been shipped off to Uzbekistan.) The result was that I grew up full of self-confidence and blessed with more freedom than I would have given me had I been the parent. Having no siblings to interact with forced me to develop and exercise my imagination, and I consider that a treasured gift.

Another perk of being an only child is you don't have to share. Yes, that sounds selfish, even churlish. But it's true; I didn't have to share attention, toys, love, my room, or my clothes. To this day, if I ever do anything even remotely smacking of selfish, my kids will turn, one to the other, and say, "He's an only child, you know"—a line they got from their mother. Lonely? Never. I was so comfortable with myself that on rainy days when the neighborhood kids were all indoors, I played by myself for hours, happily inventing games and stories. Never lonely, always content.

I breezed through grade school, with a few bumps early on because of mild dyslexia, and high school. When I got to college (Marquette University), I made the mistake of confusing my first year of higher education with party time, so I was told to not bother coming back for my sophomore year. My mother immediately went into "What will people think?" mode and my dad was disappointed. He rarely ever got mad at me. When I did something stupid or wrong, it was clear he was disappointed, and I would have rather had him mad. He said he would continue to pay for my education on condition that I go to school locally and that I actually take it seriously. I called the UMD (University of Minnesota Duluth) chancellor's office and made an appointment. I figured going through the traditional admissions process would be useless with my track record, so I decided to go directly to the top. On the appointed day, I walked into his office, handed him my transcript from Marquette, and said, "Here's the record of a failure. I'm here to ask for another chance, and if you give it to me, I want to start from scratch as a freshman." He was a bit stunned, but he agreed, and four years later I graduated from UMD.

From there it was on to graduate school in industrial relations. It was awful. The thought of a career negotiating labor contracts left me cold, so I quit and joined the navy's flight training program. After six years in the navy, with a wife and two kids, I made application to the FBI and was accepted. Twenty-two years in the Bureau then retirement. The CIA asked me to come to work for them, so I did that for three really fun years.

The point of all this is that whatever I've done, I've entered into with the sincere belief I could handle it—no reservations, no qualms. I am convinced that confidence is a major factor in begetting success. Was I hardwired that way, or is it because I am an only child? Or both? You decide.

FAITH-BASED GOVERNANCE

My wife and I were sitting in a small rural coffee shop having breakfast one morning several years ago. In walked an elderly couple. The man was clearly agitated and complaining loudly to his wife about the state of affairs in the world. He exclaimed that the country is going to hell in a handbasket. "People have forgotten this is a Christian nation," he roared.

Is it? Tell the millions of US citizens who are Jewish, Muslim, Hindi, Buddhist, Sikh, agnostic, and atheist that this is a Christian nation, and you disenfranchise them by implication. America is a pluralistic nation, and that pluralism is one of the cornerstones of our strength.

George W. Bush wears his religion on his sleeve. He proudly proclaims he is a born-again Christian and that God guides his hand in the governance of this nation. He said that God tells him what to do, including suggesting the invasion of Iraq. Mr. Bush has stated in no uncertain terms that his Christian moral compass, with God's help, guides him and informs his decisions. What he expresses is a concept of absolute moral principles, a concept many Christians have no difficulty with. But the majority of the world is not Christian. Indeed, a large segment of our country is not Christian. So how does Bush's absolutism resonate with them? Or more fundamentally, who is the final arbitrator of morality? Who determines what is moral and what is not, and on what basis? Is it possible that in utilizing narrow moral principles upon which we base our foreign policy we risk becoming a theocracy? I would prefer that when my president makes foreign policy decisions on my behalf, he base them less on his personal moral convictions and more on the self-interest of the entire nation he represents. To juxtapose one's personal moral conviction upon another who doesn't share that conviction is an immoral act, and if done by a public official comes dangerously close to dismantling Jefferson's "wall of separation" between church and state.

So, if we agree that we live in a pluralistic nation and a pluralistic world with widely varying views of morality, then is there an absolute morality?

In expressing my views about Mr. Bush's governance from a narrow and specific moral framework, a devout Christian with whom I was talking asked if I thought that pursuing a legitimate foreign policy objective through a policy of rape and genocide would be acceptable. In his zeal to put forth his very conservative Christian viewpoint, he lost sight of the fact that his very question was flawed. Any foreign policy objective accomplished through rape and genocide cannot be legitimate, and here's why. You can say that rape and genocide are immoral on religious grounds, and I have no quarrel with that, but you can just as legitimately secularize that statement by saying that rape and genocide interfere with the orderly conduct of a society, and for that reason, they are wrong, and it is precisely for that reason that people of virtually all moral persuasions agree they are wrong. To say a foreign policy based on rape and genocide is wrong does not theocracize government; it simply acknowledges concepts of commodious behavior commonly held by most societies. But not all so-called "immoral" acts share the universal condemnation that rape and genocide do, and it is the imposition of one's narrow moral view of these less extreme behaviors on those who may not share that moral view that troubles me.

We are still left with the question, is there an absolute, or perhaps more appropriately, a universal morality? I think there is, and the example above leads the way. Although humankind has warred with itself, probably since Homo erectus appeared on the scene, I think the human animal is hardwired to seek peace and stability. To achieve that, a code of conduct, a basic blueprint for societal tranquility, had to have been formulated, and it was thousands of years ago, long before the birth of Christ. This code came not from religion, although virtually every religion throughout history, many of which have had no contact with one another, has adopted it. The code came from the genius of the human mind recognizing a problem and solving it, and it arose in disparate and far-ranging societies because of the universality of the human intellect. This code is, quite simply, the golden rule. Faith-based governance beyond this centuries' tried code is unnecessary. The golden rule, tempered by national self-interest, is quite enough.

THE STORM

A Story For Kathryn Sarazin
by
Her Grandpa

There lived, many years ago, in an emerald land boarded on all sides by the sea, a little girl named Katie. Katie was a pretty little girl, with shiny brown hair cut shoulder-length, hair that bounced like a rubber ball when she ran in the fields near her home. She had beautiful green eyes that twinkled like stars in the sky when she smiled, which was very often, because Katie was a happy girl with a quick smile and an engaging sense of humor.

One day Katie's dad, with whom she lived, had to leave for a few hours to conduct some business. Katie, and her dog Stormy, would be all alone. But Katie didn't mind. It was a beautiful, warm, sunny day, and all of the flowers of spring were blooming, and all of the trees were wearing their summer leaves, and the birds were happily chirping as they built their nests in preparation for starting new life. Katie was quite content.

"Katherine," said her father as he was about to leave, "I want you to stay in the yard while I'm gone, and if you need anything call me." He paused for a moment, then turning to Stormy, who was listening intently, he said, "Stormy, you take care of Katie and be sure nothing happens to her." Stormy cocked her head, blinked once, then nuzzled Katie's hand.

Katie's favorite doll, which she had owned since she was a very little girl, wasn't really a doll at all, but a stuffed bear named Snowflake. There was a time when it was nearly as big as she, but Katie grew and Snowflake didn't, and now the difference in their sizes was just about right.

After Katie's dad left she, Snowflake, and Stormy went out into the yard to play, but first they would have a tea party. She covered the picnic bench out back with a colorful flowered tablecloth, then she got three cups, three saucers, three spoons and three napkins. "Stormy, you sit here, and Snowflake you sit right here," said Katie as she carefully arranged the seating like a young hostess, completely in charge. Stormy was a little bewildered, but obeyed, and Snowflake sat quietly where he was placed.

The tea party was going quite well and was nearly over when Katie heard a deep rumbling in the distance. It was a sound like someone hitting the metal heat shield behind the stove at Grandpa's house. It startled her for a moment. Stormy's ears perked up, then she moved over near Katie and put her head in Katie's lap. Snowflake seemed unconcerned. "What was that?" asked Katie almost to herself. She had no sooner gotten the words out of her mouth than a thundering crash shook the table and the teacups as a huge rolling cloud turned the sky black. CRASH! again. Katie was frightened, but she remembered what her dad had always told her: it's all right to be afraid, just so long as you don't let it stop you from doing what has to be done.

Katie knew what had to be done. She quickly gathered the teacups and saucers and spoons in the tablecloth and began running for the house. "Come on, Stormy! Quick!" But Stormy needed little urging, and in a moment they were both inside.

Katie had never before been alone in a thunderstorm, and she was truly scared. She and Stormy went to Katie's bedroom, got into bed, and pulled the sheet and blanket over themselves. CRASH, CRASH. The thunder shook the house as lightning flashed so brightly they could see it even from where they hid. Rain came down in such torrents that the sound of it was almost as loud as the thunder. "I wish Daddy was here. I'm scared," Katie said to Stormy, but she got no answer. Stormy was squinching as close to Katie as she could, and her eyes were tightly shut.

The storm seemed to last forever, then finally the thunder grew fainter, turned to a distant rumble, and was gone. The rain had stopped and the sun came out once again, flooding Katie's room in clean white light. Katie and Stormy slowly came out from under the covers, and they both sighed with relief knowing the storm had passed.

Suddenly Katie had a chill. Snowflake. She had left Snowflake out in the storm. Poor Snowflake. He must have been very frightened, and maybe he was hurt. Katie and Stormy ran downstairs, out the back door, and to the picnic table. Snowflake was gone. Katie's heart fell. She had left her favorite stuffed animal, her friend, out in the terrible storm, and now Snowflake was gone. Katie felt weak. She sat on the bench and began to cry. "Snowflake, where did you go?" she said through her sobs. But there was no answer.

"Hey, little darlin', why the tears? You're much too pretty a little thing to be cryin' so hard." The high-pitched, gentle voice came from out of nowhere and startled both Katie and Stormy. Katie looked up, and there standing before her on the picnic table was a little man no more than ten inches high, dressed in a dark green jacket, green tights, and wearing funny pointed green shoes and a green cap that fell over to one side with a little tassel on the end. He held a long-stemmed white pipe in his teeth. His full, white beard came nearly halfway down his chest, and when he smiled, his deep blue eyes sparkled like fireflies. "Me name's McGhenty, Michael McGhenty, and you would be Katie, I believe."

Katie was startled. "What, who are..." she stammered. Stormy was now under the picnic table lying as flat as she could, with her head between her paws.

"I'm a leprechaun. In fact, I'm you're leprechaun. Every little girl has her own special leprechaun assigned to her, and I'm yours," said Michael McGhenty with a smile. He continued, "It seems to me that you need some help. You've lost something, haven't you?"

"Yes, I left Snowflake out in the storm, and now he's gone. I don't know what happened to him. I shouldn't have left him, but when the storm came, I was so scared I just ran into the..."

"I know, I know," interrupted Michael McGhenty. "That's why little girls have leprechauns, and that's why I'm here." As he spoke there was a little poof, and suddenly Snowflake appeared next to the little man, dry and clean. Katie thought she could see just a tiny bit of a smile on Snowflake's face, but she wasn't sure. "When you ran into the house and forgot Snowflake, I took him out of the storm for you."

"Thank you, thank you!" said Katie excitedly as she hugged Snowflake. "You saved Snowflake."

"Twas nothin', darlin'," said the little leprechaun. "Whenever you need me, I'll be there for you, no matter where you are. You can count on Michael McGhenty." With that there was another poof, and Michael McGhenty was gone.

A few minutes later, Katie's dad came home. "Are you OK, Peanut? I was worried about you. That was a pretty bad storm."

"I'm OK, Dad. Stormy, Snowflake, and I will always be OK." She smiled as she gave her dad a big hug.

AN AFFAIR OF THE HEART

I grew up in northwestern Wisconsin amidst pine forests and thousands of fresh water lakes, the legacy of the last ice age. Water has been as much a part of my life as the sky, or the earth, and I have been drawn to it for all of my life as inexorably as the compass needle seeks north. My first boat, or the first boat I can remember, was a beautiful 18-foot mahogany rowboat named *Kitty Foy* after my Irish grandmother. With a gleaming white hull, red cove stripe, and a glossy varnished interior, it was the spaceship that transported a youngster whose age was still a single digit to exotic places around the lake where my parents had a summer cabin. "Stay close where I can see you," was my mother's constant admonition. And when she wasn't looking, I would sneak the *Kitty Foy* off for yet another adventure, completely lost in my imagination, utterly comfortable being on the water and part of it.

That was many years ago. The *Kitty Foy* has probably long since become ashes in someone's fireplace. We still have the cabin on that beautiful little lake, and we have boats, and I still thrill at visiting the romantic destinations of my youth. When we go back to Wisconsin each summer, I frequently go out on the water on warm starlit nights and quietly drift on the gentle breezes of my imagination, as I did so many years ago.

My youthful initiation to the water was but the progenitor of something that has become a passion beyond passions and an etching on my soul—sailing. Twenty-eight years ago I read a piece in *National Geographic* about a sixteen-year-old boy, Robin Graham, who sailed alone around the world. The story fascinated me and ignited my imagination. Why, I reasoned, if a lad of so few years could do this, couldn't I? Sailing, it seemed, was but another word for adventure, another spaceship to transport the child within. I read every book I could find about the how-to of sailing, learned the language, and began to sail. I never stopped.

I've raced a little, but it has never held much fascination for me. I try too hard to win, and in so doing, the process becomes agony. Racing seems almost to be a violation of the sanctity of sail. Most racers I've known don't care all that much about sailing, only about competing and winning. The mysticism of movement under sail, that Bernard Moitessier so eloquently captured in his writing, is lost on the race course, and replaced with a sort of hard, loud, mechanical atmosphere full of polar diagrams, target boat speeds, and trimming by the inch. Lest the racing community now scramble for their word processors to write letters demanding my head, please understand that I admire their pluck, their skill, and their fierce competitiveness, but it just simply isn't my view of sailing.

There is a basic premise associated with sailing, and that is, sailing was invented by God to transport the blessed from one place to another in a way that is enriching and pleasure-laden. This is the law of the sea and has the same weight of truth as the law of gravity. Most sailors must have an anchor constantly at the ready so they can secure themselves firmly to earth to avoid being transported bodily into heaven. That's what He thinks of sailing. When I started sailing, my view was different than it is now. The destination, a quiet cove or bustling waterfront community, was the goal. Getting there was a delight, but arrival was the prize.

I started with an old Islander 21, which I named *Carina*, and sailed it over much of Chesapeake Bay, often spending days at a time on that cramped little vessel, which I dearly loved. But always it was the destination. I rarely daysailed; there had to be a place to go—a beginning and an end—a logical progression to neatly mirror the progressions demanded of us all in our jobs and our lives.

But the greatest progression is life. It's time that herds us all into the same corral eventually, and it's time that softens the edges and illuminates the soul. I have finally learned how to sail. After all these years, I have finally learned that although the destination is important, it's not as important as the process. To paraphrase a past presidential campaign slogan, "It's the sailing, Stupid." I've known it all along, I suppose, but as the years pass, it becomes more evident to me that what Rat said in *The Wind in the Willows*, "Believe me my young friend, there is nothing—absolutely nothing—half so much worth doing as simply messing about in boats," is a truth absolute. The thrill I get each time I leave the slip never diminishes; rather it seems to increase with time. Perhaps because I understand that each sail is a gift, and as I move closer to the close of my life than its opening, I appreciate the gift more and more. To be able to escape on a boat; to transport one's self across the water largely through one's own efforts; to sit quietly and listen to the sounds, and hear the quiet; to slip deeply into one's own soul and return to face the world around without pretense, ego, or malicious intent; to appreciate and try to understand the nature that surrounds you and propels you—to do all of this is to sail. One discovers that relationships on board become deeper, because all aboard are held together in a common experience, at once intense and soothing. And when the destination is reached, it is a delight indeed, but the secret of sailing is in the journey.

As I sit quietly on dreary winter nights, wishing for the miracle of spring's awakening, I think of these things, and I long to step aboard my little vessel again to set off on another journey. I long to sail, and that longing is not unlike the ache for a distant lover. Yes, sailing is an affair of the heart.

A PROBLEMATIC YEAR

Here we are, 2012. It's just begun and already there are ominous clouds on the horizon. The Maya (they're Maya, not Mayans I've learned) calendar predicts the end of the world on December 21, 2012. I find this prospect not only troubling, but problematic on a lot of levels. On the most basic level, I don't want to die on December 21, 2012. As a matter of fact, I'm not particularly keen on dying at any time. What about the millions of dollars spent and to be spent on the 2012 presidential election? What a waste. Whoever gets elected won't get a chance to be sworn in. Will his name go down in the history books as our forty-fifth president? And if it does, so what? All the history books will be gone.

Another thing that troubles me is my new refrigerator. Will Maytag honor the warranty if it's destroyed on December 21? Will it matter?

What about my property taxes? Should I pay them by the end of July, or just spend the money until the end of December when it won't make any difference? I wonder how many months it takes for the county to auction my house at a sheriff's tax sale. If I've got five months, I'm safe. I'll have to look into that.

And speaking of money, I might as well spend everything I've got and run the credit card up to its limit. Make that credit cards; I'll get a few more then visit Provence, Andalusia, Tuscany, and Bhutan. I'll do it on my own boat, except for Bhutan. I'll buy a mega-yacht, on time of course, and sail off into the sunset (sunrise in this case) to the Mediterranean this spring and stay there until the cataclysmic event, with one side trip on a chartered Gulfstream to Bhutan.

There I am on my 135-foot motor yacht, *End Game*, tied securely to a bulkhead behind the breakwater in Piombino, Tuscany, Italy, just sixty or so miles southwest of Florence. It's December 20, 2012. My steward and chef are ashore getting provisions: fresh anchovies, squid, red snapper, pasta, vegetables, San Marzano tomatoes, wine, whiskey, more wine and whiskey. I dine that evening with my guest, the Countess Delivea, Francesco, di Contallo. We have an exquisite late dinner on the afterdeck, under the Tuscan stars—a meal begun with ziti in a delicate fresh anchovy red sauce, followed by squid and red snapper in a caper, shallot, and seasoned wine sauce accompanied by tiny new potatoes sautéed in garlic butter, all topped with white truffles from Piedmonte. For desert we have bananas Foster (which, oddly, she has never tasted), and it is all washed down with copious amounts of Castello di Brolio – Chianti classico. After dinner, and with only a gentle hint on my part, she agrees it would be foolish to drive home so late, so she dismisses her chauffer and stays on board for the night. Then, just as we are in the midst of unbelievable, wild, unbridled sex, the clock strikes twelve, my yacht becomes a pumpkin, and the countess and I are toast.

But what if it doesn't happen? Remember Harold Camping, the retired civil engineer turned Christian radio talk show host? He predicted the end of the world May 21, 1988, then September 6, 1994, then May 21, 2011, and finally October 21, 2011. Many of his faithful followers quit their jobs, sold their possessions, and waited for the end. As far as I know, they're still waiting.

What if the Maya were wrong and the world doesn't end on December 21, 2012? That is a possibility, you know. The very thought of it is beyond comprehension, so the world damn well better end on December 21, 2012, or I'm screwed.

AN E-MAIL TO AL

A l:

A US Special Forces team in conjunction with British SAS, the Mossad, and probably the CIA, capitalized on someone ratting al-Zarqawi out, by surrounding the house in which he was meeting, and calling in two F-16s, which took Zarqawi out of the picture permanently.

The operation was beautiful. That two F-16s on routine patrol could be diverted and reprogrammed to drop two 500-pound bombs on a specific house, at night, speaks to the excellence of US technology. That the US military leadership didn't waffle and decided to take Zarqawi out is a refreshing example of decisiveness.

al-Zarqawi was a highly competent, highly effective terrorist, responsible for the deaths of huge numbers of American servicemen and women and the deaths of even more Shiite Iraqis. He was power mad, even to the extent that he had become a major problem for Bin Laden. I am glad he's dead. There will be repercussions to be sure, but his death is more important than the repercussions, and is a welcome event for this moderate.

So, with that as a backdrop, I was somewhat taken aback this morning when I read your e-mail, which forwarded several pieces. In one of them, someone injected a remark, referring to Zarqawi, that the liberals had lost their idol. That remark at first angered me, then I got to thinking about it, and I realized it's a metaphor for the enormous divide in this country, and for what happens when those on the fringes of that divide engage in hubris and cease to think critically.

I suspect when you forwarded that remark you didn't seriously consider its meaning. It means that liberals are traitors to this country. It means that liberals espouse terrorism and the murder of US soldiers and innocent civilians. It means that liberals deny everything this country stands for. It means that liberals can have no voice, because nothing they say is legitimate. And finally, it means that the absolutism of the conservative voice is truth, and all else is false. The similarity of this thinking to the Taliban and to Osama bin Laden is chilling. I doubt that in your heart you believe al-Zarqawi was a hero to liberals. I am saddened that people with differing views can no longer listen to each other and have lost the ability to think with critical, open minds.

We might all do well to heed the words of Benjamin Franklin who said in 1787, "Having lived long, I have experienced many instances of being obliged, by better information of fuller consideration, to change opinions even on important subjects, which I once thought right, but found to be otherwise. It is therefore that, the older I grow, the more apt I am to doubt my own judgments and pay more respect to the judgment of others."

Just some thoughts for a Sunday morning.

Harry

COLD THOUGHTS

When I got up a few mornings ago, the temperature outside was twenty-three degrees. For those of you who skipped class that day when they talked about these things, twenty-three degrees is nine degrees below freezing. It's also about fifteen degrees colder than the inside of the average refrigerator.

I had to take the garbage down to the can in the boathouse. That's a round trip of about one hundred yards. I wore a pair of old, comfortable deck shoes and a bathrobe over boxers and a T-shirt. The ground was crunchy as I fast-paced my way through the cold. By the time I got back to the house, shivering, with teeth rattling, considerable shrinkage of some body parts had taken place.

I don't wish to sound whiney, particularly to those of you who weather the northern Wisconsin winters, but you have to understand I've been away for forty-eight years. Except for a four-year stint in Maine early on, I've been living in warm and moderate climates, and I loved it. I don't like the cold—the cold that was an unnoticed companion when I skied, and tended a trap line, and hunted on snowshoes. Now it is a highly visible evil companion who hurts.

A day or so after the twenty-three-degrees incident, I awoke to a landscape of white. That's right, it had snowed—rather a lot of snow, as a matter of fact, and of course it was cold.

My God how I used to love to build snow forts, and have snowball fights, and roll around in the snow from early morning until dinnertime. I haven't built a snow fort in sixty years, and I don't think I'm going to recreate one now. I hate the snow. Snow is my enemy, and although I can't fight its arrival, I'm not going to give it the satisfaction of meeting it in person. I'd rather curl up with a good book and a hot buttered rum, thank you.

Today it warmed all the way up to fifty-four degrees. Wow, a heat wave. I decided it was time to haul the boat. I brought it around (slowly so as to not create too much breeze) to the public landing where my wife met me with the trailer. I wore my offshore foul weather jacket, which had comfortably protected me on several Bermuda, New England, and Caribbean sailing trips. Hah, little good it did now. I was nearly ready for toe-tagging by the time I arrived at the landing.

I'm not a very good at hauling and launching small boats. Most guys are able to do it without getting even their toes wet. I usually have to go wading, so I wore jeans and my Crocks—no socks of course, just bare feet tucked into holey, water-draining Crocks.

It's too painful to go into detail about the haul-out process. Let me just say that those souls around the lake who were startled this morning did not hear screams of joy.

Later, after I brought the boat home and winterized the engine, I was sitting in the living room reading when I glanced out the window. It had grown quiet. There wasn't a ripple on the lake, and the flag hung as motionless as a monk in meditation.

It was late afternoon, and the sun was low in the west, filtering through the trees behind the house. I decided to sit on the porch. Bundled against the cold, and sipping a sundowner, I looked across the lake to the hills on the far shore to the east, as the setting sun changed the colors of the pines and naked aspens every few minutes. The ground around me was completely covered with pine needles and leaves, all soft brown and beige. Slowly, ever so slowly, the color of the ground changed to a breathtaking reddish-orange, as everything about seemed to be enveloped in a soft fog of color. Then, as slowly as it had begun, the color began to fade, the glow of the sun on the far shore disappeared, and all around me gradually drifted to gray.

It was a wonderful few minutes, and as I sat, thrilled by what I had seen, I realized how dearly I love this place. What the hell; I guess the cold isn't so bad.

CONTROL ISSUE

Cecil County, Maryland, was a paradox. Situated in the northeast corner of Maryland, with the Washington – New York megalopolis corridor running through it, it sat alone in the mid-1970s as an essentially rural county, and even today it retains much of that character.

Something else set Cecil County apart from the rest of Maryland or even nearby Delaware and southern Pennsylvania. Cecil County had virtually no middle class. There were the very rich, several DuPont families and others, and the very poor who eked out livings where they could. It is in this setting that you find your hero, happily assigned to handle all matters under FBI jurisdiction in Cecil County.

One fine, hot, summer day an urgent teletype arrived from another field office. It seems there was a fugitive, (we'll call him Tom Jones), from another state, wanted for some heinous crime that I don't recall. Mr. Jones was believed to be staying with his aunt, (we'll call her Cora Moffett), at 125 Dogwood Road in Elkton, Maryland. Jones' description followed—a young white guy, medium height and weight, etc. The lead was "Locate and apprehend," with a cautionary statement, "ARMED AND DANGEROUS."

Since my partner was unavailable, I jumped in my trusty Bureau car and drove to the Maryland State Police barracks not far from Elkton.

I commandeered a detective, Bernie, and the two of us drove to Dog-wood Road.

In those days Dogwood Road was an unpaved road on the outskirts of town, on which was located a dozen or more broken down, ramshackle houses occupied by folks well below the poverty level. Cora's pad was no different. I asked Bernie to go around back while I went to the front door. The inner door was open, and only a screen door separated the inside from the flies, or the flies from the outside, on that steamy hot day. No one answered. An interesting legal question arises here. You can enter a residence without a search warrant if you have probable cause to believe a fugitive is there, but your search is limited to where the body could be; in other words, you can't rummage through drawers or anywhere else where a person could not logically hide. The teletype was a little vague about the veracity of the information that Jones was staying with his aunt, so I concluded that I didn't have probable cause to go in the house—a close call.

As Bernie and I were about to leave, a broken-down old car driven by a woman drove up and parked in front of the house. She was slender, almost scrawny, in her late forties or early fifties, barefoot except for flip flops, and wearing a very faded cotton print dress. I approached her. "Mrs. Moffett?"

"Yes. Who are you?" she said in a tiny, weak voice.

I told her my name and identified myself as an FBI agent, showing her my credentials. "I'm trying to get in touch with your nephew Tom. Is he staying here with you?" She was holding a bag of groceries as she, Bernie, and I stood in the middle of that dirt road. She said nothing, but looked at me blankly. Then I heard the sound of water falling on dirt. I looked down and Cora was peeing right there in the road. It was obvious the stream was uninterrupted by underwear, and when it hit the ground, it stirred up little dirt devils as it splashed onto Cora's bare feet and flip flops. Through it all she remained unflappable, apparently oblivious to the fact that she was relieving herself.

Finally she spoke. "Yes, he's staying with me, but he's not here now."

"When do you expect him back?" I asked.

"'Bout half an hour," she replied.

She agreed to let Bernie and me stay in the house until Jones came back. I stashed the Bureau car around the corner, then Bernie and I settled in while Cora tended to some chores, walking back and forth on the linoleum floor, her wet flip flops making a splat, splat, splat sound with every step.

Before long a car pulled up, and two young men got out. "Is that him?" I asked Cora.

"Yes."

"Which one?"

"The first one with the green shirt," she said.

I got behind the front door and Bernie ducked into the kitchen, separated from the living room by a sheet hanging from a slender metal bar. When Jones came through the screen door, I slammed the inner door closed behind him and said, "Jones, FBI, you're under arrest." He spun around as Bernie emerged from the kitchen. Mr. Jones wanted to fight. I grabbed one arm and Bernie the other, and we drove him toward the nearest wall—a little too hard, perhaps, because we put his head through the wall. This seemed to have a calming effect on him, and I was able to cuff him, then the two of us carefully extricated him, uninjured, from the drywall.

We put Tom Jones in the backseat of my car, and Bernie got in beside him. Although the temperature was well into the nineties, there was no air-conditioning. Mr. Hoover ordered the air-conditioning units removed from all Bureau cars because he thought agents would spend too much of their time in the cars trying to stay cool.

As we drove to the jail, Bernie said, "For Christ's sake, can you hurry up?" It was then that I realized that tough-guy Jones had taken a dump in his pants, as the smell gathered to a putrid crescendo. I guess it's a family trait.

·

GOD AND GOVERNANCE

There is an interesting, albeit somewhat disturbing, trend in politics, particularly Republican politics, and that is the emergence of religious faith (Christian only) as a qualifier for the presidency. It's not likely anyone could be the Republican nominee for president unless he makes a public declaration of his deep faith in God and membership in an established Christian religion. The Religious Right, which at one time called itself the Moral Majority, has hijacked the Republican Party. The thinking is that unless you are deeply religious, you can't govern. Newt Gingrich said the other day that he could not vote for an atheist for president because nonbelievers lack the moral grounding to guide the ship of state. He also said, "How can you have judgment if you have no faith? How can I trust you with power if you don't pray?" He also likened atheists to Islamic extremists, which is akin to saying strawberries and pickup trucks are both modes of transportation. He says these things, of course, because they resonate with that far right segment of the population who believes them—the same segment that wants to bring prayer into public schools, do away with sex education, teach creationism as if it were science, bash gays, and believe only Christians have moral rectitude.

Three of the Republican candidates, Michelle Bachman, Rick Perry, and Herman Cain said God told them to run. That doesn't speak very well for God; all three of them dropped out, and collectively they scarcely have the intellectual capacity of a cabbage. Pat Robertson said recently that God told him who will win the 2012 presidential election, but God instructed him not to tell anyone. I guess God doesn't want to be caught with another loser. George W. Bush said God told him to start the Iraqi war—another disastrous call on God's part. Pope Pius IX, possibly at God's urging, had himself declared infallible, but only after he borrowed money from the Bank of Rome to bribe skeptical cardinals into voting for the proposition. Perhaps the hand of God is in reality the hand of man.

I think it's useful here to examine two things: first, the basis of morality, and second, the position of our founding fathers regarding religion and governance.

We could get tied up for days discussing the basis of morality, because frankly there is no absolute answer. I'll keep it short and simple, though, and tell you what I think it is.

Religion is not the basis of morality; it's the other way around. Religions articulate a morality that's already there then try to make you think it's their creation. Schopenhauer, in his wonderful 1840 essay, *The Basis of Morality*, says that morality has its foundations in compassion or sympathy. Kant says much the same thing when he says man exhibits egoism or unselfishness, and unselfishness begets morality. In other words, they essentially agree that morality springs from empathy. I can't disagree with that as far as it goes, but I think the basis of morality is a little more, well, basic, if you will.

Man is a social creature and has been ever since Homo sapiens formed hunter-gatherer groups some 200,000 years ago, because forming groups was far more efficient than striking off on one's own. But in order for the group to prosper, the members of the group had to get along, so they had to devise rules of conduct. I don't want you killing me or stealing from me, so I won't kill you or steal from you. This is the first moral code, and it is embodied in a simple and universal truth we call the golden rule. Christians like to think Christ came up with the golden rule, but He didn't. The principal of the golden rule has existed in virtually every society, including those totally isolated from Christianity and those predating Christ. If you think about it, the golden rule covers it all. You don't need the Ten Commandments, the first four of which have nothing to do with morality anyway, and the tenth of which relegates women to the status of property like a house or an ox. The golden rule, in one beautifully simple, sweeping sentence, mandates all moral behavior. The golden rule is not the property of Christianity or any other religion. It is the property of mankind and is, I believe, the basis of morality.

So when Newt Gingrich, or anyone else pandering to the Religious Right, says that atheists (that's code for any non-Christian) can't govern because they lack the moral credentials to do so, they are dead wrong. Most of the atheists, agnostics, and non-Christians I've known have unshakable moral compasses.

What did our founding fathers think of God and governance? Most of the founding fathers were not Christians, but deists. In case you're not familiar with that term, deism is a theological system, now out of favor, which says God exists, but once He set things in motion, He stepped back and has no hand in the daily functioning of the universe or its inhabitants, so praying to God is pointless because He's not there to listen. Our founding fathers didn't wear their beliefs on their sleeves, but rather regarded religious faith as a private matter, and vigorously fought to keep religion out of government. And by the way, America was not founded as a Christian nation. Article Eleven of the Treaty of Tripoli, which was signed by John Adams in 1797, states in part, "The government of the United States of America is not in any sense founded on the Christian Religion."

George Washington was all-inclusive regarding religious belief. Although skeptical of Christianity, he believed all religious faiths should be allowed to function without restraint. In a famous letter to Touro Synagogue in 1790, he assured America's Jews that they would enjoy complete religious liberty and not just be tolerated.

John Adams, like most of his fellow founding fathers, considered Christian dogma to be incomprehensible. He and the others rejected the virgin birth, the Trinity, the divinity of Christ, and the resurrection. In February 1756 Adams wrote in his diary about a discussion he had with a Major Green, a devout Christian, about the divinity of Christ and the Trinity. Green, apparently unable to persuade Adams, said that some matters of theology are too complex for mere humans to understand. Adams wrote in his diary "Thus mystery is made a convenient cover for absurdity."

Thomas Jefferson admired Jesus as a moral teacher, but dismissed the basic tenants of Christianity. He edited the New Testament, deleting all stories of divinity and miracles. This Jefferson Bible is available today. When he was president, he refused to issue a proclamation calling for a day of prayer and fasting. His famous letter to the Danbury Baptist Association in 1802, assuring them that the First Amendment erects a "wall of separation between church and state," is a phrase that angers the Religious Right today.

James Madison, who wrote the Constitution and the Bill of Rights, was perhaps the most vehement of all the founding fathers about the separation of church and state. He opposed government-paid chaplains in Congress and the military. He opposed government-issued prayer proclamations, and he vetoed legislation granting federal land to a church.

Our founding fathers would gag if they could see how our politics have devolved. Jefferson thought that a rational form of religion would take root in America's intellectual soil and predicted that nearly everyone would become Unitarian. That hasn't happened, and America's intellectual soil has yielded something rather toxic. Today we have a climate where religious (make that Christian) faith is a litmus test for electability and moral rectitude. We have a strident block who wants to force their religious beliefs into government, schools, business, our legal system, and every facet of our everyday lives. In other words, the Religious Right wants America to become a theocracy. So does the Taliban.

LEGACY

In Erich Segal's 1985 book, *The Class*, which gained none of the notoriety of his 1970 novel, *Love Story*, he wistfully wrote, "Fear of death is universal. But what lies beneath that fear is the terror of insignificance. Of not being remembered, not counting." *Love Story* was on the *New York Times* best seller list, at or near the top, for over a year. *The Class* squeaked on near the bottom, then after a couple of weeks dropped off and disappeared into the fog of oblivion.

That must have been difficult for Segal. You're only as good as the last thing you did, and the last thing he did wasn't quite good enough. Perhaps he sensed that when he wrote those melancholy words.

I think even those who are self-effacing or humble harbor a secret appetite to be remembered, to count for something. If we happen to be possessed of a creative talent, quite naturally we would like to make a mark in whatever field is our genre. But in the end that only works for a very few of us. Most of us are destined for quiet obscurity.

Perhaps there's more than one legacy we can leave. Perhaps there's more than one way we can count for something after we're gone. Perhaps if the legacy of creative genius is not our lot, something else is.

Jim Dearborn was a friend of mine. Early this year he contracted some sort of immune disorder, and on St. Patrick's Day he died. Jim never wrote a best-selling book, composed a symphony, painted a great picture, designed a magnificent building, or found a cure for a disease, but he was a good man. I wrote his widow a letter in which I said, "I liked Jim from the day I met him many years ago. What elevated him was that he was always a gentleman and a gentle man." Is that a legacy? Is that counting for something? I think so, and were I to leave a legacy like that, I would be quite satisfied.

Let's now take another view of legacy, one that may not be obvious, but one which I think you will see near the end of this piece is quite legitimate.

Nature, probably through the evolutionary process, has designed us to question, inquire, discover, accept, reject, and always seek truth. It's part of who we are as humans and it's the reason man has progressed from the discovery of fire to walking on the moon. Drew Gilpin Faust, the president of Harvard, was interviewed by the *New York Times* recently. She was asked, "Is there any book you wish all incoming freshmen at Harvard would read?" She answered, "Kathryn Schulz's *Being Wrong* advocates doubt as a skill and praises error as the foundation of wisdom." Thomas Jefferson, in a 1787 letter to his nephew Peter Carr said, "Question with boldness even the existence of God; because, if there be one, he must more approve of the homage of reason, than that of blindfolded fear."

Faust and Jefferson have articulated the very essence of what it is to be human; question everything and be ready to accept that your long-held beliefs may be wrong. But living up to the promise of our better nature isn't easy. Even scientists for whom that kind of that thinking is, or should be, the fabric of who they are, sometimes miss the mark. The shouting and division in Washington, at the Tea Party, in the extreme religious arena, and in nearly every aspect of our twenty-first century society screams, "I'M RIGHT. YOU'RE WRONG, AND I DON'T WANT TO HEAR ANYTHING YOU HAVE TO SAY BECAUSE YOU CAN'T CHANGE MY MIND."

This toxic mindset diminishes who we are and returns us at the speed of a thought to that time before our ancestors began to walk upright. Albert Einstein once said that a mind is like a parachute; only useful if it's open.

But what about those of us who aren't held hostage to inflexibility? Can we hone the skills our higher angels gave us to question, to accept that we may be in error and to, as Faust says, use that error as the foundation of wisdom? I think we can. I believe a life lived that way is a life that elevates the human spirit to its potential. As a bonus, a life lived that way must certainly touch and enrich others. What does this have to do with legacy? I can't imagine a richer legacy for an ordinary person than to have it said he lived his life honestly, open to diverse ideas, willing to admit error, and always seeking truth. That's a legacy worth leaving. That's counting for something.

MIDWINTER REPORT

O K, let's get honest here. When we decided to move to Wisconsin permanently, it was not without trepidation. Actually trepidation isn't exactly right, it was more like terror. You've heard me say this before, and excuse if I bore, but moving back here was a very big deal, and the big deal part of it was weathering the winter. What would it be like to fight mind-numbing, eyeball-numbing, Antarctic-like cold? What would it be like to fight white-out snow conditions with winds howling like the Hound of the Baskervilles? And what about driving? Am I going to have to negotiate my 3,000-pound car on a skating rink all winter? That thought is a little frightening. We've been here now a little over three months beyond our usual get-out-of-Dodge time, so I think it's appropriate that I report on what it's been like. If you think I'm obsessed and that the Wisconsin winter fires a major portion of my cerebral cortex, you're right.

Like a good soldier, I reasoned that I had to prepare for the battle. One of the first things I did as fall slid into the freezer and winter began to take over was to buy a heavy parka (I think it's rated to negative thirty-five degrees); a pair of heavy gloves, similarly rated; and a hat, a wool cap in this case. Then it occurred to me that I needed one more sartorial appendage: boots. When I was a kid, we wore overshoes, but I guess they don't make them anymore, or if they do their distribution is an underground activity, like cocaine and meth. I bought a pair of waterproof, insulated, heavily treaded boots. They're beautiful. They really are waterproof, warm, and heavily treaded, and in size and weight, each resembles a small Volkswagen.

Not to worry, I was told. We haven't had any significant snow here for years, they said. And as for cold, not a problem; it doesn't get real cold here anymore like it used to. Those reassurances generated one more worry. Did I just blow a few hundred bucks on a parka, gloves, hat, and boots that I won't need?

Not to worry about that either. On November 9 it snowed and froze, and conditions were so bad they closed the Blatnik Bridge. On December 2 it snowed enough that it came up above my new boots. On December 8 the temperature went down to thirteen degrees below zero, and on December 19 it went down to sixteen degrees below zero. Of course the span between the 8th and the 19th didn't constitute a warm spell.

I have been rather pleasantly surprised with the efficiency of the snow removal, so the major county, state, and US roads are, for the most part, passable after a snow. But the back roads, like the one I live on, would challenge Mario Andretti to maintain a straight line.

Oh, one more thing. Something I hadn't thought too much about before winter got a choke hold—how about walking? I broke my leg in 2003 when I slipped walking out to my car a couple of days after a snowstorm, and that was back in Maryland, so I've become a little wary of ice walking. I have to walk about ninety yards to get to my mailbox. The day after one of the snows, it melted, then rained, then froze. My trip to the mailbox could easily have been mistaken for Baryshnikov dancing the Prince in *Swan Lake*, as I executed a series of pas de chats and Grand jetes all the way out and back. My apologies to Baryshnikov; it wasn't a particularly pretty sight.

Then there's the salt. Salt, salt everywhere, and not a grain to cook. I bought a big bag of salt in the fall. I've salted the back porch, the walk to the garage, the front porch, and the walk to the driveway. There's more salt on my porches and walks than in a cod processing plant. Salt works, but it also comes in the house on those VW boots. If I don't vacuum every day, I find myself stepping on those sharp little salt crystals in my bare feet when I get up in the middle of the night to get a drink of water.

It's a little like an Amazonian aboriginal rite of passage, right up there with the face carving and ear notching.

So how do I rate this first in fifty years experience with winter? Not so bad really. But I have to be honest. I would rather be wearing a T-shirt, shorts, and sandals, with the temperature hovering somewhere around eighty degrees. When I hear friends say, "I love winter. It's my favorite time of year." I smile faintly, mutter a quiet "uh huh," as I think, why?

LETTER TO *THE BALTIMORE SUN*
11/21/05

The debate rages on. I'm referring to the so-called debate over intelligent design, and I find it curious that it's a debate at all (Saturday Mailbox, November 19, 2005). Those well-meaning souls who propose teaching intelligent design as an alternative to evolution theory miss the fundamental tenet of science. The word "theory" means an explanation of how observed phenomena occurred and/or their relationship to other phenomena based on verifiable evidence. In other words, scientists observe something then attempt to describe how it happened or what its relationship is to other observed things.

Evolution is not a theory; it is a fact. All scientists agree there is overwhelming evidence that evolution has occurred. When we speak of the theory of evolution, we refer to the explanation of how the fact of evolution occurred. Gravitational theory doesn't question the existence of gravity; it simply tries to explain how gravity works.

Intelligent design is not a theory; it is a religious belief based on faith, not on observable fact. Unfortunately belief in intelligent design ignores the fact of evolution. You may believe the world is flat, but that doesn't make it so. Most of us have religious faith, and we cherish the beliefs that derive from that faith, but we must not lose sight of the fact that a religious belief is a statement of something which has no factual basis, and which we cannot prove. It certainly isn't science.

Teaching the belief of intelligent design may be appropriate in a in a class exploring religions of the world, but it has no place in the science classroom.

OOPS

Marilyn and I started dating in 1955. On gentle summer days we would often drive out to the lake, where I now live, and water ski. In fact, we were the first to water ski on our lake, something I cannot justify taking pride in since it was, like most things in my life, the product of blind luck, not astute timing.

My dad bought a Crestliner with a 35 hp Johnson—a trifle underpowered, but enough to do the job if one had patience getting up from an in-water start. We and our friends (it's amazing how many friends you acquire when you have a ski boat) had great fun water skiing. Marilyn and I particularly liked night skiing. There was something mystical, almost magic about it. It was physical poetry. We would often pick a clear night with a full moon, then at the right time when the moon bore about 90° we would ski down the moonbeam, across the lake to Lindale Bay, a little tavern nestled quietly in a tiny cove behind the island. It was just the two of us; one would ski across to Lindale Bay and the other would ski back—no observer. Had either one of us fallen, the driver wouldn't have known for some time, and recovery would have been difficult. But when you're young, you don't clutter your mind with reason. The trip back was always a little different from the trip over because the moon refused to wait for us while we had a beer. It continued its trip across the sky; thus the moonbeam shifted, but we adapted. After all, when you don't care about the consequences of stupidity, adaptation is easy.

One summer day Marilyn and I went to Mille Lacs Lake to go swimming. I don't remember exactly why we went there, but I think it had something to do with the fact that her family used to vacation there. It was a gorgeous day. The public beach was a beehive of swimmers, and in the water ski boats were buzzing all about. We brought a picnic lunch and a blanket and whatever else one needs for a day at the beach. All was well, and we were content.

After one of our swims, Marilyn had gotten out of the water, and I was behind her a minute or so. As I stepped onshore, I heard the roar of a ski boat behind me. I turned. It had stopped and the people in the boat were motioning to me and pointing at the skis they had dropped behind them. I had no idea who they were, but I wasn't about to pass up such a magnanimous gesture. With a smile and a wave intended to convey "thank you," I returned to the water, put the skis on, grabbed the rope, and motioned the driver to let-er-rip. He did, and I was up in a second; his motor was bigger than 35 hp. He took me on a wide oval ride, then returned to our starting point where I dropped off, removed the skis, and shouted, "Thank you," which he probably didn't hear.

When I returned to Marilyn, she was doubled over with laughter. "Geez, I didn't look that bad did I?" I said, knowing the answer couldn't possibly be yes.

"That's not it," she said, gasping for air as she tried to talk through the laughter. "The people in the boat weren't motioning to you to go skiing; they were motioning to their friend who was on the beach behind you. You got to the skis before he could."

Oops.

ROUTINE MAINTENANCE

B oat maintenance, as any true sailor knows, is accomplished only by defeating the gods who decree that all objects on a sailboat which need maintenance or replacement shall be placed just millimeters out of reach. Lest you think this is sour grapes, consider this. My little sailboat, *Cyrano,* had a manual bilge pump located (bolted) in an after cockpit lazarette. (For those who may not be familiar, that is a storage locker, under the seat, at the rear of the cockpit.) Insert a handle in an opening in the cockpit, and with twenty or so pumps, the water in the bilge below is sucked up through a long hose and discharged in undulating streams out the transom (back) of the boat. It was a fine old pump, made in Ireland, and as reliable as the opening time of an Irish pub. But, after two decades of service, it gave up one day a couple of years ago.

Two fundamental truths emerged. One hates to lose a sturdy old friend who has been so unfailingly faithful, and as one grows older, roughing it takes on a new and gentler meaning. The choice now was to rebuild the pump with a kit or discard it and install a small, inexpensive, efficient electric bilge pump that requires only the flick of a switch to operate. After a full moment of agonizing, I decided on the latter course of action.

The opening of the after cockpit lazarette measures about eleven by twenty-one inches, and the pump was bolted inside the lazarette some distance from the opening. Since I am far too large to fit in the lazarette with any reasonable expectation of getting out short of a 9-1-1 call, it was necessary to remove the steering wheel, kneel in the cockpit, reach inside the lazarette with my left hand grasping a wrench, and with my right hand grasping a screwdriver, try to remove the six bolts holding the pump. This operation was done entirely by the Braille method, because I was stretching so far into the lazarette that my chin was on the cockpit seat, and my eyes could only focus on the back of the seat a few inches from my nose. This is a condition not uncommon to sailors and is usually accompanied by bloody knuckles and loud offensive language.

All the bolts were finally removed, and the pump hung only by the hoses attached to either side of it. Now it was a simple matter of pulling the pump toward the lazarette opening in order to remove the hose clamps and hoses. Enter the maintenance god. The pump would not move. The hose leading from the bilge to the pump was somehow attached to the bowels of the boat, making it incapable of movement. Not an inch would it move. I could feel the hose clamp with the fingers of my left hand, but I couldn't get a screwdriver on it to loosen it without steadying it with my right hand, which, because of the configuration of things, would have required my elbow to flex in the wrong direction.

I have the good fortune to be the grandfather of a delightful, bright, (then) eleven-year-old granddaughter who is as slender as a piece of straw. With a little coaxing and some grandfatherly bribery, Katie easily wiggled her way into the lazarette and in no time had both hoses off and handed me the pump with a studied nonchalance only an eleven-year-old who is quite pleased with herself can accomplish. Then she left to do more important eleven-year-old things.

The next task was to install the new electric pump using most of the old discharge hose. Obviously the two ends of the hose that had been connected to the old pump had to be joined. That would be no problem. Simply attach each hose to a nipple with a hose clamp, and we're in business. Enter the gods. The nipple was about 1/16 inch too big, and the next smaller size was too small, so it had to be filed down being careful not to file away too much material. The other problem was again with the way my arm is made. I could not grasp the hose in one hand and the nipple in the other without major, groundbreaking orthopedic surgery, which, since it would have been elective, I would have to pay for, and Katie was no longer available.

I'll not further detail how I managed to connect the two ends, nor will I detail the hurdles encountered in wiring the new pump, nor will I list the number of times I had to leave the project to go to the store for one small thiddlemajig I forgot to buy initially or the last time I was at the store. The project, which was begun at noon, was finished by five thirty p.m. I didn't lose nearly as much blood as I had anticipated, and since all my neighbors are sailors, none were scandalized by my language.

Wanna see the bilge get pumped dry in just a few moments? Here, I'll just flick this switch.

PURPOSE

The corkscrew I hold in my hand has a purpose, and it's quite clear what that purpose is. The car parked in my driveway has a purpose, and there's no ambiguity about it.

But what about me? About you? What is our purpose? When I was young, I was taught that my purpose on earth is to love and serve the Lord and be with Him in paradise. That's nice, but it's not nearly enough. In those days religious instruction was intended to impose point of view; critical thought was discouraged lest the authority of the church be challenged.

A deer in the woods and an eagle in the sky have purposes: to inhabit the food chain and to procreate. If you have a poetic bent, you might add to provide beauty. But we, human beings, are at the top of the food chain, and as far as beauty is concerned, we often provide instead misery, war, torture, and degradation to our fellow man, to nature, and to the planet. I refuse to be so cynical as to believe that is our purpose. Surely we have a higher purpose.

How are Beethoven, Shakespeare, and Einstein like the corkscrew? Their purpose is self-evident, and had any of them shirked their responsibility to mankind, it would have been a sin against humanity. But what about the rest of us? What about those of us who were not born with special gifts? What about the mass of humanity whose purpose isn't self-evident? Where do we fit in the cosmic scheme? Surely we aren't random creatures subject only to chaos theory. Nature is far too orderly to allow that.

To answer the question of our purpose, we can turn, at least in part, to science. New and cutting-edge research has discovered mirror neurons. The best way to describe mirror neurons is by example. You're driving down the street late at night when suddenly you happen on the scene of a house fire. The building is fully involved, and it's clear that, despite the best efforts of the fire department, it will be a total loss. There on the front lawn is a young mother and her two small children, clad in their nightclothes. The mother is sobbing, and the children are clinging to her, terrified. You suddenly feel terrible, and you're on the verge of tears yourself. But why? You don't know this woman; she means nothing to you, and she never will. But you can't help it; you feel her pain and you share it. In other words you mirror her anguish, and that's the result of mirror neurons. Although the lesser primates share with us this trait to a certain extent, it is only the human species that is able to feel so deeply, to empathize so completely with our fellow man.

I don't wish to imply that our purpose in life is empathy. What I am implying is that this phenomenon of mirror neurons allows us to paint a larger picture of our place on the planet and our purpose here. The philosopher Joseph Campbell, in his book, *The Hero With a Thousand Faces,* points out that nearly every society through the ages, even those having no contact with any other, has devised a code of conduct designed to hold the society together and promote harmony, and that code of conduct is, in various forms, the Golden Rule. If we live by no other code— no Ten Commandments, no laws, nothing—but follow the Golden Rule, we will live in harmony and peace with our fellow man.

Now let's take another tack. Aristotle taught that man's highest purpose is the search for truth. The old saying that the truth will set you free is, in fact, true. Truth not only enriches the soul of he who finds it, but it informs his life so that the conduct of it gives him greater pleasure.

And what about pleasure? Some religions teach us that pleasure for its own sake, hedonism, is evil. Only through pain and sacrifice can we expect to find happiness. I disagree. I submit that pleasure as a principle aim is a good thing, with one caveat. We must never seek pleasure at the expense of another.

Let's see if we can put this together and try to crack the purpose code. We are hardwired to empathize with our fellows, and we seem disposed to want to treat each other as we want to be treated. It is self-evident that we should always seek the truth. And we are the only species on the planet with the capacity to actively seek pleasure. What does it all mean? Perhaps it's not as complicated as we might think. Perhaps our purpose in life is to nurture and enrich our fellow man, to seek the truth, and ensure that what we do gives us pleasure. Beethoven, Shakespeare, and Einstein enriched mankind with their gifts. We enrich mankind with understanding, sympathy, and forgiveness, and we enrich ourselves with truth and pleasure. Is that trilogy noble enough a purpose? I think it is. If the anomalies among us, the Adolph Hitlers, the Idi Amins, and the Osama bin Ladens, can cause such intense suffering, then what can we do with a simple kindness, a helping hand, a quieting word in a time of need, with the joy of learning the truth and seeking that which gives us pleasure? How high can we make the spirit soar by what we do? How much joy can we bring to other human beings and to ourselves by embracing these three simple principles? I can think of no better purpose. Perhaps why we're here is indeed as simple as a corkscrew.

THE DELIRIUM OF POWER

Arnold Schwarzenegger, John Edwards, Mark Sanford, Eliot Spitzer, and Dominique Strauss-Kahn are only five in a long list of very public people who have disgraced themselves in a very public way by their seemingly stupid, and sometimes criminal, behavior. How could they, you ask? What were they thinking? These are intelligent men; how could they be so stupid? Well, I don't know, but I can guess. I can guess that they are all successful because they are risk takers and because they have utter confidence in their abilities. Then success brings fame and with it a certain sense that they are untouchable, thus the bad behaviors. What they have done, of course, has not only destroyed their own public lives, but more importantly, they have betrayed their families and caused untold grief. Schwarzenegger lost his wife, but his career may survive. Edwards lost his wife and his political career, and he's been indicted. Sanford and Spitzer lost their public careers and their wives. Then the pompous arrogant Strauss-Kahn not only lost his position as the most powerful banker in the world and likely the next president of France, but he stands a very good chance of doing some serious jail time.

Now enters the new kid on the block, Anthony Weiner, a bony little man who, and since I'm a guy I can't say with authority, is probably as attractive to women as a bag of fish guts. Weiner—isn't that a wonderful name. I don't know what he was thinking when he took a picture of his bulging wiener under his tighty-whities. Perhaps he thought he would capitalize on his name with a little show-and-tell. Doesn't the poor guy even know that women prefer boxers? Then he sent the picture to young a woman he doesn't know. I suppose he assumed the massiveness of his manliness, nestled there in his Fruit of the Loom, would cause her to swoon and yield herself to him. Instead, I suspect she wretched.

But what the hell? That was so much fun he decided to take it a step further. For Weiner's gift to the world, he photographed his Mr. Happy, free of the undies, for all to see. Now the reasoning here is clear. If a masked penis will cause the ladies to swoon, imagine what an unmasked one might do. The very thought of it probably caused intense arousal. If he walked around with an erection for more than four hours, I suspect that instead of seeking medical help, he probably had the thing bronzed.

Then when he's caught he lied. Here's a guy with an ego the size of Montana and a badly mutated common sense gene. He has become a laughing stock, the butt of a thousand jokes, and a pariah in the House and in his party. So what does he do? He refuses to resign. He lives in his own impregnable little Weinerworld, surrounded by a wall of grandiose self images. He's the Humpty Dumpty who thinks his shell is made of Kevlar. Resign? Why should I resign? What does all of this have to do with me being a member of the House? That's like Jeffery Dahmer asking what his selection of meat for dinner has to do with fine dining.

The American public can forgive indiscretions committed by its elected officials. It's a healing process that keeps the train on the track by saying, OK, you screwed up in your personal life, but we elected you to do a job, and we think despite what you've done you can do it. But, lying is unforgivable. If you lie you reveal a character flaw that affects everything you do, including the job we sent you to Congress to accomplish. We can't trust you anymore, and you should have the grace to step aside. Anthony Weiner lied. He lied repeatedly until the relentless press backed him into a corner from which he could not escape, forcing him to tell the truth. He didn't tell the truth because it was the right thing to do. He finally told the truth because he had to.

Then there's Huma Abedin, Weiner's newly pregnant wife who is an accomplished diplomat in the highest echelons of the State Department and who is a devout Muslim. I wonder how she feels that her devoted, loving husband has been waving his willie willy-nilly on the playground of the Internet. Betrayed, belittled, marginalized. To her credit she didn't show up at his confessional news conference to be even more humiliated as her slime-bag husband admitted his deviant behavior.

I don't know what's next for Weiner. He remains defiant in the face of a situation that demands humility and a plea for forgiveness. I don't know what's next for his relationship with his wife. What I do know is that he's one of a long list of egomaniacal idiots who believe their own press clippings.

THE COLD WAR

Confession, they say, is good for the soul. Don't you believe it. I've teased more than one confession out of some hapless schmuck who discovered, when the judge sentenced him to the iron bar motel, that it might have been more prudent to keep his mouth shut.

Despite that, I'm going to confess. I'm going to confess a really dumb thing I did once. Frankly, I've done a lot of dumb things, but I'm not going to confess more than one of them, because space and utter embarrassment stop me from doing that—just this one thing to demonstrate to those of you who perhaps thought me infallible that I'm not.

I was about eleven or twelve years old and taking piano lessons from Serge Brewsaw. Brewsaw was a legend in Superior. He looked like Beethoven, with a wild mien of graying hair and the bearing of a Teutonic knight. He lived in an apartment above the Trade Home shoe store on Tower Ave. The living room ran nearly the entire length of the store and was so massive that it comfortably accommodated two concert grand pianos, several couches, a gaggle of chairs and tables, French tapestries on the walls, statuary, paintings, several large expensive vases, and a number of enormous, plush Oriental rugs. It was a living room that could have been plucked straight from a nineteenth century mansion. His kitchen, bathroom, and bedroom were tiny appendages at the rear. It was in this grand living room that Brewsaw held court, gave lessons, entertained, and listened to music.

Occasionally I would arrive early for my lesson, and when I did, I was treated to the end of the lesson of the student before me, usually a girl several years my junior, flawlessly playing Rachmaninoff's *Piano Concerto No. 2* or some other enormously complicated piece. When it came my turn, I struggled through *Teaching Little Fingers to Play*. Oh the embarrassment of it all. I was a terrible student. Actually I had passed terrible and resided in abominable. Ordinarily Brewsaw would have dropped me, but he was caught on the horns of a dilemma. Those Oriental rugs and some of the furniture were loaned to him by my family, so he was forced to sit through what must have been sheer agony, listening to a snotty nosed little no-talent play each week, usually with dirty fingers that left sweaty smudges on the gleaming white keys.

I noticed, on those occasions I had to wait for my lesson, that Brewsaw always had several magazines laying on one of his larger coffee tables. One of those magazines intrigued me. I don't remember the name of it, but it was a Communist publication, complete with hammer and sickle, published in Russia and printed in English. Wow! I mean holy cow wow! Brewsaw was a card-carrying Communist, and I took piano lessons from him each week.

It was a well-known fact that Zeldorf the tailor, who had a shop on Tower Avenue down around Eighth Street, was the leader of the local Communist cell. Never mind how I knew; I just did, so you'll have to accept it. It occurred to me that if I could prove that Brewsaw was a Communist, as if the magazines weren't enough proof, and report it to the FBI, they would arrest him, and I wouldn't have to take piano lessons anymore. I devised a plan.

I went to the library, and in the encyclopedia I looked up the melting point of lead: 621.5° Fahrenheit. Ah ha, thought I. I can easily reach that temperature on my mom's stove. I had a little money from cutting lawns, so I rode my bike to Lund's sporting goods store on Tower Avenue, very close to Zeldorf's, by the way, and bought several pounds of lead twelve-gauge slugs, used in hand loading shotgun shells. Then I went to another store—I don't remember which one—and bought a small, inexpensive cast-iron pan. Next, I scrounged around alleys on my bike, looking for an old garden hose tossed in the trash by some householder with a new one. It didn't take long before I found one. I cut a length with my pocket knife, and rode home, quite pleased with myself.

The next step was a little tricky, because this entire operation required the utmost secrecy, so naturally I couldn't tell anyone of the plan, not even my mom and dad. I had to do what I was going to do when my folks weren't home, and I figured I needed about an hour or so to do it. My chance came one day when my dad was at work and my mother announced she was going shopping in Duluth and would be home in a few hours. I feigned casual disinterest, but inside I was fairly tingling with excitement. Now I could make my move.

I cut the garden hose precisely into two equal lengths, about eight inches or so. I got some pliers from my dad's toolbox, figured about how many slugs it would take to fill an end of the hose up to about three inches, turned the burner of the stove on high, and began melting the slugs in the pan I had bought. They actually melted. Holding the hose with the pliers so as not to burn myself, I held one end of the hose firmly down on my mom's cutting board as I carefully poured the lead into a small funnel placed in the hose. The kitchen filled with acrid smoke from burning rubber (I hadn't thought about that), but the hose held, and very quickly the lead set. I proudly lifted the hose from the cutting board, only to discover that the hot lead had made an indelible burn mark on the board—I hadn't thought about that either. Oh well, if she notices I'll think of something, but now I had more important work to do than to worry about a burn mark on a cutting board. I did the same thing with the second piece of hose, this time using the sidewalk as a backstop as I poured the molten lead. When the lead had cooled, I stuffed rags in the open end of each hose until they were tightly packed and I couldn't stuff anymore in. Finally, I neatly taped both ends with electrical tape, and I was done. I held my handiwork, one in each hand, proudly admiring what I had made. Two beautiful, perfectly balanced, lethal blackjacks.

Jim Neal lived just a half block away, and we were good friends. Jim was a year older than I, but we got along well, and I liked him a lot. But more important, I trusted him, and I knew I could trust him with a vital secret. I went to his house to get him. We rode our bikes to the woods behind the Pattison School where we stopped. "Jim," I said gravely, "if I tell you something will you promise you will never tell anyone?"

"Sure," he said casually.

"Look," I said as I pulled the two blackjacks from my back pocket, handing him one.

"Geese, neat. Where'd you get these?" he asked.

"I made 'em," I replied, trying to impart that, 'it's really no big deal—I do this all the time' attitude. Jim continued to handle the blackjack, swatting the air at imaginary bad guys. Then I said, "I need your help with something, but you can't tell anybody what we're doing, OK?"

"Sure, what is it?" he said enthusiastically.

I explained to him how I found out Brewsaw was a Communist and that I had a plan to expose him. Any evening we could get out (since the days are long in summer, that wasn't too much of a problem) we would surveil his apartment until he came out, hopefully to go to Zeldorf's for a Communist cell meeting. We would follow him on foot (he didn't have a car), and when the meeting started, we would listen at a window and take notes. The blackjacks were for our protection in case one of the Communists spotted us. Jim liked my flawless plan and immediately signed on.

I don't recall how many evenings it took, standing on Tower Avenue, trying to blend in with the lampposts and trash cans, as we surveilled Brewsaw's apartment. Then one evening it happened. He left the apartment carrying a small bag. Probably full of documents plotting the overthrow of the US government, we surmised. Sure enough, he headed north in the direction of Zeldorf the tailor. We had him. He got closer and closer to Zeldorf's, and as the tension mounted, we could barely contain our excitement. A dangerous Communist operative was about to be taken off the street, and I was about to rid myself of piano lessons.

Then, a block or two short of Zeldorf's, Brewsaw turned right off of Tower. He's trying to lose the tail, we reasoned, but he won't lose us. Actually, that's not quite what he had in mind. Instead of attending a Communist cell meeting that night, he went to the public steam bath.

We tried again a couple of times, but somehow it just wasn't the same. The excitement wasn't there, and with that lack of excitement came a lack of commitment, and the whole thing was forgotten as we forged on to new and larger adventures.

I kept that blackjack for years, until I threw it away during one of our many moves. I wish I hadn't. It would have been a nice memento of, well, you know.

Some years later, when I was going to school at UMD and he was an old man, I ran into Brewsaw at John Flynn's bar. He said he remembered me, but I don't think he did. We talked and immediately struck up a friendship. I visited him occasionally in that beautiful, regal living room of his. I discovered he was a brilliant, sensitive, gentle man, now so twisted with arthritis that he could no longer play the piano. But music was his passion, and he would always play music for me, from his extensive record collection, over an elaborate sound system that he built, insisting that I sit on the floor, on one of those luxurious Oriental rugs, in a specific spot, to enjoy the full majesty of the music.

Eventually I graduated and set off to distant places to seek my fame and fortune. A few years later, on one of our vacation trips back to Wisconsin, I learned that Brewsaw had died. No one seemed to know if he had any living relatives, and no one knew what became of his possessions. I made a not-too-serious attempt to track down the Orientals and furniture, but with no success. They had served a good man well, and it was fitting that they should be lost with him.

By the way, I never told him of my anti-Communist scheme years before—there was no need to.

THE RELUCTANT ROMANIAN

T he claxon-like sound of the secure phone ringing startled me. It always did, not just because of the grating abrasive noise it made, but because it didn't ring very often. Secure phones in the late '70s were about the size of a small washing machine with a telephone perched on top. They were owned and administered by NSA who provided the codes we had to dial in periodically, which encrypted the voice transmissions in the process, distorting them so it sounded like someone speaking in a barrel underwater.

The caller was Jim, the Foreign Counterintelligence (FCI) supervisor in Baltimore. He said someone identifying himself as, we'll call him George Smith, a scientist at the Aberdeen Proving Ground wanted to talk to an agent about a national security matter that he was reluctant to discuss over the phone. I was tasked to interview George. This will be fun. Another McCarthy-like conspiracy-infused idiot who sees a Communist behind every bush. I've been through this drill before.

George Smith was a physicist in his early fifties. He was born in Romania and moved to the US as a teenager with his parents, before Romania became part of the Soviet Union. He had been a naturalized US citizen for decades and held a top secret clearance with the army. It was obvious early on that he was a bright, engaging man, not given to flights of fancy.

He explained that he has a lifelong friend, who we will call Andrei, who was an ophthalmologist living in Romania. They hadn't seen each other in years, but corresponded from time to time. Andrei contacted George recently, saying he was going to travel to New York, arriving in about ten days, and that he may want to defect. Andrei, said George, is very, very nervous. "Does he have a family?" I asked. Yes, a wife and two daughters, but they won't be with him because the Romanian government won't allow entire families to leave the country at the same time. "OK," I said. "Give me his itinerary, and I'll pass it along to State who will make arrangements, probably through you, to contact him when he gets here." George was clearly not a conspiracy nutcase, but a defecting Romanian ophthalmologist with no obvious intelligence value isn't something I was particularly interested in, and in that case, it's State's purview.

"Oh, one more thing." said George. "Andrei is Nicolae Ceausescu's personal physician." Now George had my attention. The president of Romania's personal physician isn't just another defecting doctor; this is a doctor worth his weight in intelligence gold.

"I assume you will be contacting Andrei before he leaves for the US?" I asked. He nodded yes. "When you do, please don't say anything about his defecting. That can wait until he gets here. Meantime, I'll make some arrangements and get back to you. Are you comfortable with that?" He nodded again, solemnly this time, as the weight of what was about to happen sank in. "How is Andrei's English?" I asked. George indicated that Andrei speaks virtually no English. "By the way," I said, "why does Ceausescu have an ophthalmologist as a personal physician?"

"I have no idea," said George.

I drove directly to the office in Baltimore and met with Jim. We mapped out a game plan. I would go to New York with George who would contact Andrei and tell him to come to a specific hotel (the FBI has a number of secure hotel rooms scattered throughout the city just for situations like this). I would be introduced as a representative of the US government—no mention of the FBI, which might frighten him. I wanted a Romanian speaker from the New York office present, but no other agents; I didn't want to overwhelm Andrei. I also wanted New York to do a countersurveillance on Andrei to be certain that the Securitate

(Romanian secret police) wasn't surveilling him. Finally, if we were going to make this thing work and flip Andrei into becoming an asset, I had to have the authority to promise him certain things: first, extraction from Romania for him and his family when the time came; second, education for his daughters; and third, a substantial stipend. The reality was he probably couldn't very easily get a license to practice medicine in the US, particularly given his inability to speak English. Fourth, I needed to be able to promise him a new identity for him and his family if he so desired. Finally, the CIA would be cut in only after my meeting with Andrei was over. Jim agreed, and the wheels were set in motion.

FBI headquarters, where ambition is routinely mistaken for ability, bought the whole package, amazingly without any of their usual helpful suggestions as to how we in the field can benefit from the wisdom of those who spend their entire days behind desks. New York also agreed to provide everything we asked for, including Andrei's favorite tea.

George and I flew to New York and went directly to the secure hotel room. Waiting there for us was the Romanian speaker and two more agents. Not much use in arguing with them at that point. I was on their turf, and I needed their help. I also learned that the New York FCI supervisor decided that a countersurveillance wasn't necessary. Aw shit. These idiots…oh well, nothing I can do about that now.

George called Andrei at his hotel and gave him directions to ours. The plan was for George to meet him in the lobby of our hotel, talk to him for a while to calm him down, then bring him up to our room and introduce the four of us as representatives of the government who have the authority to negotiate with him. George would stay in the room to bolster Andrei's comfort level.

George and Andrei knocked on the door, and I let them in. Andrei was a squat, rather pale man in his midfifties. On the sartorial teeter-totter he tilted toward the tacky. He had the look of a peasant. He carried a rectangular box about three inches on a side and a foot long. He was shaking all over and was obviously terrified. I asked him if he was all right, and he replied that he was afraid Securitate might have followed him. If they knew he was talking to representatives of the US government, he and his family would be killed. I assured him that we had established a counter-surveillance, and he was not followed. I hated to lie, but the stakes were too high not to. He relaxed a little, but not much. It was clear from the outset that Andrei was having second thoughts and was convinced he had made a mistake by meeting with us. We talked for over two hours. I did everything I could think of to convince him to remain in place and talk to our people in Romania from time to time, but he was adamant. The promises of money, education for his girls, and a new life in America couldn't overcome the terror he was experiencing. Then suddenly, he opened the box and took out some slides to show me. This simple gesture seemed to calm him a little; he had moved into his comfort zone. What he showed me was eye research he was doing in Romania, and he was very proud of his work. I explained that I was not a doctor, but I was sure his work was very important. It was not the reaction he expected. Then he wanted to leave. I convinced him to stay a few minutes longer while I extracted all of the intelligence about Ceausescu I could get: his physical and mental condition, the strength of his hold on power, any dissatisfaction in the inner circle, who was next in line to take over, and on and on. Andrei said Ceausescu was in poor health and was grooming his eldest son, who was even more vicious than his father, and probably psychotic. I learned later this was unknown to US intelligence.

On the way back to Baltimore, I reconstructed the events of the day, trying to figure out why I had failed. Then it hit me. If I had had the foresight to bring with me an internationally known ophthalmologist from Johns Hopkins to schmooze with Andrei and praise his work, things might have gone differently. I never got a second chance.

WINTER OLYMPICS

It wasn't really a surprise. After all, they had been forecasting it for a couple of days, but when I got up yesterday morning and saw seventeen inches of snow beautifully draping everything in sight, the scene elicited a quiet "Wow." That's a two-part wow, by the way. The first part is obvious—it was a beautiful sight. Every limb of every tree, every flat surface, and some not so flat, were frosted with snow, like a winning entry in a baking contest. The other part of the wow was the realization that someone—me—had to shovel that damn stuff.

Yesterday was also the second full day of the 2006 Winter Olympics. I love the Olympics, summer and winter; although I think winter has a slight edge. What is more awesomely graceful than an athlete soaring one hundred or more meters through the air, bent low over his skis held in a V to ensure he "flies" the maximum distance? A hundred meters: my God, that's farther than a city block.

So, I decided to watch the Olympics; the shoveling could wait. We had plenty of food and a well-stocked cabinet full of medicinal spirits. Nope, no need to go anywhere; just watch the Olympics and enjoy.

Michelle Kwan appeared early on in what was probably the best performance of her life. Showing a maturity far exceeding her twenty-five years, she withdrew from the games. Her groin injury prevented her from being her best, and she didn't want to drag the US team down, so with grace, dignity, and sadness, she withdrew. I was impressed.

Chad Hedrick won the gold for the US in the men's 5000-meter speed skating event. His long, fluid strides propelled him around the course with an easy grace that belied the enormous effort this finely tuned athlete expended.

Frode Estil, the Norwegian skier, had an accident at the start of the men's thirty-kilometer cross-country, and wound up in the back of the pack with a broken ski. But, he didn't give up; he didn't even hesitate; he pressed on, and in the end, he had passed more than seventy competitors to win the silver. Sheer guts, sheer determination, sheer athleticism—these are the qualities of an Olympic medalist.

Then there was nineteen-year-old Shaun White—the Flying Tomato—with his Herculean mane of red hair and a wide engaging smile. As he listened to AC/DC on his iPod, he soared like a huge, graceful bird in the half-pipe, momentarily suspending the laws of gravity and reason, to fly and twist his way to a gold medal. And when it was over, he embraced his mom, as tears streamed down both their faces.

Then it was time to shovel. Our neighbor, who has a jeep with a plow blade, graciously does our driveway, so I didn't have to worry about that. But, I did have to clear the walk and shovel a path around the car so we could get in and out and unload whatever might be in the trunk.

I started with the walk Mindless, repetitive tasks cause the mind to wander. As mine wandered, it soon occurred to me that this wasn't a mindless, repetitive task at all; it was like an Olympic event. It requires athleticism, strength, strategy, finesse, and coordination. And here I was, someone who had been in training for years. Having grown up in Wisconsin and lived for a time in Maine, I've shoveled tons of snow, using a variety of shovels. I've perfected techniques for dealing with all sorts of snow: deep and not-so-deep, powdery, wet, slushy, and all intermediate grades. Shoveling requires careful planning. When shoveling the walk, you must not throw the snow ahead of you, and hopefully not behind you. If you're shoveling around a car, is it better to sweep the car off first and do one shoveling, or shovel to clear an area, then sweep the car and shovel again. Maintaining competitive advantage precludes me from disclosing my strategy.

Yes, I thought, as I neared the end of the walk, shoveling is indeed an Olympic event. It can be broken down into five elements: strategy, scoop and toss style, heave distance, neatness, and elapsed time. It can be graded on a point system, each element receiving a maximum of ten points, for a perfect score of fifty. The more I thought about it, the more furiously I shoveled; after all, elapsed time counts. But as I did, I began to pay more attention to style. Should I change lead hands from time to time? That might impress the judges. Without noticeably grunting, I tossed each shovelful a little farther than the last—distance counts too. I cut the banks meticulously square and cleanly—no one was going to beat me on neatness. As for strategy, I had that mapped out even before I began, and I was pretty certain I would lead on that element too. Before I knew it, I was done. I surveyed the result and was pleased.

I didn't have to wait long. The judges awarded me 48.5 points, more than enough for a gold medal. I went back into the house, hugged my wife, and stood mentally on the top level of the podium as the national anthem drifted through my mind. Yes, the years of training paid off. I won the gold and a place in the record books. I'll be back in four years.

THREAT

Around the western tip of Africa, along that stretch of coast that runs east-west, about 6° above the equator, lies the nation of Togo, a sixty by 310-mile phallus nestled between the loving hands of Ghana to the west and Benin to the east. Togo, with its 6.6 million inhabitants, is slightly smaller than West Virginia.

If you've never heard of Togo, you're not alone. I hadn't either until this news item appeared recently in the paper:

The female wing of a civil rights group is urging women in Togo to stage a week-long sex strike to demand the resignation of the country's president.

Women are being asked to withhold sex from their husbands or partners as of Monday, said Isabelle Ameganvi, leader of the women's wing of the group Lets Save Togo…. "We have many means to oblige men to understand what women want in Togo," Ameganvi said.

This is a tactic used before. In 2009 it was tried for a week in Kenya for political reasons, with no success, and again in Liberia during 2002 and 2003 to end violence. Eventually the civil war ended, but not for a couple of years. And of course all men know that the threat of no sex is a singular arrow every wife or partner keeps in her quiver.

The withholding of sex is not a modern exercise. Aristophanes's play *Lysistrata*, first staged in Athens in 411 BCE, tells of women withholding sex from their husbands to force them into peace talks during the Peloponnesian War.

This unfortunate phenomena bears examination on several levels. First, the gender thing. It's always the female who withholds sex from the male, never the other way around. The implication is clear. Women don't care about sex and men do. I find that troubling, disheartening, even disconcerting. But as a man, I have to admit that it may be partly our fault. We perceive the vagina as the holy grail of female genitalia, because that's where we put our minivans (some guys think they drive buses) for a few minutes of rock 'n' roll leading up to the crescendo, where tympanis reverberate, horns blare, violins play forte, and we are convinced we own the world. Meantime, our partner is only a fraction of the way on her journey to world domination. We guys all know how to do it right, but we're usually too horny to take the time. There is, however, a dichotomy. Worldwide sales of personal lubricants are about $1.32 billion. Some women are doing it. Don't sell your KY Jelly stock.

Then there's the emotional level. Sex is thought of as the glue that binds two people together—the ultimate expression of love. In many cultures a marriage is not considered final until it is consummated. What does the couple do after the wedding, after the reception? Do they play tennis or watch reruns of *The Simpsons*? No, they sequester themselves in a room somewhere and get it on. Human beings, dolphins, bonobos, and a handful of other species are the only animals that engage in sex for pleasure, and pleasure is a big deal as any $2,000-a-night escort can tell you. In ancient Rome and Greece, sex was considered a gift from the gods, such as Venus, Cupid, and Dionysus. The first line of Vladimir Nabokov's epic novel, *Lolita*, is "Lolita light of my life, fire of my loins."

Finally, there's the physical level. The women of Togo want to withhold sex for one week. Really? They consider this a major inducement to get the men to act? Really? OK, we can play that game too. My suggestion to the men of Togo is that they hide the vibrators and dildos for a week, lest those self-righteous women are tempted to cheat.

My hat's off to the men of Togo who are apparently doing it so often that a one-week forced abstinence will spur them to political activism.

I'm reminded of the wonderful orgasm scene in *When Harry Met Sally*, when Billy Crystal and Meg Ryan are in a restaurant and she fakes a very loud and physical orgasm. The camera then cuts to Estelle Reiner who says to the waiter, "I'll have what she's having." I'll have what the men of Togo are having.

TO THE *TELEGRAM*

I am writing in response to Lydia Chorpening's letter to the *Telegram* on December 4. I applaud Ms. Chorpening's sincerity and obvious passion, but her admonition that we have "lost the God of our roots" collides with my sense of history and fair play.

Ms. Chorpening makes the common mistake of believing that the United States was formed as a Christian nation, or indeed that it was formed as a nation embracing any religious belief. She quotes a passage from John Adams' diary extolling the virtues of the Bible. That is, in fact, an accurate quote. But John Adams, Thomas Jefferson, and many other founding fathers were not Christians; they were deists. In a letter to Jefferson, Adams wrote, "I almost shudder at the thought of alluding to the most fatal example of abuses of grief which the history of mankind has perceived—the Cross. Consider what calamities that engine of grief has produced!"

The word "God" does not appear anywhere in our Constitution. The antiestablishment clause of the First Amendment of the Constitution prohibits the establishment of religion by the state. The third paragraph of Article VI of the Constitution prohibits any sort of religious test for qualification to hold public office.

On June 7, 1797, the US Senate unanimously passed the Treaty of Tripoli, which was then signed by President John Adams. Article Eleven of the treaty reads in part, "the Government of the United States is not, in any sense, founded on the Christian religion."

Finally, Thomas Jefferson, in a letter to the Danbury (Connecticut) Baptist Association on January 1, 1802, in referring to the First Amendment of the Constitution, said that it is "a wall of separation between church and state."

Ms. Chorpening says that in the 1960s "we ruled out prayer and Bible reading in our schools." Quite so, and for very good reason; the state sponsors schools, and the state cannot sponsor religion. Then she takes the amazing leap of linking the ruling out of prayer and Bible reading in schools to increases in crime, sickness, and disastrous weather. I doubt she can provide a credible scientific basis for that one. It is unfortunate when those of faith confuse their faith with fact.

I applaud Ms. Chorpening's right to practice any religion she wants, any way she wants, but I object to her imposing her religious principles on the rest of the nation. We are a nation comprised mostly of Christians, but that doesn't make us a Christian nation. We are a nation of diverse religious beliefs, and when someone calls this great republic a Christian nation, I wonder how diminished must those who are Jews, Muslims, Hindi, atheist, or persons of any other belief feel.

Harry Sarazin

THE REPUBLICAN PARTY

The Republican Party is now like a huge beach ball that someone has pricked with a pin; and with a noticeable hiss, it's losing its structure and collapsing into a heap of wrinkled "what used to be." The party's chief spokesman, a radio entertainer and former drug addict with the thought processes of an alligator, said he hopes Obama fails, which of course means he hopes the country fails—a low point in American politics.

Now the Republican leadership is whining that with a Democratic majority there will be no checks and balances. Mitch McConnell, Republican minority leader in the Senate, said, on the Senate floor, his only job was to see to it that Obama is a one-term president. Really? I thought his job was to do the people's work. He also said the Democratic majority was "a threat to the country." How ironic. Perhaps they've forgotten that for eight years under the little emperor from Texas, aided by his Svengalian sidekicks Cheney, Rumsfeld, Rove, and the rest, any semblance of checks and balances, in addition to the Constitution and rule of law, were thrown out the window. Condi Rice was questioned this week by students at the University of California. In replying to a student's question as to whether or not waterboarding is torture, she said, "By definition, if it was authorized by the president, it did not violate our obligations under the Conventions Against Torture." Sound familiar? Remember Nixon's famous statement during the David Frost interview when he said, "When the president does it, that means that it is not illegal." How's that for hubris, folks.

We need a Republican Party because we need a loyal opposition; we don't need a disloyal opposition for opposition's sake. Arlin Specter said this morning on *Face the Nation* that he has voted in Congress thousands of times, but for one vote he cast supporting the president's economic package, the Republican Party declared him a traitor and threw him under the bus. As the beach ball continues to deflate, the party childishly and blindly opposes every initiative the Democrats propose, while failing to come up with alternate proposals of their own.

So long as the party continues to move further and further right, and embraces as its core philosophy the Taliban-like religious extremism our founding fathers understood and were so wary of, the Republican Party will continue to shrink in relevance and power. It is being consumed by the super-virus of single-minded ideologues who want to see our government as a Christian theocracy. In the meantime, Obama, who promised change, has instituted more change in his first one hundred days than any president in recent history. We don't know if his economic policies will succeed, but they seem to have slowed the decline. Even Warren Buffet, the consummate pragmatist for all matters economic, said this week that Obama was doing the right thing.

I hope, for the sake of the country, the Republican Party regains its moral compass and reinstitutes adult-like behavior in Congress. Otherwise I'm afraid it will dissolve into a footnote in history.

WINTER RESPITE

Although undiagnosed, I believe I am slightly dyslectic. As a youngster I had difficulty learning to read, and even now, as an adult tripping happily through geezerdom, I occasionally stumble over words. I make this public confession with the expectation that it may explain the story I am about to tell you. I ask not for your pity, but simply for your understanding, although a little well-placed pity from time to time can be a good thing.

It was late November of 1959 when I graduated from advanced flight training at Corpus Christi, TX, and won my navy wings of gold. I was assigned to VP-26, an anti-submarine patrol squadron, at the US Naval Air Station, Brunswick, ME. Back in those days, brand new green pilots started out as navigators, then worked their way up to copilot, and finally, after rigorous testing, became a PPC, patrol plane commander. The plane flown in VP-26 was a P2V, a rather odd, Rube Goldberg-like aircraft, first built in 1945 and modified a number of times since. Our planes, P2V-5F (fifth modification), had two reciprocating engines and two J-34 jet engines, an afterthought made necessary after an already cramped plane was made even more uncomfortable by the addition of more and more electronic gear and more crew, making a total of twelve. Without the jets it's unlikely a fully loaded bird could have lifted off, which would result in a very uncomfortable conclusion to a takeoff run.

After checking into the squadron, I was given a short briefing and told I would be assigned to a flight crew and a collateral job in a few days. Meantime, I was to show up for work every day. My first act each morning was to check the ops board to see if I was assigned to a flight. Fair enough; after all, they were paying me. And so it came to pass that a few days after I arrived at VP-26, I checked the ops board and lo, there was my name, Ensign H. Sarazin, assigned aboard LK-4 the following morning at 0800 for a flight to Argentina. Argentina! Oh my God. It's mid-December and I'm going to Argentina. I can cavort on the pampas in my T-shirt and shorts; I can learn the tango; I can consume vast quantities of Argentinean beef; I can, I can, well, do all sorts of things one does in Argentina. Wow, the gods were smiling on me.

When I went home that night, I was as excited as a teenage boy in Hooters. Marilyn helped me pack; short-sleeved shirts, shorts, one pair of slacks (probably necessary for the tango lessons), light jacket—after all, it can get chilly on the pampas—and a camera.

I was on the flight line wearing my brand new flight suit, sea bag in hand, well before 0800. They're not going to leave me behind; I'm on my way to Argentina.

The interior of a P2V is cramped with equipment. The seating, were it on a commercial aircraft, would justify asking for your money back. The only visibility out is from the nose cone, the cockpit, and a couple of small waist windows; otherwise, one is encased in an aluminum tube with no amenities.

This is going to be a long flight, I thought; after all, Argentina is a long way from Brunswick—so far that we will fly from winter in the Northern Hemisphere to summer in the Southern Hemisphere. Perhaps the PPC will let me get some right seat (copilot) time; after all, I've got to learn how to fly this bird. Wow, Argentina.

About four and a half hours after we took off, the PPC announced over the intercom that we should prepare for landing. That's odd; we can't be in Argentina already, so why are we—of course, we're going to refuel.

When the plane came to a stop, the crew began to disembark. Exiting a P2V is via a short ladder in the nose gear well. I thought it best that I let everyone else get out first; I wasn't sure what the protocol was, but

I figured if I was last I couldn't go wrong. When I got to the ladder, a rush of very cold air hit me, then I dropped to the ground. There was snow piled all around, and the air was biting. I turned to look at the operations building and there, in huge gold letters, was a sign: US Naval Air Station, Argentia, Newfoundland.

GABE AND ROSE
A Short Story

"Gabe. Gabe your dinner's ready." She wasn't sure her small voice would carry through the rain, across the lawn, onto the dock, and down below on the boat, but she called anyway, as she had hundreds of times before. The old fool will work on that little boat until midnight, she thought with a smile, and he's too stubborn to come and eat even if I go get him.

That boat. That beautiful little boat. Gabe had named it *Rose*, his wife's name, not to placate her, but because he loved her and he loved the boat, so it was a natural thing to do. She was 32-feet overall, somewhat more if you included the long, slender bowsprit. She was plank-on-plank longleaf pine with white oak frames, built to withstand time and any seas she may encounter, and over the nearly thirty-five years of her existence, she had done both. *Rose* had the lines of a Bristol Channel Cutter, although she wasn't one. Her shear was ever so slightly more pronounced, her rig taller, and her bowsprit a little shorter. Her history was lost with the sudden death of her third owner. His wife, who hated the boat, quickly rid herself of it to the fourth owner who kept it only two years before selling it to Gabe. But whoever drew her lines, and built her with such care and craftsmanship, clearly had a Bristol Channel Cutter in mind. Now her gleaming white hull lay quietly to the dock in front of Gabe and Rose's home near Dun Cove, as she had since Gabe bought her nine years ago.

"Hi. Dinner ready yet?" said Gabriel Murphy as he let the screen door close gently behind him. "I guess I got carried away down there, Rosie. There's always so much to do to get her ready to go. My God, whatever that is it sure smells good."

Gabe had been a tall, muscular man in his youth. Now, in his seventy-first year, he had lost much of the muscle and some of the height, but was still an imposing figure, with thick, wavy, white hair, clear blue eyes, and the round Irish face that could charm the devil or frighten a saint. He had been in the CIA before his retirement at age sixty. His years in a variety of overseas stations had shaped the volatile Irish kid fresh from Johns Hopkins into a skilled professional. His reputation throughout the Agency as a charmer and master storyteller was legend. Now, with his wife of nearly fifty years, he was living out the sunset of his life in quiet happiness.

Gabe met Rose at Hopkins, and it was clear to both of them from the beginning that they would spend the rest of their lives together. Rose, the daughter of a rather well-known ocean racing sailor from New England, had virtually grown up on a sailboat. She taught Gabe to sail and along with the instruction had managed to impart her love of the sport to him. Among the many gifts she had given him over the years, one he treasured as much as any was the gift of sailing. Her enthusiasm fired his, and it quickly became a passion they shared. For the past forty-eight years, they sailed together in places all over the world, as Gabe's assignments scattered them happily from continent to continent. Now, settled in Maryland, their sailing was confined to Chesapeake Bay because of age, although Gabe, with his Irish confidence and pride intact, would never admit such was the case.

Most of their sailing on *Rose* was done together, for long weekends, longer weeks, and occasionally a month or more. But Gabe had a stirring in his soul. He was gregarious by nature—a people person—but there was in him a need to sail alone every now and then—a need to single-hand. He had long since concluded that it was the sense of adventure in him that compelled him to challenge the sea from time to time. It was as if Joshua Slocum or Bernard Moitessier were whispering in his ear, "Go do it; see if you can."

Rose, on the other hand, concluded Gabe needed to go single-hand-ing (and she noticed he did it more and more as he grew older) because he felt age shadowing him, and his fragile male ego needed to be reas-sured that the old guy still has what it takes. No matter. For whatever reason, Gabe had to get his single-handing stints in about twice a season, and Rose understood. But lately she began to worry. His health was good, and his mind was as sharp and clear as ever, but he was no kid anymore. What if something happened out there? What if he got hurt, or sick? "Rosie, you worry too much, I've been taking care of myself for seventy-one years, and by this time I should have it down pretty pat. I'll be just fine," and with that he would put his arm around her still shapely waist, kiss her gently on the cheek, and the subject would be dropped.

"Now Gabe, I want you to call me, even if you anchor out. Please let me know where you are. The kids worry about you, you know."

"No Rosie, you worry about me. I'll call, and I won't be gone more than about a week—less if the weather turns lousy, but I don't' think it will. There's a good long-range forecast. Of course if it's really nice, I may just slide out the mouth of the Bay and call you from Bermuda." She knew he was joking, of course, but she knew Gabe. His fertile imagi-nation might, at any moment, snatch an offhand comment and build it into a quest. Don Quixote could have taken quest lessons from Gabriel Murphy.

It used to be very important for Gabe to get away from the dock early, but no longer. The sense of time urgency that was the warp and woof of his life for most of it had dissipated like morning fog in the hot sun, as retirement gradually shifted his priorities. There still remained a gener-alized, gnawing sense of urgency. "How much longer can I sail—how much time left—how much time?" But he attributed this to growing older and for the most part dismissed it. He was truly relaxed now, as he had never been when he was working. Rather than feel a sense of worth-lessness when he retired, as so many do, he had a feeling fulfillment, of arrival. He had always taken his work seriously, but he also realized that not long after he left, few would remember, and none would care. That's just the way life is. So most of the really important things lay outside of work, unless the work is creative, and Gabe had no illusions that the work of a bureaucrat is creative, so the important things for him were family, home, friends, sailing, and the hundreds of little things he did that enriched his existence. Being able to concentrate on these was true fulfillment, so retirement released him from time urgency, and gave him contentment.

"Well, I guess that's everything Rosie, time to shove off." The new morning was crisp and clear, as the first evidence of fall demanded a light sweater.

"Don't you have any idea where you're going? You must have..."

"Rosie," he interrupted, "I never have any idea. It doesn't matter. That way I can sail, or hole up, or do whatever I want, and I don't have to be stuck with any sort of schedule. You know I never plan these things—it's more fun that way. Don't worry. I'll call."

Rose Murphy watched the clean little cutter glide slowly around the point, and when it was out of sight, she returned to the house with an uneasy feeling. It will crush him when he can't sail by himself anymore, she thought. She understood how this proud, gentle man thought and how he would react, and it worried her.

The first few hours of every single-handed adventure Gabe Murphy took were always tinged with a little apprehension. It wasn't the sailing that made him apprehensive; it was the sense of what the adventure might hold, and there was the ever-present edge of guilt over leaving Rose. But he knew she understood. The lack of a schedule created an open-ended potential for adventure, making the whole excursion sweeter, and that's why Gabe did it in the first place.

It was 1240 as he passed Bar Neck on his way out the Choptank to the Bay. What a beautiful day, he thought. One of those rare late summer days when the sun makes crisp, clean shadows, visibility bounds beyond the horizon, and the air is clean and comfortable. The wind was WSW at 9 knots, and Gabriel Murphy was at home in his element.

Might as well sail to Hudson Creek off the Little Choptank, he thought. A short day, and a quiet anchorage. Time enough to read, fix a nice meal, and listen to some music (Rose had slipped a new tape of sea chanteys in Gabe's sea bag, which he would discover later to his delight).

Gabe never got bored. He could sit for hours in an airport waiting for a delayed flight and enjoy himself watching people. He was always content with himself and was constantly entertained by his imagination and memories. So sitting on a sailboat, in the middle of nowhere, watching the birds and water, and even spiders as they built their marvelously engineered webs, was a pure delight.

It was Tuesday, and as he had expected, there were no other boats in the creek—good. Total emersion in aloneness was a good way to start a single-handed venture. It was, in fact, the only proper way to start.

Gabe liked to spoil himself the first day out, so dinner would be Caesar salad, shrimp and scallops over pasta with his own secret, carefully crafted marinara sauce, and a bottle of Chardonnay. Yes, Gabriel Murphy, the seventy-one-year-old ex-CIA officer turned full-time retiree and sailor, was indeed content.

Wednesday morning was different. It was unusually hot and hazy for this time of year. More like a typical midsummer day on the Chesapeake. What little wind there was, was out of the SSE, and there seemed little promise of more as the day matured. Oh well, thought Gabe, may as well go to Solomon's today. Ought to make it in a few tacks, and if the wind collapses altogether, well, that's what they make engines for.

The wind on the Bay was a little fresher, at least enough to sail without ghosting, so Gabe settled back, trying to hold the favored port tack as long as possible without pinching.

A late lunch of pita bread, chicken salad, and cran-raspberry juice came and went. The sky grew thicker, as it had been doing most of the morning, and now it was dark gray, nearly black, like the bottom of a thunder cell—but no thunder cells here, just dark clouds from horizon to horizon, and probably full of rain.

By 1500 the wind had increased to force 4, and *Rose* slid along nicely, heeled on her lines, as happy as her master.

The suddenness of the change startled Gabe. Without warning the wind increased to 20 knots, then quickly to 30. *Rose* was overpowered and nearly out of control before Gabe could react. Almost as quickly, the seas became steep and confused, as water broke over the bow and drove horizontally back to the cockpit where Gabe, soaked and cold, struggled to roll up the yankee. *Rose* heeled excessively, water washing over the lee rail and along the deck. Rolling up the yankee proved to be more of a task than he had expected, and it left him weary. If I get a deep reef in the main and leave the little staysail up, she should get back on her feet and punch through the seas, he thought. Gabe learned long ago that the only convenient way to reef the main alone was to heave to. Having done this, he eased the main sheet and halyard then went forward to attach the deep reef cringle to the hook. It was raining now, and the wind drove it in blinding sheets, which felt like a sandblaster on the face. *Rose*, despite being hove to, rolled and pitched wildly in the seas, as the sound of the wind and rain nearly obscured thought. Gabe made his way forward cautiously, crawling along the side deck on his hands and knees. When he reached the shrouds, he grabbed hold, pulled himself up, and began to step up on the coach roof. But before he could heave himself all the way up, his foot slipped and he fell, striking his head on the edge of the coach roof, then landing with most of his weight on his left shoulder. He lay on his back, wedged between a lifeline stanchion and the side of the doghouse, dazed and aching. The wind and rain produced an unending background cacophony as he wavered between consciousness and insensibility.

He didn't know how long he had lain there. He only knew that blood from his throbbing head was being washed away by the rain, that his left arm was numb, and his shoulder probably broken. He knew he was in trouble. He managed to roll over and painfully get up on his knees, using his good right arm. Inch by agonizing inch, he crawled back to the cockpit. He couldn't reef, he had too much canvas up to sail, and he had no sea room to run off, even if he was able to manage the boat, which he doubted was possible. He was dizzy and his vision seemed blurred, although maybe it was the ceaseless rain. He needed help. Never in his years of sailing had he ever asked for help. He prided himself on his ability to be self-sufficient, but Gabe knew this time he needed help.

Getting below was more difficult even than he had expected, but he made it, and he managed to pull himself up onto the nav seat. "Mayday, mayday, mayday, this is the cutter *Rose*. I am approximately two miles northeast of Cove Point. I am injured and need assistance." He released the mic button and waited.

"Vessel calling mayday, this is Coast Guard Station Taylor's Island. Say again the name of your vessel and your exact position."

"This is the cutter *Rose*. I am hove to approximately two miles northeast of Cove Point. I'm injured and need help."

It was several hours before the Coast Guard 41-footer from Taylor's Island spotted a white sailboat hove to about a mile and a half ENE of Cove Point. The name "Rose" was painted neatly on each quarter. There was no one in the cockpit or on deck, so with some difficulty, the 41-footer came alongside and put a man aboard. The seasoned veteran of more than one rescue at sea made his way carefully below, bracing himself against the somewhat unfamiliar motion of a small sailboat hove to in strong winds. Before reaching the bottom step of the companionway ladder, he saw the white-haired old man, with dried blood in his hair, slumped over the nav table. The VHF radio mic was out of its holder and lay on the table next to him.

Later, when they gently lifted him onto a litter, they noticed the old man had been lying across the open log. A coastguardsman picked it up and read the last entry, which was scrawled in a large, uneven hand across an otherwise blank page: "Rosie, I love you."

JOURNEY

Several months ago I began a journey—not one of my own doing, but one imposed upon me. It's a journey some of you have taken and one many of you will take. It's a journey through the desert of death, and it began when my wife died on February 25, 2011.

I want to share with you some of my memories, thoughts, and feelings as I travel down this road. Nothing I say here will be profound or even new; it would be difficult to improve on 200,000 years of human evolution.

Marilyn and I started dating when we were both in college, she at St. Scholastica and I at UMD. She graduated in 1955 and I in 1957. It should have been 1956, but ahhh, I'll explain that some other time. She got a job as a social worker with Catholic Charities in Superior, and I went on to graduate school at the University of Minnesota in Minneapolis. I hated graduate school. Industrial relations was clearly not the field I was cut out to pursue, so to regroup and consider my options, I withdrew from school after the first quarter and was promptly drafted because I forgot that my student deferment would expire if I was no longer a student. Perhaps you can see now why it took me five years to pursue a four-year undergraduate course. After some maneuvering (it didn't hurt that Marilyn's father was head of the draft board), I managed to get out of going into the army, and joined the navy.

Off I went to Pensacola, Florida, for preflight training. Marilyn and I had decided before I left that we would be married when I was commissioned. Here is an excerpt from a letter I wrote to her on November 12, 1957: "All last night and today I've been bothered by a mad compulsion to marry you and move out to the lake [Barnes, WI] permanently. I could work for the town, or start some small business or something like that. We wouldn't be rich, in fact we may even starve, but it sounds kind of appealing anyhow. I hope someday we can live out there, hon. I can think of no place I would rather spend the rest of my life."

On Saturday, May 10, 1958, the day after I was commissioned an ensign in the United States Navy, we were married in the chapel at the US Naval Air Station, Pensacola. On Monday I started flight training.

I had decided to make the navy a career, but in a sudden shift of game plan, I left the navy in 1963 to join the FBI. As with all major decisions in our lives, she never complained or balked. I always sought her counsel, but she usually agreed with me. During our married life, we lived in Pensacola, Florida; Corpus Christi, Texas; Norfolk, Virginia; Topsham, Maine; New Orleans, Louisiana; Glen Burnie, Maryland; and Havre de Grace, Maryland; and along the way we had two beautiful children, Ann and Jim, who both live with their spouses in Baltimore, Maryland.

In the fall of 2006, I noticed the first sign that something was wrong when Marilyn drove off the road and into the woods just outside Gordon on a clear, sunny day with no traffic around. Fortunately she wasn't hurt, but she had no explanation for the accident. She had another unexplained accident in Maryland in the winter of 2006. Over that winter we talked about selling the house and moving to Barnes. In March of 2007 we sold, moved to Barnes, and undertook a major remodeling project. After fifty-eight days out of the house, we finally moved back in September.

Marilyn's condition continued to deteriorate slowly but steadily. She would suddenly, and without warning, fall while talking to someone. Before long, and after a brief period with a walker, she required a wheelchair.

By mid-2010 she could no longer care for herself and had to be bathed and fed. She could neither stand nor talk, and it wasn't certain if she recognized me or the kids when they came to visit.

I began practicing for her death. I knew I would either wake up beside her one morning and she would be dead, or I would go in the bedroom at some point to get her up for a meal and she would be gone, so I practiced the scenario over and over in my mind that I might be prepared. I somehow thought this would ease the shock.

On the night of February 24, 2011, after I put her in bed following dinner, she opened her eyes and looked at me for a very long time—something she hadn't done in months—then she went to sleep. The next morning I went in the bedroom around ten fifteen to check on her, and she seemed all right. When I went in at ten fifty-five to get her up to start the day, she was dead. I now believe that looking at me as she did the night before was her way of saying good-bye.

Practicing her death did help soften the shock, but there was another component I hadn't reckoned on: loss. I thought I had become accustomed to her loss since for months all that remained of her was a shell. But when she died, I experienced a profound sense of loss and loneliness, and that I had not foreseen.

No two people grieve the same way, and there is no right or wrong way to grieve. The time of grieving is not set in stone; it's different for everyone, but I think I can say with certainty that although time softens the jagged edge of grief, it never erases it.

I'm doing well. My family and some very dear old friends have helped me on this journey, and for that I'm grateful. But this is a journey one travels alone. That's terrifying at first, but I have come to feel a certain strength in being alone, so it's OK—not ideal—but OK.

The hole in my heart will never completely heal, but the soft memories of her are the salve that stops the bleeding.

THE OTHER HALF

I stand now alone.
The half of me that was the other half
Has slipped away as lo I moan,
Because the half of me who used to, can no longer laugh.

I knew it was nigh.
I dreamed it, trying to make the journey soft.
But on the day she gave her last sigh
I sank into a maze of disbelief, and viewed myself as from aloft.

That was scarcely two score days ago.
As I sit here alone, cradled in nature's breast,
My mind from time to time will go
To the half of me that's now at rest.

And when, like the sword of Damocles, hangs the grief,
Awful, crushing, choking; dashing any hope of cheers.
I shudder in utter disbelief
As I am overcome and surrender to the tears.

The half of me that was the other half
Was one as soft and gentle as morning fog aflow.
She bolstered me and made me laugh.
The half of me that was the other half—I love her so.

A BEAUTIFUL ENDING

Days have become muted as the sun rises and sets further and further to the south, and the wedge of daylight between those events keeps getting smaller and smaller, as if some giant rat is eating it from the fat end. A chill has invaded my summer reverie, like a gunshot in the middle of the night, stark and unwelcome. Accompanying this change is the annual miracle of fall colors, nature's mockery of the Great Masters, her way of letting us know where beauty and wonder truly come from.

So it was last week that I decided to take a drive to see for myself the dichotomy of chill and beauty. I chose a particularly wonderful back road. Those from New York City, Philadelphia, Chicago, or Los Angeles would say every road here is a back road, but we know better. I chose Lake Owen Drive, a beautiful, serpentine ribbon of asphalt snaking its way for about fifteen miles through the forest from Drummond, WI, to near Cable. The day was crystal clear and calm. I chose to drive it around one p.m. when the sun would be at its highest. I wanted maximum light penetration through that dense woodland. The colors were at their peak and more vibrant this year than any year I can remember. I drove at a snail's pace—not much chance of holding anyone up on that stretch of road. The shrill beauty of the colors, contrasted with moments of bright sunlight and others of deep shadow, made for a sort of psychedelic experience—LSD without the LSD.

When I was a little boy, I fought bedtime like all little boys, because when you're a little boy that's one of your jobs. The truth, which I would never admit to my parents, is that I kind of liked bedtime. My bed became a vehicle—a rocket ship, submarine, race car, fighter airplane— that transported me to another world, an exciting world full of adventure and danger. But in the far reaches of my mind, I always knew I was safe; I was safe in my bed, in my home, and with my parents. My imagination allowed me to experience quixotic adventures in which I was the hero, without the danger of being clobbered by an errant windmill. It was in this way that I imagined myself to sleep nearly every night. Now, decades later, and scarred by the realities of life, I ride down this lovely road, and I get a sense of being nestled and protected by the vivid canopy of trees surrounding me. I am once again happy and safe and securely out of harm's way.

But there is another thought that crosses my mind. As magnificent as all of this is, it foreshadows an ending. The leaves that are so glorious now will dull, wither, and fall to the ground, leaving grotesque skeletons of trees reaching to the sky in vain attempts to reclothe themselves. I am reminded of the final movement of Mahler's ninth symphony. That quiet, haunting, ethereal music that can conjure feelings of solitude and peace, but only briefly, because in the overarching meaning of the music, it is a symphony of death.

Thus, it is on Lake Owen Road, on an idyllic day in early October, I take a journey of solitude, of beauty, of safety, of joy, but one portending the death of summer. What does one do, smile or cry? Perhaps both.

CHRISTMAS LETTERS

The first Christmas letter was written by St. Paul who, as you know, was a prolific letter writer. In 1948 a letter from St. Paul dated December 12, 0058 was discovered by biblical scholars in a cave near Qumran. It was addressed to St. Paul's cousin, Goldfarb of Galilee, who was a sandal maker. In the letter Paul tells news of his family with an emphasis on the accomplishments of his children, Irving the doctor and Sherman the lawyer. Paul wishes his cousin a very merry Christmas and expresses hope that sandal sales are brisk over the holiday season. Thus with that letter, written 1,954 years ago, the tradition of the Christmas letter began, and it remains little changed today.

Throughout my adult life, I have received Christmas letters from people I scarcely know, bragging about their kids, grandkids, nieces, nephews, dogs, and gerbils and, I suspect, so have you. All these family heroes are referred to by their first names only, and the connections between them and to the letter writer are shrouded in mystery. I don't care what these faceless creatures have accomplished, and if I knew them, I probably still wouldn't care. So the Christmas letter, instead of an instrument of joy and good cheer, becomes a nuisance and object of dread during the holiday season.

In 2003, to retaliate, I made up a family—first names only, relationships undisclosed. Their accomplishments far exceed anything one could possibly hope for in one's own family, except for one member who is a bit of a black sheep, but lovable. I skipped the "family" letter in 2004 and got so much flack from friends and relatives that I was forced to reinstate it in 2005 and beyond. The 2010 letter is missing for personal reasons. What follows are all of the letters about my "other" family.

CHRISTMAS 2003

Dear Friends:

Here we are once again at that wonderful time of year when the dreaded Christmas letters flood the mail. So, in the spirit of shameless disregard for your sensibilities, here is ours.

I broke my leg in February. When asked, I say I was on my way from Camp 5 with my friend, Sherpa Zutang Norgay, grandson of Tanzing Norgay, to summit Mt. Everest, when I fell into a forty-five-foot-deep crevasse onto the rocks below. If the book deal falls through, I'll tell what really happened. I slipped on a patch of ice in the driveway next my car while on my way to get a haircut—no book deal there. Toward the end of the sixth week in a cast the leg was so gamey dogs wouldn't come near me, and one day after driving by the Baltimore Zoo I am told all the camels fainted. Marilyn, on the other hand, remained accident- and disease-free for the entire year, unless crankiness can be classified as a disease.

Now for news about the rest of the Sarazin family. Buffy was admitted to the Astronaut Training Program in May. As you can imagine, she is thrilled, but with some melancholy. She is saddened to leave her job as chief astrophysicist at the Johns Hopkins Applied Physics Laboratory, but she has been assured they will have a place for her when her astronaut days are over. Buffy, Rick, and the twins moved to Houston in May. Rick was fortunate to get a job as chief of neurosurgery at the Texas Medical Center, so they are comfortably settled. Sarah and Timmy have adjusted well, but being the only eight-year-olds in their senior class in high school initially caused some raised eyebrows among their classmates.

Michael will soon finish his triple PhD program at Oxford. He has loved his time there and made a number of friends whom he cherishes. He's still single, but has been seriously dating a wonderful young lady, Martha Blair, daughter of Prime Minister Tony Blair. We met her and her parents during our trip to London in June. They seem to be lovely, charming people.

We are particularly proud of Tommy. Since the trial he has worked very hard and is now in charge of the prison library, a job he loves. The guards hold him in high regard, so all is well with him. How gratifying to know he will be comfortably settled for the next ten to twenty years.

Marilyn and I are well, happy, and still somewhat in touch with reality.

A Very Merry Christmas and Happy New Year to you all.

Harry & Marilyn

CHRISTMAS 2005

Dear Friends:

Well, we've made it to another Christmas, and that's no mean accomplishment.

Marilyn is doing well, and after about a year and a half remains cancer-free. Ann and Jim are still gainfully employed, they tell us, and content as clams as they both work very hard. There have been no tragedies, setbacks, major events (good or bad), or other notable phenomena in our lives over the past year. Marilyn and I spent another six months plus at the Lake, and each year we do that, it just gets better—we love it.

Some of you have inquired about the rest of the Sarazin family, so here's an update. You will recall that Buffy was admitted to the astronaut program in May of 2003. She did well and enjoyed the challenges of the program, but in late 2004 she decided that being an astronaut wasn't for her. Perhaps it was the acrophobia. She resigned, and she, Rick, and the twins (now ten) returned to Maryland. As promised, the Johns Hopkins Applied Physics Laboratory reinstated her. Since she's been there, she has become interested in particle physics, and as a result, in June of this year, she completed Kaku's string theory equation, which now describes the eleventh dimension. It is said in some physics circles that this is the equation that describes the universe. There's talk of a Nobel Prize. Meantime, Rick was appointed chief of neurosurgery at Johns Hopkins with a full professorship at Hopkins Medical School. The twins, Sarah and Timmy, have enrolled at St. John's College in Annapolis where the curriculum is based on the great books of intellectual achievement over the past two thousand years. The freshman reading list includes Homer, Sophocles, Euripides, Plato, Aristotle, Fahrenheit, Proust, and much more. They love it and are thriving, although social integration is a bit challenging.

Michael finished his PhD at Oxford and is now doing post-doc work at Harvard. He and Martha Blair were married in June of 2004 and live in Cambridge, MA. It was a lovely wedding in London, but Martha's father, Tony, was only able to attend briefly due to pressing affairs of state. They are getting along well, but Martha had a bit of difficulty adjusting from Ten Downing St. to a one-bedroom apartment in Cambridge. Michael will finish his studies in January and has been offered a position as chief economist at Goldman Sachs in New York. He's not sure if he wants to do that or teach. Harvard has offered him a professorship.

Finally, Tommy is getting along well and is still in charge of the prison library. He tells us he now has a special friend, Spike, who will also be there for ten to twenty years. We're so happy for them both.

A Very Merry Christmas and Happy New Year to you all.

Harry & Marilyn

CHRISTMAS 2006

Dear Friends:

Well, we're still here, on earth, that is, although, sadly, we've lost some good friends during the past year. That's what we get for growing older.

Marilyn remains cancer-free (just over two years). Ann and Jim continue to get paychecks and assure us they aren't under state or federal indictment. We have nothing spectacular to report, good or bad. Perhaps we live lives of insipid desperation. We spent a wonderful seven months at the Lake, and enjoyed the best weather we've ever had.

As for the rest of the Sarazin clan, there have been a few changes. Buffy continues to work at the Johns Hopkins Applied Physics Laboratory, but she has become disillusioned with string theory. Following the recent measurements of cosmic microwave background energy, which tend to confirm the Big Bang, she is now concentrating on dark matter. She had a rather unpleasant incident in July. A colleague, with whom she has sharply differed on the probability that there will ever be a grand unification theory, and she were discussing the effect of neutrino oscillations on the standard model of particle physics, when he suddenly became enraged and tried to choke her. She hit him in the groin with an eight-inch stainless steel paperweight shaped as $E=mc^2$. That ended the incident. Her colleague has since been contacted by the Vienna Boy's Choir.

In early August, Rick was about to perform a delicate neurosurgical procedure when the anesthesiologist inadvertently administered laughing gas to the patient instead of the regular anesthetic. When the patient began to giggle, he jerked his head, which resulted in an unwanted lobotomy. He probably would have sued, but he couldn't remember why.

Sarah and Timmy, the twins, are in their second year at St. John's College. Their first year was a great success academically, but their social life is wanting. Timmy, who is now thirteen, is particularly bothered because he's entering puberty and the hormones are churning, but none of the girls will give him a tumble. Sarah is a little more mature about it.

Michael and Martha are still in Cambridge, MA, while Michael completes his post-doc work. He is leaning toward accepting the professorship Harvard offered; however, Martha's dad, Tony, thinks he could do better at Goldman Sachs. Of course Tony will be out of a job in a few months, so he may be looking for a prosperous son-in-law.

Tommy and his friend Spike had a serious spat this fall and didn't speak to each other for nearly a month. They've now made up, and all is well. Tommy continues to run the prison library, and he loves it.

That's about it. Merry Christmas and Happy New Year to you all.

Harry and Marilyn

CHRISTMAS 2007

Dear Family and Friends:

Greetings again from paradise. As most of you know, we sold our house in Maryland this past spring, and did some extensive remodeling to our cabin here in Wisconsin, so we now have a year-round permanent home. We're going to try a winter here, but if it gets too brutal, we may beat feet for warmer places.

All is well with us and with our kids. Other than the sale of the house and all that followed, our year has been largely event-free.

As for the rest of the Sarazin clan, it's been a pretty good year. Buffy was promoted to group leader of a group studying black holes at the Johns Hopkins Applied Physics Laboratory outside Baltimore. You will recall that Buffy and a colleague got into a rather violent argument last year (she had to clock him in the crotch with an $E=mc^2$ paperweight). He was so distraught by her promotion that he attempted suicide by lying on the sidewalk and putting his head over the curb at a bus stop, hoping a passing bus would squash him into eternity. None appeared; apparently he had an old bus schedule. The police took him away before he harmed himself. He now resides at Sunny Shadows, a home for the seriously confused. Buffy and her team are trying to develop a workable formula for precisely determining the rate of change as time slows between the event horizon and singularity in a black hole. This will, in turn, predict the warping of space-time. It will also help measure gravitational waves, which can provide detailed maps of black holes. This is truly pioneering theoretical physics, and it builds on work done by Campanelli and Luosto at the Rochester Institute of Technology. Buffy thinks she is close to a solution, and she's quite excited about the whole thing. If she's successful, there's a Noble in there for sure.

Rick remains as chief of neurosurgery at Hopkins. Earlier this year he was named the Gugleheiffer Chair in neurology at the Johns Hopkins Medical School. It's a lot of added work, but he feels honored, and it admits him to the academy, which means a little higher class of cocktail parties.

Sarah and Timmy are now in their third year at St. John's Col- lege in Annapolis. Their reading list includes Cervantes' *Don Quixote*; Galileo's, *Two New Sciences*; Hobbs's, *Leviathan*; Descartes's, *Meditations, Rules For the Direction of the Mind*; Milton's, *Paradise Lost*; Spinoza's, *Theological-Political Treatise*, and much more. Each of them has main- tained a 4.0 average. They are now fourteen, and have integrated rather well into campus social life, which largely consists of discussion groups with copious amounts of coffee.

Michael and Martha are still in Cambridge, MA. He finished his post-doc work, turned down the offer at Goldman Sachs, and accepted a full professorship in economics at Harvard. Martha's dad, Tony, since leaving office, seems to be prospering as Quartet envoy to the Middle East. Martha is a little sad that her parents had to leave Ten Downing St., but she realizes politics is fluid.

Tommy fell into a deep depression after his friend Spike got paroled in March. His work at the prison library began to suffer, and he was threatened with removal. Then, and if you believe in God this is clearly divine intervention, he got a new cellmate, Bruno. They are now insepa- rable. Tommy is ecstatic because Bruno won't be getting paroled any time soon. Actually, he won't be getting paroled at all.

Merry Christmas and Happy New Year to you all.

Harry & Marilyn

CHRISTMAS 2008

Dear Family and Friends:

Greetings from the great north woods. Our first winter here in fifty years wasn't as bad as we (I) thought it might be, although we were told it was one of the snowiest and coldest in over a decade. We were warm and cozy in our (mostly) new digs. OK, the truth is it was colder than hell, and I nearly froze my kahunas off when I was outside, but it was cozy inside, so we survived.

As most of you know, Marilyn has Alzheimer's. Each day is a struggle for her, but she's tough, has tremendous spirit, and never complains. In early October I was diagnosed with prostate cancer. We're handling it, and it's going to be OK. On balance, life is good, very good.

Now for news of the rest of the Sarazin clan. Buffy, who is at the Johns Hopkins Applied Physics Laboratory outside Baltimore, is well along in her study of black holes. She and her team have not yet been able to develop a workable formula to determine the rate of change as time slows between the event horizon and singularity in a black hole. She has, however, discovered a gravitational anomaly in which gravity disappears in rapid pulses over a very narrow band at constant radius from the event horizon. These pulses appear randomly along the circumference of that radius. She is now trying to develop a theory to explain this observation. One possibility is that in those nanoseconds after the Big Bang, when all the laws of physics were established, the enormous forces involved caused a partial fracturing of gravitational waves. If this is the case, it may lead to a refinement of the theory of gravity and it could render parts of Einstein's General Theory of Relativity in error. Stephen Hawking has contacted her, and he wants to meet to discuss her discovery. Her colleagues have named this gravitational anomaly the Buffy Blink.

Rick loves teaching neurology at the Johns Hopkins Medical School. Unfortunately, he has had to scale back somewhat on surgery. One interesting case he had involved a Saudi prince who suffered from a rare non-malignant brain tumor on the temporal lobe, deep inside the Sylvian fissure. It was necessary to keep the prince conscious during the operation to ensure his speech functions were not disturbed. Although he spoke halting English, he was asked to speak every minute or so. At one point, as Rick was excising the last remnants of the tumor, the prince suddenly began to sing "Che gelida manina" from Puccini's *La boheme*, in a strong, beautiful tenor voice, although he apparently had no musical training. He has since appeared at La Scala and is booked into the Royal Opera House and the Met.

Sarah and Timmy, now fifteen, are in their last year at St. John's College in Annapolis. This year's curriculum includes Tolstoy, Hegel, Marx, Kierkegaard, Cervantes, Kant, Dostoevsky, and much more. Sarah has decided she wants to go into the Foreign Service and has been admitted to the Nitze School of Advanced International Studies at Johns Hopkins. Timmy wants to pursue a career in theoretical physics and has been admitted to MIT's graduate program in physics.

Michael loves teaching economics at Harvard and is more than ever convinced he made the right decision when he turned down the offer by Goldman Sachs. Martha has become involved in Cambridge politics and now sits on the city council. Her dad (Tony Blair) is very proud that she's following in his footsteps.

Tommy is getting along exceptionally well. He and Bruno are not only cellmates, but Bruno is now working in the library with Tommy. They are very close. Tommy won't be coming up for parole until 2025, but he's quite content with his life. In June he won the prestigious Con-Lib award from the National Association of Prison Libraries for his administration of his prison library. We're all very proud of him.

Merry Christmas and Happy New Year to you all.

Harry & Marilyn

CHRISTMAS 2009

Dear Family and Friends:

We weathered another winter in the great north woods, no worse for the experience. I have discovered, however, I really don't like cold. So why are we here? Because we love this place—go figure.

Marilyn's condition has deteriorated still further. She is barely communicative and unable to do anything for herself. She has been in rehab since September with severe pressure sores. She'll be home by the end of December. My prostate cancer has been successfully taken care of, and I have no problems, except people tell me I'm a little grumpier than I used to be. Balderdash, and to hell with them.

Now, about the rest of the Sarazin family. Buffy is deeply involved in her study of black holes at the Johns Hopkins Applied Physics Laboratory. She is concentrating on super massive black holes. She has made startling progress and recently found a link between sigma (the speed at which stars at the outer edge of galaxies are moving) and super massive black holes at the center of those galaxies. The stars of sigma are too far away from the galaxy's black holes to be affected by them, but the link she found suggests that at one time the black holes had an effect. But discovery doesn't come without problems. One of her colleagues, another woman, deeply jealous of Buffy's accomplishments, recently spiked her hot chocolate with a massive dose of a powerful laxative. As a result Buffy had several embarrassing and uncomfortable accidents in the lab. She confronted the woman, and a physical fight broke out that had to be broken up by other members of the lab. Buffy did, however, manage to break the woman's nose. The harassment stopped.

Rick still teaches neurology at the Johns Hopkins Medical School and does neurosurgery on a limited basis. He had a close call in the OR one day last June. He was operating on a professional wrestler, a giant of a man, with only local anesthesia so they could communicate. Rick had just excised a malignant brain tumor and was about to replace the section of skull he had removed, when the man suddenly leapt off the operating table and got Rick in a take-down hold. It took three orderlies and two cops to get him under control and back on the operating table so Rick could replace his skull bone.

Sarah started at the Nitze School of Advanced International Studies at Johns Hopkins, and she loves it. Her decision to go into the Foreign Service has been reinforced by her graduate school experience so far. Timmy started this fall at MIT in the theoretical physics graduate program. He has already caught the attention of his advisor and professors by discovering an error in a complex equation in one of his textbooks.

Michael has been granted tenure at Harvard and has been named vice chairman of the Economics Department. Sarah is pregnant and continues to serve on the Cambridge City Council.

Tommy seems more content than he has been for years. He and Bruno continue their deep involvement with one another, which is good for both of them. The Maryland Department of Corrections gave Tommy a special award for his work in the prison library. We are all happy for him and very proud.

Merry Christmas or Hanukah and Happy New Year to you all.

Harry & Marilyn

CHRISTMAS 2011

Dear Family and Friends:

As most of you know, Marilyn died peacefully here at home one cold morning in late February of this year; I don't think she suffered. It's been a journey since her death, a journey that gets slightly easier with each passing day. My family, my friends, and a constant search for intellectual stimulation have sustained me, so on balance, all is well, and I'm back on track—mostly.

Jim and Connie and Ann and Bill are doing well as are the gaggle of grandkids. None has filed for bankruptcy, been indicted, run over by a cab, or had any major diseases, so I guess we can be grateful for that.

Buffy was shocked in late September by the announcement that Swiss physicists had beamed neutrinos (subatomic particles with no charge) from Geneva to Italy, a distance of 454 miles, and that they traveled sixty nanoseconds faster than the speed of light. One of the bedrocks of scientific belief is Einstein's Special Theory of Relativity (published 1905), which stated that nothing can travel faster than the speed of light. In an attempt to replicate the experiment, Buffy intends to beam neutrinos from her lab near Baltimore to a target in West Virginia, where no known intelligent life forms are thought to exist.

Rick continues as chairman of the neurosurgery department at John Hopkins as well as with his professorship at John Hopkins Medical School. He went on a fishing trip to Canada with some friends this past summer. While on a remote lake, and a considerable distance from shore, a sudden thunderstorm with violent lightning descended on them. Before they could scramble to shore, lightning hit the water near their aluminum boat. It fried all the electronics on the boat and blasted a hole in the hull, which they temporarily patched to get ashore. Rick seemed to have been unhurt, but shortly thereafter he developed a craving for chainsaw art. He bought a Stihl chainsaw, several large pine logs, and began carving during all his spare time. His first three carvings were of The Buddha, Harry Truman, and Aretha Franklin. He's quite proud of his work; unfortunately, they all look alike.

Sarah got her master's, magna cum laude, from the Nitze School of Advanced International Studies at Johns Hopkins, and, although she's been offered a number of jobs in the private sector and with the State Department, she decided to get her PhD. She has already met her advisor, whom she really likes, and she intends to accelerate the process, probably getting her doctorate in mid-2012.

Timmy also got his master's in theoretical physics, magna cum laude, at MIT and has started his doctoral studies. He has been asked by Dr. Frank Wilczek of MIT, a 2004 Nobel Laureate and one of the world's leading theoretical physics, to be a laboratory assistant. One of Wilczek's areas of interest is quantum chromodynamics, an area in which Timmy is particularly interested.

Michael was asked by President Obama to serve on his Council of Economic Advisers, so he will be devoting a little less time to his teaching duties at Harvard. He and Martha had a little boy in August of 2010, who they named Winston. Martha was reelected to the Cambridge City Council last year.

Tommy and Bruno appear to have an ever-deepening relationship. But it's tinged with sadness. When Tommy is paroled in 2026, their relationship will be over because Bruno is a lifer. Tommy continues to run the prison library and won a second special award for his work from the Maryland Department of Corrections. I'm very proud of him and happy for him and Bruno.

Merry Christmas or Hanukah and Happy New Year to you all.

Harry

Made in the USA
Lexington, KY
07 April 2013